GIMP

GIMP

mark zupan

and tim swanson

when life deals you a crappy hand,
you can fold—or you can play

HarperCollinsPublishers

HarperCollins books may be purchased for educational, business, or sales promotional use. For information, please write: Special Markets Department, HarperCollins Publishers, 10 East 53rd Street, New York, NY 10022.

FIRST EDITION

Designed by Nicola Ferguson

Library of Congress Cataloging-in-Publication Data is available upon request.

ISBN-10: 0-06-112768-X

ISBN-13: 978-0-06-112768-7

06 07 08 09 10   ID/RRD   10 9 8 7 6 5 4 3 2 1

I will light a match this morning, so I won't be alone
Watch as she lies silent, for soon light will be gone
I will stand with my arms outstretched, pretend I'm free to roam
I will make my way through one more day in hell
How much difference does it make?
How much difference does it make?

I will hold the candle until it burns up my arm
I'll keep taking punches until their will grows tired
I will stare the sun down until my eyes go blind
Hey, I won't change direction and I won't change my mind
How much difference does it make?
How much difference does it make?
How much difference...

I will swallow poison until I grow immune
I will scream my lungs out until it fills this room
How much difference
How much difference
How much difference does it make?
How much difference does it make...

The lyrics to "Indifference," a song by Pearl Jam that Mark Zupan listened to
thousands of times in the months after he became a quadriplegic.

GIMP

prologue

I dream about running all the time. My spine vibrates with the impact of each step, my heart plays a drum solo in my chest, and my lungs feel like fire. Sometimes I'm sprinting in my old football uniform, scanning the blue sky for a pigskin that's about to hit me in the numbers. Or I'm dribbling down a basketball court, my feet pounding the hardwood as I shake my defender, pull up, and drain a three. Or I'm on a grassy soccer field about to destroy the dreams of a striker with a nasty slide tackle.

Other times, I'm just running down a street near my house in Austin, Texas, and my wheelchair is rolling next to me, keeping the pace, mile after mile, as if some marathon-running ghost is pushing it. Some nights, I can outrun it. Other nights, I can't.

These are not bad dreams.

Then I'll wake up and pull back the bedsheets and stare at my legs. They look like your average thirty-one-year-old legs, but I can tell how much the muscles have atrophied since the accident. Back when I was playing soccer in college, my mom used to joke that my thighs were thicker than tree trunks and twice as strong. These days, I can't really move my legs, and I have to take antispasm medication to keep them from shaking involuntarily.

Still, I'm thankful.

One thing you learn when you become a quadriplegic is that everything is relative: fear, pain, strength, courage. And luck. Here's an example. When I broke my neck, I ruptured the disk between C6 and C7 and damaged my spinal cord. The human body has seven cervical vertebrae in total. In general, the higher up you break your neck, meaning the closer to your skull, the less function you have in your extremities, like your arms and legs. And if you snap it around C2, forget about it. That's known as the hangman's fracture. It's usually lights out after that. Goodnight, Irene.

My injury occurred a ways down my neck, and while I have impairment in all four of my limbs, which technically makes me a quadriplegic, I'm far from being totally paralyzed like the actor Christopher Reeve, who was probably the most famous quadriplegic before he passed away in 2004. I can actually get up out of my chair and stand for short periods of time to pull on some pants, reach a dish out of the cupboard, or put gas in my car. I can even take a few slow steps as long as I have something to hold on to.

Mind you, this is after years and years of hard work and painful rehabilitation. I have good function in my trunk, and my chest and arms are strong enough to bench-press 240 pounds four times. I'm unable to close my right hand completely, which sucks, because I used to be right-handed. Although I've lost the use of a muscle in my left shoulder, I have pretty good strength in my left arm and hand. Overall, I consider myself to be lucky. In fact, I am a goddamn lottery winner.

But more on that later.

Here's my story in a nutshell. When I was eighteen years old, I was in an accident, one that I could have easily avoided. I nearly died and will now spend the rest of my life confined to this chair. Those are the cold, hard facts and they can't be changed. I know this because I have relived the accident a few million times in my mind, second by painful second. I've played out every scenario in my head, thought of all the things I could have done differently, should have done differently, but the reality is always the same.

Over the years, I've come to understand why the Monday morning quarterback is never the guy throwing the football on game day. While hindsight may be 20/20, the truth is that most of us are more like Ray Charles when it comes to everyday life. When I was younger, common sense usually spoke to me a little too softly and a lot too late. As I've gotten older, I've learned to listen. I guess wisdom really does come with age.

My life changed forever more than a decade ago, on October 14, 1993. I had been in college at Florida Atlantic University in Boca Raton for a handful of weeks, living with a good friend of mine named Chris Igoe. In high school, we played football together, lifted weights together, partied together, listened to music together, acted like idiots together—all the stuff you do when you are young and dumb and your future stretches out before you like a red carpet at a Hollywood premiere. I remember feeling that we were like brothers back then, but I had no idea how close we would eventually become.

Even though I was only a freshman, I had earned a starting position on FAU's Division I squad. I wasn't exactly Freddy Adu, but I had a pretty nice touch, great defensive skills, and a bazooka of a shot. I was fast, aggressive, and willing to outwork and outplay anyone on the pitch. I had the determination and desire to win. Basically, I would do anything to put the ball in the back of the net.

At FAU, we had a saying: "Win or lose, we booze." So after we won an early evening game, the team headed to a local bar called Dirty Moe's, famous for its nickel beers, dollar shots, and lax policy when it came to carding. Igoe wasn't on the team, but he loved sports and would always cheer us on from the sidelines. And he was with me at the bar that night, glass in hand, hitting on women. The place was packed with people who had been at the game, so I didn't have to buy a drink all night. At one point in the evening, I had four drinks lined up in front of me—cocktails, beer, shots, whatever. I drank them all.

This is where things get a little hazy. I know I left the bar stumble drunk around midnight. I was probably feeling sick from all the alcohol or was worried that I was making a fool of myself in front of the ladies. It was drizzling outside. I was shithoused and just looking for a quiet place to pass out. Igoe's black Isuzu pickup was in the dark parking lot. Despite the rain, I climbed into the truck's bed, curled up in a ball, and fell asleep.

Fourteen hours later, firemen would fish my crippled body out of a shallow canal near the freeway. My temperature would be eighty-eight degrees and my heartbeat would have slowed to thirty beats per minute. I'd have both hypothermia and pneumonia from being in the cold water for so many hours. But that wouldn't even be the bad news. My neck would be broken and it wouldn't seem very likely that I would ever walk—let alone run—again.

But like I said, more on that later.

You see, I've been an athlete all my life. Soccer, basketball, baseball, golf, tennis, football: you name it, I played it before the accident. Now I've become known as the guy with the goatee, shaved head, and tattoos who plays murderball, also called quadriplegic rugby—quad rugby for short. It's not so different from other full-contact sports, except that we go to war in specially designed wheelchairs made from thick-tubed aluminum that look like something from a Mad Max movie. The object of quad rugby is to beat the shit out of the other team for four quarters while trying to get a ball across some lines and into a goal. It's a blast to play. But for me, it's more than a game. It's the sport that saved my life.

When I was growing up, sports meant everything to me. So you can imagine how I felt when it became clear that I was going to spend the rest of my life in a wheelchair. I thought I would never be able to play again—or drive a car, or have a job, a girlfriend, a house, a family of my own—you get the point. Keep in mind, I was only eighteen years old when I became a quadriplegic, much more a boy than a man. I had a lot to learn about my life at that point. I still do.

There's a quote by distance runner, philosopher, and author George Sheehan that explains how I feel about athletics and why I love to play:

Sport is where an entire life can be compressed into a few hours, where the emotions of a lifetime can be felt on an acre or two of ground, where a person can suffer and die and rise again on six miles of trails through a New York City park. Sport is a theater where the sinner can turn saint and a common man become an uncommon hero, where the past and future can fuse with the present. Sport is singularly able to give us peak experiences where we feel completely one with the world and transcend all conflicts as we finally become our own potential.

Traumatic injury can have a similar effect. It's a giant lens that makes you refocus your life. It's an X-ray for the guts and soul, the ultimate bullshit test. It forces you to inspect what you're truly made of, past the fatty layers of self-deceit and denial, clear down to the bone and marrow of your true being. Break your neck and you'll quickly get to know yourself. Intimately. You'll learn who your true friends are. You'll figure out what family really means. You'll stop worrying about stupid shit. You'll become thankful for moments that most people would consider inconsequential. And like Sheehan says, you'll finally become your own potential.

People have called the way I've dealt with my injury "inspiring" and I hope that it is, but really, that's not for me to say. The one thing I can say for myself is that I've always approached my injury as a challenge. I have learned that the true measure of a man is not necessarily the adversity he faces, but how he faces adversity. I've also learned that regrets suck a whole hell of a lot more than apologies. My goal is that when you read about what I've gone through, it will change the way you think about people in chairs, about friendship, and about life, because that's what it has done for me.

Traveling all over the world playing and promoting quad rugby, I've been asked a lot of questions about what it's like to be in a wheelchair. It probably seems like your worst nightmare come true and, at times, it is. Your mom is always warning you when you're young that if you're not careful, you'll break your neck (she was right, by the way). So what makes my story different from the stories of other disabled athletes? In some respects, there isn't much of a difference. But then again, how many quads do you know who have crowd-surfed at a Pearl Jam concert, or sung onstage with Eddie Vedder, or been skydiving, or won a Paralympic medal in Athens, or shaken hands with the president of the United States, or chugged beer with Johnny Knoxville? How many quads do you know who play a sport where they knock each other on their asses? Better yet, how many people do you know who have done any of that stuff?

In truth, my accident has been the best thing that could ever have happened to me. I'm not trying to be glib when I say this, or rationalize my mistakes, or offer you a steaming bowl of bullshit-flavored chicken soup for the soul. What I am saying is that it has been the single most defining event of my life. And without it, I wouldn't have seen the things that I've seen, done the things I've done, and met so many incredible people. I wouldn't have become a world-class athlete. I wouldn't have come to understand and cherish my family and friends the way I do, and feel the kind of love they have for me and I have for them.

In other words, I wouldn't be me, plain and simple.

Learning to live with limited function has forced me to take a good hard look at myself. When something catastrophic like this happens, the anger, frustration, and despair can become overwhelming. Often, you take these emotions out on the people closest to you and on yourself. There have been times that I have stared in the mirror and hated what I saw. I have more shameful, embarrassing memories, moments of stupidity, of rage, of selfishness, and of weakness, than I care to admit. But injury can be like a rebirth, because you learn that you can't live in the past. Either you move on with your life or you wither away and die.

Going back and revisiting some of the desperate and destructive times after my accident will be like ripping the scab off a deep, wide cut that never completely healed. I promise I won't preach to you, or glamorize or sanitize my life, or try to make it seem I was smart or tough when I wasn't. But at the same time, I am not going to pull punches. I'm going to talk about life, death, pain, joy, forgiveness, and other heavy shit. I'll probably even talk about penises and vaginas at some point. I'm hoping that my experiences will speak for themselves. And I am asking you to forget everything you think you know about quadriplegics, and just think of me as a human being and a competitor, because that's exactly what I am.

This past year, I was fortunate to have several articles written about me because I was one of the people featured in the documentary *Murderball*, which won the audience award at the 2005 Sundance Film Festival and was nominated for an Academy Award. The adjective that people most frequently used to describe me was "fearless." I like that because it's true. I'm not trying to brag, but I am pretty fearless. But not for the reasons you think. Most people fear pain. I've learned that not feeling pain is a much more frightening proposition than actually feeling it. In fact, there are times when I'm playing that I actually enjoy it.

The other thing I've read about myself is that I play quad rugby with so much intensity that people forget I'm disabled. This bothers me a little bit. I get what they are trying to say and thank them for the compliment, but the two concepts aren't mutually exclusive. That's like saying that Denzel Washington is such a good actor that you forget he's black. I can be disabled and still play really fucking hard.

Apologies. I should have warned you that I'm not the most politically correct guy in a chair.

By the way, I hate being called handicapped. Fucking hate it. Call me a cripple, or if you want to be polite, call me disabled. I'm not completely sure why the term rubs me wrong. Well, okay, maybe I am. It has something to do with the idea that a handicap in sports is when a person is given artificial advantages to help them compete. I don't want any advantages given to me. I can win on my own, both on and off the field.

But here's the bottom line: At some point, life is going to give you a swift, hard kick to the nuts. You can't control everything that happens to you, but you can try to understand it. For me, this has been just one of the many things I've learned in this painful, beautiful, crappy, exhilarating, stupid, rewarding life that started the day I landed in this chair—which I thought was my cross to bear, but was actually my salvation.

rearview mirror

Kurt cobain was singing about teen spirit. I cranked up the volume and pulled onto the freeway. The year was 1993 and Nirvana's *Nevermind* was still getting heavy rotation on the radio. That August in Coral Springs, Florida, was hot and humid beyond belief. Breathing felt like sucking air through a sweaty sock. Mashing on the gas, I angled my black Ford Mustang, which was loaded with clothes, CDs, and soccer gear, into the fast lane. This was a big moment in my life, one of those crossroads that misty-eyed adults are always telling you about when they reminisce about their youth, and I knew it. I was heading off to my first semester of college at Florida Atlantic University in Boca Raton, one of five freshmen invited to play on the school's Division I soccer team.

The FAU campus was a short thirty-minute drive from Coral Springs, where I had graduated from Marjory Stoneman Douglas High School. Sandwiched between Fort Lauderdale and Boca Raton, Coral Springs is a wealthy community where the Everglades have been battling with concrete-covered strip malls for decades and losing. But like most small towns in southern Florida, the place has retained its own special kind of quirkiness. Cranes, flamingos, and even an occasional alligator will lounge in the hundreds of drainage canals that crisscross Coral Springs. Fishermen still sell stone crabs fresh from the Atlantic on folding card tables not far from gated communities housing million-dollar mansions. And in true Florida fashion, senior citizens hungry for their early-bird specials pack the restaurants at 4:30 p.m.

Heading north to Boca on I-95, I thought about what I was leaving in the rearview mirror. Starting with my graduation in June, it had pretty much been the best summer of my life. I had done fairly well for myself academically, despite an admitted lack of effort. I ranked forty-three out of a class of around five hundred at Douglas High, with a 3.8 GPA. I had excelled in math and science. My mom and dad, who have always been really cool, down-to-earth parents, let me throw a party for about twenty of my friends on graduation night. We lived in a rambling single-story ranch house in a development called Eagle Trace, complete with a screened-in swimming pool, near a golf course where my dad, little brother, Jeff, and I would play together. Mark "Super" Duper, the former Miami Dolphins wide receiver, one half of the famous "Marks Brothers," lived just down the block from us. Whitney Houston also owned a house nearby. Let's just say her place was a lot bigger than ours.

My parents knew we were going to be drinking on graduation night, so instead of burying their heads in the sand, they allowed us to get loaded under their supervision, as long as everyone gave up their keys at the front door. All my buddies came to raise a glass, hang out, and celebrate this early milestone in our lives: Steve Nelson, a left-footer from my high school soccer team who I worked with at a restaurant called Chowders; Jeff Nickell and Frank Cava, two guys I had become close with while playing football my senior year at Douglas; and of course, Chris Igoe, Douglas High's resident class clown and self-proclaimed "pimp."

Tall, lanky, red-haired, and coated with a shotgun blast of freckles, Igoe had been a polarizing force at Douglas. You either loved or hated him. There was absolutely no middle ground. He was funny, smart, brash, and completely out of control. Igoe was obsessed with gangsta rap music, especially N.W.A. and Snoop Doggy Dog. He regularly dressed in Nike track suits, occasionally with a small travel clock hanging around his neck, which he had purchased during one of his two stints at military school. He would walk through the halls at Douglas singing "I-G-O-E" to the tune of Snoop's "What's My Name?"

His senior year, Igoe would wear what he referred to proudly as his "Black Power" glove on his right hand during football games. He would ball his hand into a fist and raise it above his head for a few seconds before each kickoff. What did the gesture mean? Who the hell knows? It was really just a driving glove that he had to hide from Coach Mathisen, who said he would boot Chris off the team if he ever wore it at a game again. Of course, Chris kept wearing the glove.

Equal parts arrogance and insecurity, Igoe acted like he was the star of a raucous sitcom and we were his laugh track. My other buddies from the football team—Cava, Nickell, Ari Levy, the McCarthy brothers—were no angels, and we all had a certain amount of mischief and mayhem lurking inside us, but we were nothing compared to Chris. No one was. Igoe was the type of guy who would go to a high school party, steal bottles out of the parents' liquor cabinet, try to have sex with someone's girlfriend in the bathroom, start a fistfight, and then take a shit in the washing machine, which was all pretty hilarious, as long as you weren't the person who had to clean up after him the next day.

Igoe didn't get into much trouble on graduation night, beyond body-slamming me headfirst into my bed, a bit of liquored-up brawling that left me wounded and woozy. But that hardly mattered. We drank enough beer to kill a mule, wrestled in the pool, blasted "I'm Gonna Be" by the Scottish group the Proclaimers over and over again, singing the infectious "I would walk five hundred miles" chorus at the top of our lungs, much to the discomfort of my neighbors.

My dad, who has worked in the food business for most of his life and is a genius in the kitchen, partied with us, working the grill, barbecuing steak and chicken all night long. At one point, he was giving my friends and me some "wise" words to live by. "When you are ready to pick a wife, never marry a girl with fat ankles," he said, only half kidding. "If she has fat ankles as a young woman, you know she is going to be a big lady when she gets older."

Later, he was half in the bag himself when he helped us concoct a drink that we called the Goodnight Irene. Here's the recipe: Pour four or five fingers of vodka into a tumbler. Add ice. Stir. Drink. Repeat. After a few of those, it was goodnight Irene.

The night ended with beer cans, plastic cups, and empty plates littering the patio. People were sleeping on every available couch or chair while my dad, Nickell, and Igoe floated around on air mattresses in the pool, drunk as lords, pontificating on the past, present, and future. My dad is a stocky guy and looks like a hairy fire hydrant with arms, legs, and a stiff, round belly. He doesn't talk a whole lot, unless it's about cooking or golf, and isn't big on emotions, but when he speaks, he says exactly what he means. That night, he congratulated my friends on their accomplishments and then got strangely serious, offering up this bit of advice, which, true to his nature, was short, sweet, and to the point.

"Life is going to be hard, guys," he said softly as dawn splashed pink streaks across the flat, dark Florida sky. Igoe and Nickell were listening intently, probably staring down at their own blurry reflections on the water's surface. My dad took a sip of his Goodnight Irene and said, almost wistfully, "You have no idea what you're in for."

I wish I could have heard my father's speech. He's a self-made man from a blue-collar background who doesn't open up very often. His childhood was a lot harder than mine. Unfortunately, I had passed out on my bed.

what was i like during this period of my life? Compared to my friends, I wasn't as sensitive as Steve, as morally insane as Igoe, as academically disciplined as Nickell (who got straight As in the advanced prep classes we shared), or as kindhearted and caring as Cava, who was ferocious on the football field but a big teddy bear in real life.

My friends would probably tell you that I was quiet, intense, loyal, and very physically fit. While most kids hated practice, I took training seriously and knew if I put my time into strengthening my body, it would pay dividends on the field. At the end of my senior year in high school, I was five feet nine, 172 pounds, and strong for my size. I could run the fifty-yard dash in 4.7 seconds and would often jog six miles home after lifting at the gym. A mile circuit around Eagle Trace took me five minutes and change to complete.

I was also a workaholic. During summer training for football season, we would run drills in the morning and lift in the afternoon, then I would hop in my car, drive to the soccer field, and practice with my club team in Boca for a couple of hours in the evening.

While I loved playing football and watching it on TV with my dad and little brother, soccer had always been my primary sport. Igoe likes to refer to it as "commie ball," but there is a reason that it's known as "the beautiful game." Soccer is truly a thinking man's sport, where intelligence and finesse are often rewarded over aggression. But then again, nothing equals the brutal beauty of football. Burying your helmet into another player's chest and knocking him on his wallet is one of the best feelings in the world. With football, you get to mainline intensity with hot shots of adrenaline. While soccer is more free-form, fluid, and organic in pacing and the way the play builds, football is more scripted, regimented, and organized, like a military campaign. If soccer is jazz, then football is rock and roll with the volume turned to eleven. My experience on the soccer field made me a better player on the gridiron, and vice versa. Each game spoke to a particular part of my personality.

But what I liked most about both sports was the team camaraderie, the lifelong friendships forged on the field. To win at either game, you often have to sacrifice yourself for the ultimate benefit of your squad. At the same time, every team needs a superstar to make the big play when it counts. If you're truly a good player, your time on the field is a tightrope walk between selfishness and selflessness. You have to pick your shots carefully or risk alienating your teammates. The best guy on a squad always makes the people playing with him look better. This is the glorious democracy of team sports. With both soccer and football, it ultimately doesn't matter how good an individual player is. No one player can win a game by himself. The whole is always greater than the sum of its parts.

That summer between my senior year of high school and my freshman year of college, I was in love with more than just athletics. Her name was Kati Hanson. She was a green-eyed brunette with tawny skin, a quiet laugh, and perfect white teeth, the type of girl who would draw a small heart to dot the "i" in her name when passing you a note.

Kati was a year younger than I was and she was on the swim team. We had started dating my sophomore year, when I moved to Coral Springs from Pewaukee, Wisconsin. She would make me peanut butter and banana sandwiches and leave them in my car so I had something to eat between football and soccer practice. While most of my friends would be out raising hell on the weekends, I would often stay home with Kati and watch a movie. Or we would double-date with Steve Nelson and his girlfriend, a petite brunette named Dana Lewis, who worked at Chowders with us. After a while, I got Kati a hostessing job there as well.

After work, I would follow Kati home, park my car down the block, walk back to her house, and knock softly on her window. You can imagine what we did after that. The next morning, I would sneak out of her room and hide in the garage until her parents left for work.

As a graduation present, my dad used some of his frequent-flier miles to take our family to St. John in the Virgin Islands. My brother invited a friend of his and I asked Kati to come along with us as well. The night before we left, Steve and I worked a shift together at Chowders. Having a job and earning my own money meant a lot to me, and I took the responsibility seriously. My parents had instilled their strong work ethic in me—I started delivering papers when I was fourteen years old and we lived in Minnesota, then moved on to working in restaurants a few nights a week. My parents did fine financially and always provided us with every opportunity they could, but we weren't as well off as other families in Coral Springs. So it felt good to make a little walk-around money for myself.

As a busboy, my job was to bring out the bread and butter, fill up water glasses, and pick up the plates. I quickly realized that it was more fun to hang out by the bar, so I started bar backing when the restaurant was slow, washing glasses in a tiny silver sink and carrying big buckets of ice to the bartenders. At the end of our shift, Steve and I convinced one of the line cooks to give us a bottle of Goldschlager, a ridiculous brand of hard liquor that supposedly contains actual flakes of gold. It tasted like cinnamon and gave you a hell of a hangover. We stayed up all night getting bombed on the stuff with some friends. The next morning, I woke up on a strange floor with my brain in a vise. I looked at my watch.

"Oh fuck," I said.

I jumped into my car, raced home, and pulled up to our house, bleary-eyed and reeking of alcohol. My mom and dad were in the driveway with my little brother and his friend, talking to Kati and her parents. All their suitcases were stacked neatly in the car. My mom stopped worrying about where I had been all night and became apoplectically angry. My parents had always been pretty lenient with me, as long as I didn't do stupid shit and get myself in trouble. If I did, then the hammer came down. Hard. My mom once grounded my brother, Jeff, for four solid months for lying to her. This time, I knew I had crossed the line. I started to make excuses. My dad interrupted me.

"Are you still drunk?" he asked. "Never mind. Don't say another word. Get in the car."

I did. We barely made our flight. Later, I apologized for staying out all night and making my parents worry. I promised never to do it again. They eventually cooled down enough to enjoy themselves. We stayed at the resort for a full week. Kati and I had our own room with a king-size bed in my family's condo. We swam in the turquoise ocean or lounged by the pool, ordering food and tropical drinks with hunks of fresh fruit and umbrellas in them. Despite my lapse of judgment the night before we left, I remember feeling like I was an adult for the first time. I also remember enjoying the closeness that I felt with Kati.

"I'm really going to miss you when I go away to college," I said. We were on the beach, lying stomach down on towels, digging our toes into the vanilla sand. I noticed that her bare shoulders had turned a beautiful bronze and her eyes were unusually bright.

"I'm going to miss you too," she said.

We kissed, but for the first time in our relationship, I felt a twinge of heartache.

kati was a big reason why I chose to attend college at FAU. At one point, Duke had been on my wish list, but that seemed like too much of a long shot. During my junior year, my parents had taken me on a tour of Atlantic Coast Conference schools to check out the campuses and talk to various coaches. My SAT scores had been pretty good, but not stellar. During senior year at Douglas, I had been co-captain of the soccer team. My play had gotten me some notice in the local papers and won some awards. I had been recruited by a few other universities, including FAU, but was hoping that Clemson in South Carolina would offer me an athletic scholarship with admission. They didn't. The coach said I could try out as a walk-on. I told my parents that I was sure I could make the team. We looked at brochures and crunched the financial aid numbers. At the end of the day, we would be looking at close to six figures of debt. They were willing to make the sacrifice, but I decided to pass.

I narrowed my focus to in-state schools, which would save my parents money on tuition. I thought about attending the University of Florida four hours north in Gainesville with Nickell and Cava. Florida State in Tallahassee was also a possibility. Ultimately FAU, which had offered me an athletic scholarship and had recently moved up from Division II to Division I in sports, seemed like the best bet. It was close to home, which meant close to Kati, and it was relatively inexpensive. It didn't have the best academic reputation, but at that point, academics weren't a priority to me. I wanted to play college soccer. Period.

Igoe, who was test smart but had a grade point average that might as well have been in the negative digits, was also thinking of enrolling at FAU in the fall. He had also been accepted to the University of Central Florida, where he could possibly play on the football team. It took a while, but I convinced him to go to FAU instead. I was going to help him with calculus and chemistry. Igoe, who certainly has the gift of gab, was going to help me write my English papers.

"Together, we'll be unstoppable," Igoe said. "In a few weeks, we're going to run the place. Just you watch."

My friendship with him continued to grow once we knew that we would be attending the same school. For all Igoe's bravado and bluster, he was a pretty cool guy with a good heart, and hanging out with him was always entertaining, as long as we didn't get arrested. During the day we would lift weights or swim at the beach with friends. At night, if Kati and I weren't hanging out, we would drive around and get loaded with our football friends. There wasn't much more to do in Coral Springs.

Igoe got a black Isuzu pickup truck for graduation from his father, who owns a banking software company. His dad was working overseas at the time of the ceremony and wasn't around to watch Chris walk across the stage in a cap and gown. Igoe would joke that the truck was "a gift of guilt." Igoe's old car, a piece-of-shit yellow Cadillac El Dorado that we called "The Cadu," was an automatic with red ants and roaches living in the air conditioner and a faux white convertible top that would occasionally blow off on the freeway if you didn't have someone in the passenger seat holding on to it. Igoe's new truck was a stick. He didn't know how to drive a manual transmission, so I taught him how.

Igoe always wanted to listen to rap. I liked rap too, but made it my goal to broaden his horizons and show him there was something beyond, bitches, hos, and heavy bass. My love affair with music had started a few years back, when metal ruled the radio. The first concert I went to was Kiss and White Lion. I saw Poison live three times. I got my friend's older sister to buy me Motley Crüe's *Dr. Feelgood* album the day it came out. They wouldn't sell it to me because of the explicit lyrics. When Megadeth or Iron Maiden or Guns N' Roses came to town, I had tickets and pushed through the crowds of long-haired kids to the front of the stage.

In high school, my tastes changed and matured. Grunge replaced metal. I got into Metallica, Tool, Stone Temple Pilots, Alice in Chains, Pearl Jam, and Nirvana. The poetry of the lyrics spoke to me as much as the guitars. I would listen to these CDs as I ran mile after mile around Eagle Trace, pushing myself, building up my endurance and stamina for the upcoming soccer season. My musical predilections began to rub off on Igoe. I even introduced him to some of the classics, like the Doors, which totally blew his mind. At the end of the summer, I asked him if he wanted to room together at FAU.

"Sure, man," Igoe said. "That would be fucking awesome."

chaptertwo

come as you are

Welcome to the first day of practice, gentlemen." FAU soccer coach Kos Donev was issuing us our marching orders. "You
will be expected to complete two miles in less than twelve minutes."
Training camp had started promptly on Monday at 5:30 a.m., a clear
sign that Donev wasn't screwing around. He wanted to win. He also
wanted to know who had followed the conditioning program he had
sent to us during the summer, and who had slacked off and spent
their time chasing girls and slurping beers at the beach. The reality
was that the majority of the guys had probably done both. Nevertheless, this morning's run around the soccer fields was going to be a
serious gut check.

Donev was from Macedonia, part of the former Yugoslavia. He
had come to Florida as a teenager and had played at FAU himself. I
had shaken hands with him a couple of times before, when he had
attended my club games to scout and recruit local players. In his
mid-thirties, Donev was a gregarious guy who talked so fast that his
accented words seemed to get caught in his teeth, piling up on each
other like cars crashing on a freeway during rush hour. He knew the
game well and was very big on fitness, more so than any of my previous coaches. He knew the FAU Owls would be fighting an uphill
battle this year, having moved up a division in the Trans America

Athletic Conference. Soon, we would be facing off against strong soccer schools like University of North Carolina Greensboro, Florida International University, Georgia State, College of Charleston, and University of South Florida. If we wanted to be competitive, we had to put in the sweat and sacrifice.

"After we finish the two miles," Donev told the crowd of sleepy-looking players standing around the soccer field, dressed in shorts, T-shirts, and cleats, "we will have another thirty-minute timed run. Now, let's stretch it out."

The team had come to school a few weeks before the rest of the student body to prepare for the fall season. Donev had scheduled "triples" for us— three practices a day, five days a week, with lighter workouts on the weekend. We would condition in the morning before the humidity became too unbearable, run drills in the scorching afternoon, and scrimmage in the evening. We would be eating, breathing, and sleeping soccer.

Fine by me, I thought. I was in the best shape of my life, and was beyond stoked just to be there. I had watched college sports on TV with my dad and brother for as long as I could remember. Competing at this level was like living a dream.

After losing a lot of players to graduation the previous year, the team was rebuilding, and it seemed possible that the young guys would do more than just practice and ride pine. In the past, FAU had relied heavily on junior-college transfers when it needed seasoned players to beef up the roster. This year, Donev had invested in the future by handpicking five freshmen, including me, to grow and mature with the squad.

We circled up in the middle of the dew-soaked soccer field, and Donev led us through a series of stretches, starting with the lower legs and on through the other major muscle groups. I looked around at the other four freshmen. I was friends with one of them. His name was Chris Shafiei, and we had played club ball together in Boca for a few years. He was living in the same dorm suite where Igoe and I had a room, and was one hell of a midfielder with incredible ball handling skills and a shot like a thunderbolt. It was clear that competition to earn a spot on the starting eleven was going to be stiff.

The morning light changed from blue to gold as we warmed up. Everyone had their best game faces on, but I could see the anxiety in some of the new guys' eyes; hear the butterflies flapping in their stomachs. Many of them were out of their comfort zone, away from home for the first time, and having to prove themselves in front of a group of strangers. They were intimidated. I wasn't. Being an outsider had become the norm for me. My family moved around a lot, and I had changed schools and club teams four times in the past five years. Being the new guy didn't bother me. I just kept my head down and worked. I felt I had developed an extra reserve of inner strength for just these situations.

Once we had loosened up, the team lined up on one corner of the field and got ready to race. "Gentlemen," Donev said in his buzz-saw English, "get set. Go!" We took off like quarter horses out of the gate. I shot to the front of the pack, pumping my knees and elbows, jockeying for the pole position. After a lap, I found my stride.

For those of you who haven't spent much time on a track, completing two miles in less than twelve minutes is no small feat. You have to run just a shade off of an all-out sprint. The group ballooned at first, then thinned and separated into clusters, like a globular organism dividing itself several times over.

The race quickly became an exercise of attrition, and it became clear who was in shape and who wasn't. My summer training was paying off. My muscles felt loose and my body was covered in a warm sheen of sweat. Despite the rapid pace, I was breathing deeply and comfortably. As I finished the first mile, I moved into third place, chasing this gazelle in soccer shorts and a dark-haired guy with a face full of stubble, whom I recognized as Jeff Sharon, a fifth-year senior and team captain. A few seconds later, I pulled up next to Sharon. He turned his head, looked at me, and grinned.

"Hey man," he huffed, laboring to talk while legging it. "Where you going so fast?"

No reply. I wasn't there to talk. I kept running.

"What's your name?" he asked.

"Mark Zupan," I said.

"Jeff Sharon," he said. "Nice to meet you. You a freshman?"

"Yup."

I moved slightly ahead but Sharon remained in my shadow, running just behind me, step for step. I couldn't get him out of my back pocket. The guy had lungs like an opera singer. *He's probably a midfielder*, I thought. Middies run up and down the field all day, playing on both the offense and defense, creating the link between the forwards and fullbacks. I also played in the midfield, as well as center defense and marking back, which is an outside fullback position. Then I remembered hearing that Sharon played in the back, running the defense, the same position that I played in high school.

I wondered if I would be taking his spot once the season started. *Highly unlikely*, I thought, but the idea still made me smile to myself. I was one cocky son of a bitch.

We ran in silence. Then a few laps later, he pulled even with me. There was plenty of distance left in the race. It was clear that we couldn't catch the gazelle in front of us, and no one was close enough to overtake us from behind. We were running neck and neck, straining for second place, a respectable finish considering there were about twenty-five players out for the first day of practice. I prepared myself for a fast finish. I figured Sharon and I would just have to duel it out with a sprint at the end. Even though I was fatigued, I felt confident that I was quick enough to beat him. He must have read my mind.

"Hey, man," Sharon said, panting while he spoke. "Just so you know, the freshmen usually let upperclassmen like me come in a little front of them. It's a sign of respect."

I looked at him like he had just puked on my shirt. *Fuck this guy*, I thought. *If he wants to win, he's going to have to earn it just like anyone else.* I wasn't about to give anyone a free pass, not even the captain of the team. Not on the first day.

I downshifted in my mind, upped my RPMs, and forced my legs to accelerate. My eyeballs bounced around in my skull with each step. My calves and quads turned to napalm, my blood became battery acid, and I somehow developed a quarter-size hole in my lung that was allowing all the oxygen to escape at an alarming rate. Still, I propelled myself forward through the physical discomfort. Pain has never bothered me when I work out. In fact, if I don't suffer, that means I'm not working hard enough.

Even after all that, Sharon was still right next to me.

"How about this?" Sharon said. He was motoring along like he still had half a tank of gas, but he had started to wheeze like a bagpipe with a bullet hole in it.

"Why don't we ease off this pace a little and cruise across the finish line together?" he said. "That way, we'll both take second, and we don't have to kill ourselves."

It seemed like a fair proposition, even generous. As much as I wanted to beat everyone out there and make a name for myself early on, I also wanted to be liked by the older players who were the starters on the team. And to tell the truth, I was worried that I was going to be totally spent after this run. I knew that we still had more conditioning to do, the other thirty-minute run that Donev had mentioned, and then most likely wind sprints. The sun had finally made its debut in the east, round and orange, and the light suffusing the field was bright and intense. The humid air was beginning to boil like water in a teakettle. I was dumping so much sweat, I looked as if I had just stepped out of a swimming pool.

"Cool, man," I said, shortening my stride, slowing down just a little. "We'll cross the line together."

We hit the final stretch. Donev was standing about ten yards from us, head down, looking at a stopwatch and calling out times: "11:10, 11:11, 11:12 ..." We were a few feet from the finish line when Sharon jackrabbited several steps in front of me. He caught me completely off guard and there was no way I could react or catch him. I watched the back of his head cross the finish line, and I swear I could hear him laughing. I wanted to punch him in the mouth and tip my hat to him at the same time.

"Nice job, gentlemen," Donev said as we passed. "Well done."

I sat down on the dew-soaked grass and caught my breath. I had smoked every other freshman out there, and almost all the veteran players. Third place was not a bad showing. I should have been proud. Instead, I was pissed because I had been outsmarted.

Sharon walked up to me as the other guys were crossing the line and offered me some of his water. "Thanks, Zupe," he said, "for giving an old guy a break."

That made me laugh. "No problem," I said.

We slapped hands. At that moment, I knew Sharon and I were going to become good friends. I also realized that I was going to have to use more than just my body if I was going to successfully make the transition from high school to college ball.

no one is going to confuse FAU with Harvard. You won't find any ivy-covered brick buildings there, no stone gargoyles or leaded-glass windows, or anything with a peaked slate roof. I remember someone telling me that, decades ago, FAU had been converted from an old air force base, and the aesthetic is definitely midcentury military. The nondescript beige rectangular buildings that cover the campus seem far more institutional than academic.

Every edifice seems to have been made exclusively from concrete blocks and right angles. About 23,000 students attend school there (including graduate students), and it's largely a commuter campus. While the architecture hardly inspires enlightenment or higher learning, at least the landscaping isn't totally depressing. Palm trees, which sway above the student body like unconcerned parents at a cocktail party, line the miles of wide concrete sidewalks and broad lawns that checkerboard the grounds.

Igoe and I lived on the second floor of an anonymous brown breadbox. It was a typical dorm room with two metal-framed beds, one big closet that we shared, and a large window that overlooked a grassy area containing a barbecue setup with picnic tables and a sand volleyball pit where students would hang out on the balmy, tropical evenings.

Eight people lived in our suite, which consisted of two bedrooms on each side and a common room that connected to a bathroom with three toilets and a shower. My teammate Chris Shafiei lived in the room next to Igoe and me with some European dude, who was really

muscular and would strut around the suite in these tight man pant-
ies. When Igoe and Shafiei saw him naked— which happens when
eight guys share one shower— and learned that he was uncircum-
cised, they would tease him mercilessly, calling him "The Anteater."
He ended up dropping out of school before the end of the first semester.

Igoe and Shafiei became fast friends and decided to decorate the
ledge that ran around the ceiling of the common room with empty
cans of Skoal chewing tobacco. It would take Igoe about three days
to go through a tin. He constantly had a wad of tobacco packed into
his lower lip, and he would leave empty beer bottles brimming with
chew spit all over the suite. Igoe said that he planned to line the entire ledge by the end of the semester.

"It's always good to have goals," I told him.

Our dorm suite smelled so bad that it would have offended a
zookeeper. I wish I could say that I was the clean one, but I was
definitely part of the problem, leaving muddy shorts, sweat-stained
shirts, and smelly socks on the floor. I had never lived away from
home and wasn't used to cleaning up after myself. I would try to
straighten up from time to time, but I wasn't about to take on the
toilet, which, after being shared by eight eighteen-year-old guys,
was decorated with splotches of dried yellow urine, brown sludge,
random pubes, and traces of vomit left over from the many nights
of binge drinking.

If the gravy stains in the bathroom weren't enough to cause a gag
reflex, there was always "the booger wall" next to Igoe's bed. It was a
tradition started by "the booger locker" at Douglas High. As was the
custom, each day before we left the suite, we would pick our noses
and then smear snot on a certain spot, which, after a while, started to
resemble the top layer of an old sausage pizza.

Yeah. I know. Charming stuff.

As messy as we were, Igoe was curiously fastidious in certain respects. I was still getting up at the ass crack of dawn for the early
morning mini-marathons with Coach Donev and the rest of the team.
When I returned, Igoe would have picked up all my dirty clothes and
put them in the hamper. He would also make my bed for me, pull-

ing the sheets and blankets so tight that you could have bounced a quarter on them.

Maybe he did learn something at military school after all.

The weeks passed and Coach Donev continued to try to kill us with his relentless training regime of triple practices in the high heat. We ran mile after mile on the muggy mornings, sprinted lines on the field, performed endless dribbling exercises between cones, worked on volleys and traps, took shots on the keeper, ran half-field offensive-against-defense drills, developed set plays for free kicks in front of the goal, and engaged in small-sided scrimmages where we could only one-touch the ball, to enhance our quick passing abilities. "We have to push ourselves if we want to win," Donev would say. "It is up to us to prove that we belong in this division."

I was doing more than just holding my own in the scrimmages, though not standing out on offense as much as I would have liked. The way the team was shaping up, it seemed as if I would be playing marking back, which is the same as saying outside fullback. It would be my job to shut down the other team's outside forward, eliminating breakaways and disrupting attempts to cross the ball from the side-line to the center near the goal. The great thing about soccer is that the defensive players can also participate in the attack. When our team had an offensive corner kick, I would advance down the field to crash the box and try to head or volley the ball past the keeper.

Donev had told me that I was playing "with the strength of a bull." Whatever I lacked in technical ability and ball skill, I tried to make up for with my athleticism and determination. But at FAU, everyone was talented and disciplined. The competition made me train even harder. In my few off hours between practices, I would hit the weight room to work on my legs and upper body. I would go out to the field by myself and run drills. I had my sights set on making the starting eleven for our first game against Central Florida.

Weeks went by and we became stronger, faster, and more cohesive as a unit. By early September, as the weather cooled from scalding to sweltering, the team had successfully gelled. A lot of that had to do with our off-field bonding. Just like my football team in high school, the FAU soccer team liked to drink as much as they liked to play.

A few of the older guys, including Jeff Sharon, lived together at the off-campus soccer house, a dilapidated coffee-colored structure with a red adobe roof surrounded by dark green mangroves. We called the place Club Royale, because they had an old neon sign hanging near a thrift-store couch in the dank living room that said "Royale." The two-story house was about five minutes from the fields. After evening practices during the week and on weekends the team would congregate there with various members of the women's team to barbecue, drink cases of cold beer, and hang out.

The soccer team had started to feel like my fraternity. It's weird how well you can get to know a group of guys in such a short amount of time when you are playing sports together six days a week. There were frats on campus, but I had no interest in pledging. During rush week, they would scrawl their odd-looking Greek letters in colored chalk on the wide sidewalks that ribboned the campus. Whenever Igoe would see this, he would take great offense, clearing his throat and hawking a giant Skoal-flavored loogie onto the pavement that would slide across the pastel letters like a brown slug. Igoe said he hated all frat guys on principle. He thought they were unoriginal and boring.

Still, the soccer team had its own ridiculous hazing rituals that you had to endure if you wanted to be part of the pack. One night when we were getting soused at the Club Royale, Sharon showed up with a set of clippers, some Bic razors, and shaving cream. It was time for the annual rite of passage known as shaving the freshman players' heads and making them look like idiots.

"Who's first?" Sharon asked, pulling up a chair. The older guys on the team yelled and clapped. No one volunteered.

"Oh, come on," Sharon said. "What are you guys, a bunch of pussies? Every guy on this team has gone through this."

Why rituals of humiliation and gallons of alcohol bond groups of men, I'll never know. I stripped off my shirt and sat down in the chair.

"Take it all off," I said. "Just don't nick me."

The clippers buzzed my reddish blond hair down until it was just a shadow on my scalp. The razor took care of the rest. The results weren't pretty. I have fair skin, and my pale head looked like a white Q-tip for the first week of classes. But my pride has always won over my vanity.

"I knew Zupan would step up," Sharon said as he finished the job. "This kid has no fear."

igoe and i were leafing through the FAU course schedule together, deciding what we would take, trying to avoid anything before 8:00 a.m. Triples had ended by now, and I wanted to get some much-needed sleep. Knowing that math and science were my strong suits, I declared my major as premed. I hadn't really given much thought to studying medicine. It wasn't like I had always dreamed about working with sick or injured people. It just sounded impressive if you said it out loud, especially to girls. I enrolled in calculus, English, macroeconomics, and an honors preparatory course, a heavy load considering the amount of time I was spending on the soccer field and in the bars.

Early in the semester, Igoe and I discovered that there was a campus pub within walking distance of our dorm. Calling the Rathskellar a bar is like calling a bottle of Thunderbird a nice wine. The Rat, as we referred to it, was a real shithole, a dark, cavernous room with filthy pool tables and a lot of kegs. It also had a kitchen that served greasy burgers and fries. Through some sort of administrative glitch, you could use your student meal card to buy beer there. Igoe had always eaten like whatever was in front of him was his last meal, and had convinced his parents to line him up with the biggest food plan available, $3,000 per semester, which he used to purchase plastic cup after plastic cup of cheap suds.

Students ran the taps at the Rat, and it wasn't like they were really checking anyone's ID to see if they were twenty-one years old. Most nights we would be in there, punishing our livers. We started having contests there to see who could drink the most beer without leaving the bar. If you split to take a piss, you were out of the game. Igoe circumvented this problem by dragging over a plastic trash can, pulling down his pants, and relieving himself in front of everyone. No one seemed to notice or care.

One night when Igoe and Shafiei were stumbling home from one too many rounds at the Rat, they ran into a basketball player we had previously met at a campus party. FAU didn't have a football team at that time, so the basketball players were the big men on campus, both literally and figuratively. He gave them a nod as he walked by.

In high school, Igoe had developed the unfortunate habit of addressing people— black, white, Asian, whatever—by saying "What's up, my nigga?" No one took offense at Douglas because everyone knew Igoe and his larger-than-life personality. And if they did take offense, well, tough shit to them. There weren't too many students at Douglas willing to heads-up anyone who played on the football team.

Igoe's joke didn't go over so well at FAU. The basketball player, who happened to be a skyscraper-tall Caucasian guy with large hands, and knuckles the size of walnuts, couldn't believe what this drunk freshman had just said to him. Without uttering a word, he stepped up and hit Igoe with a sledgehammer right that split the soft skin above his left eye and left a ring indentation in his face. From what I heard, Igoe took the punch like a champ. His head snapped back, his knees buckled from the blow, and a crimson geyser spurted from above his brow, but he kept his feet, refusing to go down for the count.

Shafiei stepped in and separated the two of them. Surprisingly, instead of swinging back, Igoe offered his right hand to the basketball player. "You've got a hell of a shot," he said with genuine admiration in his voice. "A hell of a shot."

They shook hands like businessmen meeting at a sales convention, and then Igoe limped back to the dorms by himself, blood streaming down his face, wondering if he should go to the hospital to get stitches. If I remember correctly, that was pretty much the end of his black power phase.

fau had no shortage of available women: short girls, tall girls; girls with tan, firm bodies; fat girls, homely girls; loud girls with big hair who would drink too much jungle juice from the plastic-lined trash cans at dorm parties and end up spending the rest of the night with their arms wrapped gently around the sturdy neck of a white toilet.

Igoe made it his mission to love them all, every single one of them. He would find a way to make himself the center of attention at parties, and women would end up flocking to him. Between beers two and eight, Igoe was funny, dynamic, charming, and engaging. He was a one-man party machine. He would walk up to women with supreme confidence, introduce himself, and engage them in flirtatious conversations that would often end the next morning when they tiptoed softly out of his dorm room, high heels in hand. We would call their early morning exit the "the walk of shame."

"No, gentlemen," Igoe would say. "That's the walk of fame."

But when Igoe's beer count hit double digits, he would often transform. We called this rude, angry, destructive person who would unexpectedly punch people in the face, steal stuff, throw drinks on women, get kicked out of clubs, and piss in public, his ugly cousin "Igor." As you can imagine, Igor didn't have much luck with the ladies.

For all intents and purposes, I was Igoe's sidekick at parties, his silent wingman. It wasn't like I was shy around women, but being a quiet person by nature, I just had a harder time initiating conversations. I wouldn't know what to talk about. But that never stopped Igoe. He would draw them in with some sort of outlandish opening line like "Do you believe in love at first sight? Or should I walk in again?" For some reason, most women loved the attention and ate this shit up. Igoe would introduce me, and then there would be plenty of girls to talk to. He'd tell them that I was a rising star on the soccer team. That always piqued their interest.

I would flirt, but I never took any of these women back to spend the night in my dorm room. I certainly had my chances but I always passed. I wasn't looking for a girlfriend because I already had one. Kati and I had promised each other that we would remain faithful while we were apart. I would look at a picture of her—her pretty hair and smile, all silk and ivory—and wonder if she was still into me, or if she was hanging out with other guys while I was gone. Jealousy would make me pick up the phone and call her to find out what she was doing.

While the attraction and affection we shared was real and substantial, we had recently started to love each other with an immature desperation, reciting what we thought were romantic lines from movies we had seen on cable, instead of talking about what we were feeling. We were trying to maintain what had essentially become a long-distance relationship, even though we were basically still living in the same town, and our love wasn't structurally sound enough to bridge the space between us.

Kati had started her senior year at Douglas, and I would drive to Coral Springs whenever I could to see her, which wasn't as often as I would have liked because of my hectic schedule. I would tell myself that we were going to be okay, that this was just an adjustment period, but the reality was that we were slowly growing apart and I felt powerless to stop it. We were just in very different places in our lives at that moment, and we were having a difficult time relating to each other. I did everything I could to keep the relationship going. I would call her on the phone almost every night and we would talk about nothing for hours, neither one of us wanting to hang up when it was time to go. Clearly, we still had strong feelings for one another.

But I was obviously conflicted, and maybe not totally honest with her. I never invited her to come visit me and stay in the dorms. I know it was a double standard, but part of me didn't want the other girls at school to know that I had a girlfriend. As my dad would say, "You don't bring sand to the beach." And I certainly didn't want to subject her to the filthy accommodations or Igoe's drunken behavior, which seemed to worsen each week.

When I was in back Coral Springs seeing Kati, I'd stop by the house to visit my parents and Jeff, who was in his junior year at Douglas and was playing on the football team. My mom and dad were concerned because Jeff had started to party too much and skip school. As his big brother, I had always looked out for him, and that wasn't going to stop just because I was away at college. One Saturday night when I was back at FAU, I called to check on him because our parents had gone out of town for the weekend. The phone rang a few times and then some girl picked up.

"Who the fuck is this?" I said.

"No one," she said, giggling foolishly.

"Put my brother on the phone. Now."

Silence. Then jostling of the receiver.

"Hello," Jeff said. His voice sounded weird.

"Jeff," I said. "What the hell is going on?"

"Nothing," he said. At first, I thought he was fighting with his girlfriend or something. Then I could hear other loud voices in the background and music blaring.

"Are you throwing a party in Mom and Dad's house?" I asked.

"Mark," he said. "It was just going to be me, my girlfriend, and I was going to let my boys hook up with a few chicks they invited. Next thing I know, there's like sixty cars parked on the street and a hundred people in the house."

"How did they get past the gate?" I asked.

"One car went through and then left it up for everyone else," he said.

I suddenly had visions of all the houses my football friends and I had essentially destroyed back when we were going to Douglas. Once at a party, Igoe and Nickell had taken raw hamburger meat out of the refrigerator and gently inserted handfuls of it under the various cushions of couches and chairs, where it would stay undiscovered for weeks, putrid and rotting.

"Don't you let them disrespect our house," I said. "You tell them I'm coming home and if they aren't gone, I am going to kick someone's ass. Starting with yours."

I slammed down the phone, jumped in the car, and drove to Coral Springs with the needle on my speedometer pegged at eighty, swerving my Mustang in and out of traffic like an ambulance driver. When I got there about twenty minutes later, the toilet was broken, as were a few of my mom's good glasses, but the house was still standing. It was also completely empty except for my brother and some of his good friends. Jeff swears that after he hung up the phone, he turned off the music and made this announcement:

"My brother Mark is coming home in a few minutes. He says you all need to get the fuck out. You can either leave now or deal when him when he gets here."

They chose to leave. I still had that kind of reputation at Douglas.

I ended up being the designated driver that night for a few of Jeff's friends, making sure that everyone got home safely. Jeff was pissed that I had ruined his party, but I didn't care. I wasn't about to let my baby brother get drunk and do some stupid shit that he would later regret.

chapterthree

fade to black

F au was scheduled to play its first match of the season on
Sunday, September 5, at home against the University of Central Florida. Before the game, Donev called a team meeting to
give us the starting lineup and hand out the dark blue and white
jerseys, socks, and shorts. The atmosphere in the locker room was
electric, and no one could wait to suit up and step on the pitch.
We wanted to know if the long days of practice and training were
going to pay off or if we would be overmatched and outclassed in
our new division.

Donev and the assistant coaches had laid our kits neatly on the
floor, and we picked jersey numbers. This was a bigger moment than
you might think. Most players become accustomed to having a certain
number on their back when they play and are very territorial about
certain digits. A strange number can make you feel hinky on the field.
It's almost like a superstition, and many players believe wearing a
foreign number can bring you bad luck.

I wanted number five, because that was the number I had so
much success with, both at Douglas and on my club team. I didn't
get it. The veterans selected their jerseys first, and Jeff Sharon
took number five. I was the last person in line and got stuck with
sixteen. The number held no sentimental significance for me, ex-

cept to remind me that I was a fucking rookie on this squad.

It's just a jersey, I told myself. *Don't worry about it.*

But that was only the first setback of the meeting. Donev had dia-grammed the field on a blackboard and began to announce positions. We would be running what's known as a 3-3-4, which means that there would be three strikers, three midfielders, and four defenders, with the goalkeeper behind them. It's a good lineup because it spaces out the field nicely and gives you an extra man on attack, so long as your midfielders are fit enough to run nonstop and successfully tran-sition the ball from back to front.

To give extra support in the middle, Donev said, drawing circles and arrows with his chalk, one forward would drop back and the center defender would step up, giving us essentially five men in the middle. Donev continued to explain in detail what he wanted from each position and then announced the starting eleven players. Sha-ron, who had been a starter for the past three years, would again be team captain and in charge of running the defense. My suitemate Chris Shafiei would be playing in the midfield.

Donev never called my name, which meant that I would be mak-ing my college soccer debut on the bench. Later, the trainer wrapped white athletic tape around my ankles as I sat on a table in the locker room. I felt hot faced and embarrassed.

This is bullshit, I thought to myself.

I had been playing soccer since I was five years old and had come to expect that I would be on the field when the first whistle blew. I had just busted my ass for an entire summer, and the reward for my efforts was a free trip to the bench.

When I walked to the field, I saw that more than three hundred spectators had packed the metal bleachers, including Igoe, who was already yelling obscenities at the opposing team from the stands. The fans started applauding and cheering loudly as we approached the pitch. It was a gorgeous day, eighty-seven degrees, with the high sun partly obscured by puffs of white clouds that were colored with the fall shade of rust around the edges. The warm breeze carried a slight smell of wood smoke, salt, and seaweed.

I stepped on the grass and my heart swelled with pride and felt like a clenched fist in my chest. My fingers and toes tingled with adrenaline and anticipation.

What's your problem? I asked myself. *Get your shit together. You have no reason to be angry or embarrassed. You need to get your head ready for this game. This is D I, the highest level in collegiate sports. You're suited up and you're going to get some playing time today. Who cares if you're starting or not? Just play your game.*

I took my own advice. As soon as I got my chance, I would prove that I belonged on the field.

After Sharon and the other cocaptain, a midfielder named Warren Metzer, led us through some stretches and warm-up runs, the announcers introduced each player, their position, and their hometown. Out in the center circle, the refs checked player cards and the bottoms of cleats and asked us to remove any earrings so they wouldn't get ripped out during the game.

In the minutes before the game started, we huddled around Donev. "Central Florida does not think that you belong in this division," Donev emphatically told the team, amping us up for the upcoming ninety minutes of battle. "They think that we are young, weak, and untested. They will take it to us early, hit us hard, and want to have their foot on our necks in the first half. We will not let them. You must not let them intimidate you. You must not let them score first." We placed our hands in a circle and yelled "FAU" in unison.

The center referee checked his watch and blew his whistle to start the game. Donev was right. Central Florida wanted to stomp us into submission right from the kickoff. We fought back, refusing to submit. There were midair collisions for 50/50 balls and high slide tackles that caught shins and knees instead of the ball. Jerseys were pulled from behind. Elbows were thrown. Shit was talked. The fouls stacked up as we held our ground. Both defenses acted like impenetrable walls in front of the goals, and scoring opportunities were few and far between. Most of the action was in the middle third of the field, which we controlled with the help of the shallow forward and center defender.

Then, in the twenty-seventh minute, we capitalized on their defensive lapse. Our left forward, Jason Rocke, juked his defender and dribbled the ball down the sideline. As he neared the goal line, he crossed the ball into the middle of the box, where Jeff Pollock was crashing the six-yard line. With a defender riding his back, Pollock pulled the floating ball out of the air with his right foot and slotted it in the corner just past the diving keeper's fingers.

The crowd exploded from the stands as we drew first blood. The team ran to Pollock and smothered him with hugs and high fives. Donev, sweaty and grinning, looked like a proud mother who had just given birth to a healthy baby after a long labor.

We continued to keep their offense in check for the next eighteen minutes. They took shots, but we gave up corner kicks instead of goals. At half time, we were still up 1–0. "Do not snatch defeat from the jaws of victory," Donev said as players chugged Gatorade and dumped ice water on their heads to cool off.

"Continue to shut them down in the back," he said. "If we can keep them from scoring, we will win this game."

This was easier said than done. The physical play intensified in the second half, as UCF grew desperate and dangerous, realizing they might lose their opener to the FAU underdogs. Minutes slowly ticked off the clock, and I started to feel anxious on the bench, watching the action and wondering if I was going to get into the game. Then in the sixty-second minute, a UCF player was ejected for intentionally fouling our forward Jason Rocke. Four minutes later, FAU captain Warren Metzer retaliated with a hard tackle and earned his own red card and a one-game suspension.

Both teams were now playing a man down, and fitness would be the deciding factor.

Donev peered down the bench. "Zupan," he said. "Get ready. You're going in."

I stood up and jogged in place to get the blood flowing as Donev signaled for a substitution. The lineman raised his flag, and during the next throw-in, the center ref allowed me to enter the game. I sprinted to my spot at marking back. *This is your shot,* I said to myself. *You may not get another one. Don't blow it.*

I didn't. For the final twenty minutes of the game, I played my guts out, hoping to impress Donev and work my way into the starting rotation. The man I was marking was more than a half step slower than me. I took advantage of him with my fresh legs, beating him to every loose ball and eliminating his options when he would receive a pass and try to turn toward the goal. I'd leap over him for headers and trap him against the sideline. I'd give him a little extra shove when the referee wasn't looking, to remind him who he was playing against. It wasn't like I was a dirty player trying to hurt someone. Sometimes in sports you have to play between the rules. It was just a way to beat him mentally.

"Don't even think about scoring," I told him. "I fucking own you."

At the ninetieth minute, the center referee signaled that time had expired. He blew his whistle and the crowd cheered loudly as if we had just won the Super Bowl. The final score was FAU 1, UCF 0. Our defense had done its job, locking down our final third and limiting UCF to a paltry three shots for the entire game and a big, fat goose egg in the goals-for column. Pollock had scored the only goal for us, but we had other opportunities, including a rocket launched by Shafiei from the top of the box that nearly found net.

By winning our first game against UCF, we had proved that we belonged in the Trans Atlantic conference and the first division. Afterward, we went to the soccer house and celebrated with a couple cases of cold beer.

"Gentlemen," Sharon said, holding his Budweiser high in the air, "to our first win and to a season that we will never forget."

"Cheers," we said loudly, toasting one another, smashing our cans together, and spilling beer all over the floor. "To a season we will never forget."

the following friday we played Mercer University from Macon, Georgia, at home. Because of his red card, Warren Metzer had to sit out the game. We felt lucky because usually when you receive a red for a violent foul, you're out for three to five games.

Considering my performance against University of Central Florida, Donev told me that I would be replacing Warren in the starting lineup. "Thanks, coach," I said, trying to keep a poker face, but in

truth, I was beyond ecstatic and forgot how embarrassed and upset I
had been at the beginning of the season opener.

Instead of playing marking back as I had in the previous game,
Donev had me playing a position that better matched my skills: roam-
ing defensive center halfback. My job was to mark Mercer's best goal
scorer, wear him like a tight, ugly shirt, and to render him useless as
an offensive option. I would also help distribute the ball through the
midfield to the strikers. I told Donev that I wouldn't let him down. Before the match, I put on my headphones and listened to Rage Against
the Machine's "Sleep Now in the Fire" on my Discman, blocking
out all distractions in the locker room and focusing on what I had
to accomplish that day. By the time the song reached its screaming
crescendo, I was pumped.

It was another beautiful day for a home game, sunny but not too
hot. As we took our spots on the field, I told myself that I wasn't
about to relinquish the position anytime soon. I was going to give
110 percent in this game and make sure that the man I was marking
went scoreless. I decided to stick him with a slide tackle as soon as
the whistle blew. I had learned that if you foul certain players hard
from the beginning of the match, they become timid and ineffectual,
scared to hold the ball for too long and find the right passing outlet or
shot. I wanted to intimidate this guy to see how he would respond.

The first time he received the ball, I hit him like a Mack truck and
force-fed him some turf. "Get up, bitch," I said, standing over him,
as the referee called me for a foul. I offered him my hand, which he
ignored. I grabbed him by the arm instead and roughly pulled him up
off the grass. "You're in for a long day," I told him.

Unfortunately, I was the one who was going to be in for a long day.
My intimidation strategy had worked and my man didn't want the
ball when I was around, but Mercer's other forwards weren't drinking what I had on tap. A scramble in our penalty box and a miscom-
munication with our fullbacks and our keeper led to Mercer's first
goal in the twenty-second minute. Later, their offense connected on
a rainbow cross from the left side of the field, and they put another
point on the scoreboard.

In the second half, Shafiei received a chip from our midfield in the seventy-second minute and ripped a shot through the keeper's hands, making the score 2–1. We were hoping to equalize, but Mercer put a tie out of our reach once and for all when one of their forwards broke away from our fullbacks and beat our keeper with a one-on-one in the box, with three minutes left in the game.

We ended up losing 3–1, a real disappointment because we out-shot them nine to five and had many quality looks at the goal but couldn't convert. Mercer was not a top-shelf team. Nevertheless, they had exposed our immaturity as a unit and our inability to come back from a deficit.

That night we went back to the soccer house to drown our sorrows. This time there were no speeches, no optimistic toasts to the rest of the season, just silent, steady drinking out on the patio and staring contests with our shoelaces and cracks in the cement.

We returned to the pitch that Sunday afternoon to play Georgia State, ready to redeem ourselves. Metzer returned to the starting rotation and I was back on the bench, but I didn't care. I had proved that I was good enough to start and was the first to sub in. That day, we put the hurt on Georgia State for the entire ninety minutes. Jason Rocke scored a gimme goal in the first thirteen minutes off an assist from Shafiei. After that, we opened up the floodgates. We ended up beating them 5–0, a blowout as far as soccer scores are concerned. Georgia State became so frustrated by the relentless drubbing that they started to foul us, and the ref pulled more plastic than Paris Hilton on a shopping spree, warning them with five yellow cards and ejecting two of their players with reds.

The season progressed and we hopped on the bus for our first away game, traveling to Jacksonville and beating them in overtime. We lost a close one to the University of South Florida in Tampa, one of the better teams in the conference. I didn't start the game but came in as a right midfielder and banged in my first goal of the season at the beginning of the second half, showing the team I was a versatile player who could make an impact on offense as well as defense. Later, I got my first assist when I hit Metzer with a floating cross from the right side and he headed the ball into the goal.

After that, I was officially in the starting lineup.

We continued to cross games off the schedule, traveling to Charleston Southern University in South Carolina three days later, and then on to the College of Charleston. Staying in hotels and eating in restaurants made me feel like a professional athlete. The fact was, I was a student as well, but I wasn't spending much time with my nose in books.

My professors would load me up with homework before I left for away games, and they'd work with me to reschedule exams that I was missing while I was on the road. I attended mandatory study hall and arranged for friends to take detailed notes during lectures that I later planned to copy, but I never really did. I had the best intentions to study during the long, boring hours on the bus as we traveled north through Georgia and to South Carolina. But after a while, someone would cut a loud, aggressive fart or shove smelly feet in your face, and the next thing you know, you're wrestling with a teammate, laughing hysterically as your textbooks are sliding around under the seats on the floor of the bus.

I became better friends with all my teammates on these trips, especially Sharon, but I can't say that my time away from campus did anything for my grade point average. We were only a month into school, and I worried that I was actually going to fail some of my classes. I had never received an F on anything in my life. At Douglas, I never had to study. It all came naturally to me. All I had to do was attend class once in a while and I somehow learned through osmosis. While I was able to fake it with calculus because I had taken it back in high school, English was killing me, even with the help of Cliffs-Notes.

When I got back to school, I was going to have to find a better balance between soccer and studying. And my relationship as well.

I would call Kati when I could from pay phones on the road. "Hey girl," I'd say. "How are you doing?"

"Fine," she'd say.

Her voice always sounded small and very far away.

by early october, the team was stuck in its first losing streak. Going back to South Carolina for another tournament, we got our asses handed to us in an ugly game against the University of Akron when the Ohio boys slapped us with a humiliating 7–1 loss.

A week later, we were down in Miami facing off against Florida International University, which was dominating our division. They destroyed us 4–1. We went back to Boca Raton and spent the next few days recovering and licking our wounds, resting our weary bodies and regrouping. So far this season we had registered four wins, five losses, and one tie, putting us in the bottom portion of our bracket.

Back at school, I tried to study, but I felt I had missed too much and would never be able to catch up. I would sit in the enormous classrooms, surrounded by hundreds of students, and listen to the steady drone of the professor. I found it impossible to stay interested, and my mind would wander or I would fall sleep in my seat. I would try to force myself to go to the library and study in the evenings after practice, but it was much easier to go to the Rat and blow off steam with a burger and pitchers of draft beer.

Igoe wasn't exactly the best influence. "Put your purse down and start drinking!" he'd say to me, showing up at the dorm with a half rack of beer on a random weeknight. I'd tell him I had too much work to do. "Tonight we drink," he'd say enthusiastically, handing me a bottle. "We'll study tomorrow." But of course we didn't. I'm not sure if he had been to class more than a handful of times since school started. I would try to beg off when he would invite me to midweek parties, but found that I didn't have the willpower to say no. I would end up shitfaced at the end of the night, puking my guts out in the wastebasket next to my bed or leaving a puddle of piss on the floor. Our plan to help each other succeed academically had failed miserably. Midterms were in a month, and I was going to have to ace my tests if I wanted to stay off academic probation.

On Wednesday, October 13, we had an evening game against Barry University, an exclusive Catholic private school. There was a long-standing rivalry between FAU and Barry that had basically become a class war. We saw them as the rich spoiled kids who thought they were too good to attend a public university. To them, we were the heathens, the poor victims of a sad social experiment known as public education.

We had a light practice that morning, and at the end of it, Donev told the team that we needed to step up our efforts and band together if we wanted to put an end to our two-game losing streak. "I can't do it for you," he said. "You need to figure out how to win as a team again." Barry was a smaller school than FAU, but had a decent athletic program. We all knew that we should beat Barry that evening, but no one wanted to jinx the game by saying it out loud. With five matches left in the season, there was no way we could win our division, but it was a point of pride to finish with at least a .500 record.

The night of the game, the stadium lights buzzed overhead, illuminating the grassy field with a garish white glow as the announcers read the starting lineups over the loudspeaker. The afternoon had been nice, hazy but breezy, with a dusky orange sun hanging low in the western sky. Then storm clouds moved in. It was getting dark earlier these days, and the rain started to pour down during the sour gray twilight.

When my name was called, I ran out to the center of the field and felt the droplets on my face as I looked into the stands. There was a small crowd in attendance, around sixty people, the numbers obviously limited by the shitty weather. My dad, who had left work early to come up from Coral Springs and watch me play, waved to me, as did Igoe, who was once again heckling the other team in a loud, abrasive voice.

Igoe had been drinking beer in our dorm since early afternoon, well before I left for the locker room to tape up my ankles. I hoped he could keep his shit together and not make a jackass of himself in front of my father. I felt like it was a special night because my dad had come to the match. He'd been watching me play different sports for as long as I could remember. When I was a kid, he'd usually take me for a burger or ice cream afterward, and we would take our time, deconstructing the game play by play. My dad knows a lot about sports, and his opinions on how I'd performed always mattered a great deal to me.

It wasn't much of a match. We overpowered Barry early on, with Sharon getting his first goal of the season in the twenty-third minute. Barry could barely string together two or three passes, and we pinned them against their goal with shot after shot. The field was slick from the constant rain, and the ball would skip across the muddy turf like a flat rock over water.

I was playing right halfback and spending more time on offense than defense. In the second half, I found myself at the top of the box when a cross came in from the left. It was one of those moments when time slows and you know that you're in the zone. The ball floated like a giant helium balloon, and the laces on my shoe were the size of a tennis racket. Raising my leg and swiveling my hips, I nailed a perfect side volley. The ball sailed off my foot and into the upper V of the goal where the crossbar and post connected.

This was highlight-reel material, a Sports Center clip, the goal of a lifetime. As the ball cascaded down the back of the net, I started to go ape shit with my teammates. Then I noticed that the sideline referee had his flag up. The center referee went over and conferred with him. He came back and pointed down to a spot in Barry's penalty box.

"No goal," he said. "Offsides." One of our forwards by the far post had been standing a step behind his defender. I was crushed when the referee said my goal didn't count. I needed my dad to see me succeed at this level. He didn't have the chance to play sports as a kid and would tell his friends that he lived vicariously through me when I was on the field. After starting the season on the bench, I wanted to show him how far I had come in such a short period of time. I wanted him to be proud of me.

We continued to pound Barry, but I didn't get another shot like that. By the end of the game, we had scored three more goals, including one from a penalty kick. After losing our composure for two games, we had regained our poise and confidence and played as a team again. The final score: 4–0.

"That's more like it, gentlemen!" Donev said after the game, slapping each of us on the back as we walked by to grab our bags and get out of the wet weather. "Good show."

I changed out of my cleats, gathered my gear, and went up into the stands to say what's up to my dad. I was still soaked and caked in mud.

"Glad you could make it," I said, shaking his hand. My dad wasn't big on hugging. Igoe walked over from where he was sitting and joined us. I thought that he reeked of stale beer, but he seemed relatively calm and sober.

"Glad to be here," my dad said. "You guys kicked the shit out of them. Four to nothing. Jesus Christ. That was a hell of a volley. Too bad it got called back. You were playing like a man out there. You weren't letting those older guys get the best of you."

I nodded and then had an idea.

"Hey, Dad," I said. "We're all going out for a beer in a little bit. You want to come and have a couple cold ones with us?"

He looked at his watch and shook his head.

"Can't," he said. "I have to get home to your mother and get some dinner and go to bed. I have an important meeting first thing tomorrow, and I can't stay out too late." He rolled his eyes. "Your mom would kill me."

I laughed and said, "Fine. More beer for us."

I gave him a nod good-bye. "Tell Mom and Jeff I'll see them soon."

"I will," he said. "Great game, son."

the team planned to pre-function at the soccer house for a few hours with the women's team and then go to Dirty Moe's for nickel beer night. I usually walked to the fields for the games, but because it was raining, I had driven my Mustang, and Igoe rode back with me to the dorm, where I showered, shaved, and changed my clothes.

I thought about getting some dinner, but I wasn't really hungry. It was close to eight, and they had stopped serving at the dining commons. I was tired and my legs were sore from running all night, but I was feeling good about the way I played, and I decided to dress up a bit for the evening, wearing some nice shorts, a blue Polo shirt, black Nunn Bush shoes, a braided leather belt, and a Guess? watch. I splashed on some Drakkar cologne and grinned at my reflection in the bathroom mirror. I made the devil's horns with my fingers and stuck out my tongue. My hair was finally growing back from when Sharon had shaved it down, and now I had about a half inch of dark peach fuzz. My short hair made me look a little older and a lot meaner, as did the new goatee sprouting from my chin.

Before we left, I checked to make sure that I had my ID and cash. I had only ten dollars in my wallet. I did the math in my head. The cover charge to get into Dirty Moe's would be five bucks. With the remaining five, I could buy literally 100 ten-ounce beers at a nickel apiece if I wanted to.

Clearly, it was going to be a long night.

We left the suite and walked downstairs to the lot where my Mustang was parked. Students were walking along the concrete paths, hurrying off to different destinations. Wednesday, also known as Hump day, was a huge party night at FAU, right behind Friday and Saturday. There would be dorm-room keggers and house parties, and the nearby bars and clubs would be filled to capacity.

"I'll drive," I said, walking up to my car.

"Outstanding," Igoe said

I popped the locks and Igoe climbed in on the passenger side. I sat down behind the wheel and then jumped back out of the car.

"Shit," I said, turning around and checking to see if I had a water stain on my butt. I had forgotten that I drove home from the game in my sopping uniform, and the cloth seat was still damp and muddy.

"I'm going to run back to the room and grab a towel to put over my seat so I don't fuck up my clothes," I told Igoe.

"Forget about it," he said, shutting the car door and pulling his keys out of his pocket. "My truck is right over there. I'll drive."

we drained a few beers at the soccer house before caravaning with Sharon and the rest of the guys to Dirty Moe's. The aptly named bar was located smack in the middle of a dingy strip mall about ten minutes away from campus, just outside the Boca Raton city limits, in an unincorporated part of West Palm Beach County that was mostly swampland, train tracks, warehouses, and industrial parks. Igoe was getting better at driving stick and managed to navigate the dark, winding side streets without stalling his truck once.

Entering the parking lot, Igoe slid his Isuzu into an empty space next to a light post. I got out and took a moment to peer up into the dark clouds that completely smothered the moon and stars. It was still drizzling as we walked across the glistening asphalt to the back of the line that had formed in front of the bar. A bouncer was checking IDs with a flashlight and fastening plastic bracelets around wrists to indicate if you were over eighteen or twenty-one years old. In truth, the bands were just a formality. They really didn't matter that much once you were inside. If you were underage, you couldn't order alcohol from the bartender or the cocktail waitress, but you could always get someone to order it for you. The management made its money by catering almost exclusively to a college crowd that was largely under twenty-one. If you wanted to get hammered at Dirty Moe's, no one was going to stop you.

As I handed the bouncer my Florida driver's license, the beers I had pounded at the soccer house hit my empty stomach, and I started to feel warm, loose, and pleasantly buzzed. The guy looked at the photo on the license, which was taken when I was a baby-faced sixteen-year-old.

He held it next to my face and then asked me when I was born.

"May 20, 1975," I said.

He gave me a scrutinizing look that lasted more than a few seconds.

"Five dollars," he said, finally. I handed him the ten-spot and he gave me the change, wrapped some plastic around my wrist, and waved me through the door.

"Hey, let me see that," Igoe said, screaming in my ear over the throbbing dance music as we entered the bar. He held his arm next to mine.

"Look," he said. "He gave you the wrong wristband. This means you're over twenty-one."

"No shit," I said. "This must be my lucky night."

We weaved through the hundreds of students who packed the place, which was darker than the moonless night outside, save for some rotating spotlights that swept across the walls and floors, highlighting random faces caught in mid-conversation.

Wednesdays at Moe's were off the hook, and it seemed like most of FAU was there. A long wooden bar divided the gymnasium-size room in half, with rows of booths on either side. We hung a left as soon as we could and grabbed an empty booth near the small stage, which gave us front-row seats to the bump-and-grind fest on the dance floor. A few of my teammates crowded in with us and marveled at my wristband.

"I'll order," I said, signaling the cocktail waitress. In return, my buddies without bracelets said they would pick up the tab. We started with twenty beers and five shots of a fruity drink called Sex on the Beach, which is made with peach schnapps, vodka, cranberry juice, orange juice, and pineapple juice. It tastes like jelly beans soaked in grain alcohol, and at Dirty Moc's they served it in plastic medicine cups instead of actual shot glasses.

The waitress returned with twenty-five drinks on a large oval tray. The order barely fit on our table, and it took her a full minute to un-load everything. Because I had the wristband, I got two shots instead of one, and came up with the bright idea of chasing the first shot with another shot, followed by an entire beer.

"One, two, three, drink!" we said in unison.

We pounded the cocktails, crushing the plastic cups in our fists when we were through. The shots had a slightly acidic taste that re-vealed the cheapness of the vodka. As I chugged my beer, my throat closed like a clogged drain, and liquid reversed up into my mouth and nose. I did my best to swallow it back down again, but some spilled down the front of my shirt.

I looked around to see if anyone had noticed and then took a few deep breaths. My belly rumbled intermittently like the aftershocks of a severe earthquake, and saliva flooded my mouth. I spit on the floor. Hot sweat glossed my forehead, and I wiped it away with a cocktail napkin. I had drunk enough in my life at this point to know that I needed to slow down and take it easy, or I'd pay the price. I was get-ting too loaded too fast and was probably going to puke before the night was over, but at that point, I was too drunk to care.

I was staring at the plastic cup full of beer on the table. The round surface was vibrating in sync with the bass in the loud dance music, and the amber liquid was rippling in small concen-tric circles against the sides of the cup. I became entranced by the small, foamy waves, lost in my booze-addled brain, isolated by my own oblivion.

"Maybe I should eat something," I said suddenly. The words fell clumsily out of my mouth like heavy oblong objects, and I realized that I was slurring almost incomprehensibly.

Somehow Igoe understood what I was saying and asked the waitress for a menu. Dirty Moe's specialty was raw oysters on the half shell, and he ordered a half dozen that came on a plate of crushed ice with various condiments. I eyed them suspiciously. I had never eaten oysters before. I picked one up and sniffed it, inhaling the pungent briny scent.

"You're supposed to eat these things?" I said, looking at what appeared to be a gray slimy mass of membrane and muscle. "They look fucking disgusting."

"It's an acquired taste," Igoe said, "like eating pussy." Using his tongue, he sucked the goo out of its shell. "Delicious," he said. "Eat it. It'll put some lead in your pencil."

I slathered the oyster with a thick coating of Tabasco sauce and horseradish before I knocked it back. One was plenty for me. Eating it felt like chewing a slice of the booger wall. I lost my appetite and drank another beer, hoping to settle my upset stomach.

By this time, the table was ready for another round, and we went with the same order as before—twenty more beers, five more shots. We knocked them back one after the other, urging each other to keep drinking at this furious pace, not because any of us really wanted to, but because that's what we thought we should do. We were in college and we were drinking recklessly at a college bar. At this point, I never thought to question convention.

Belly full of booze, Igoe was getting antsy sitting at a cramped table with a bunch of dudes. "Fuck this sausage party," he said. "We need some snatch over here." The transformation was complete; ugly cousin Igor was officially out and on the prowl.

Scanning the bar for females, he noticed two cute girls in tight T-shirts and miniskirts sitting at a booth behind us. They were holding hands and appeared lost in an intimate moment. "Ladies," he said, turning in his seat and hanging his hands over the back of the booth. "Excuse me. Ladies. Please, come have a cocktail with us."

They giggled and waved him off. "You're wasting your time," one of them said defiantly. "Get a clue. We're lesbians. We're not interested in you guys."

As if to reiterate their point, they engaged in a long, deep French kiss, their pierced tongues flopping around outside their parted lips like fish with silver hooks in their gills.

"Personally, I have no problem with your alternative lifestyle," Igoe said deliberately, as if he were teaching an English as a Second Language class full of space aliens. "We do not discriminate at this table. I wholeheartedly support what you ladies do in the bedroom. In fact, some of my favorite porn stars are lesbians."

No laughter from them. Not even a crooked half smile.

"Come on," he said imploringly. "You're at a bar. You obviously came here to drink and meet people or you would have stayed at home. Let us buy you a round."

It took a little more coaxing, but Igoe eventually convinced them to join us. As they were picking up their purses and moving to our table, Igoe hit me with an urgent high five.

"Fucking lesbians!" he whispered loudly, holding his fingers about an inch apart in front of my face. "I am this close to being balls deep in a threesome. I. FUCKING. LOVE. COLLEGE!"

They crowded into the booth and joined us for yet another shot of Sex on the Beach.

"You know," Igoe said, wrapping his arm around the shoulders of the nearest lesbian and giving me a conspiratorial nod and a wink, "Mark and I are very good at what we do. There is a strong possibility that if you decide to come back to our place and have hot, nasty sex with us, we might be able to un-gay you. Or at least make you bisexual."

I don't remember her response. The night became a vortex of high-decibel noise, a swirl of shadows, a slide show of out-of-focus images: Igoe dry-humping lesbians on the dance floor; the soccer team getting into a shoving match with some frat boys near the stage; pissing on the floor to the side of the urinal in the bathroom and laughing about my bad aim; shots of Goldschlager at the bar with me mumbling about my family's trip to the Virgin Islands.

After that, my brain officially disconnected from my body, and I zombie-walked out of the bar around midnight. I don't remember what I was thinking or where I was planning to go. I might have been contemplating a hike back to the soccer house, which was only about fifteen minutes away by foot. Maybe I was looking for a pay phone so I could call Kati, to tell her that I still loved her even though I knew we were drifting apart and it was killing me, or to a store to buy some food that wasn't anything like those raw oysters.

It doesn't really matter at this point. All I know is where I ended up: curled up in the fetal position, passed out in the back of Igoe's truck, the steady rain soaking my nice go-out clothes.

Too bad I was the only one who knew I was there.

"beat it, kid. we're closed. "

Igoe picked his heavy head up off the bar, rubbed his eyes, and looked around. The house lights were up, and the once-dark Dirty Moe's was now bright, cold, and quiet, like the frozen food aisle in an all-night supermarket. The cleaning crew was busy stacking chairs, picking up the plastic empties, and sweeping the sticky floors.

"Where am I?" Igoe mumbled to the bouncer who had roused him from his slumber. "When did I pass out? Where did everyone go?"

"Home," the bouncer replied sternly. "You have to go home. It's after two a.m."

Igoe poured himself off the stool and stumbled out of the bar. Standing by the front door, he surveyed the vast parking lot, trying to remember where he had parked his truck. It was next to the light post, right where he had left it five hours earlier.

Weaving as he walked, he crossed the lot, put his key in the lock, opened the door, and climbed into his truck. The windshield had fogged over with humidity from the rainy evening, and Igoe smeared a small circle on the glass with the palm of his hand. He rolled down both windows, cranked the ignition, and turned on the defroster for a while. He even opened the sliding window in the rear of the cab to let more air in. But he didn't see me, nestled against the wheel well, lying prone on the plastic bed liner, even though there was nothing else in the back of his truck.

Igoe took a few minutes to clear the cobwebs before he drove, sucking fresh air in through his nose and exhaling out of his mouth. He knew he was drunk—blind, stinking, stupid drunk—but the dorm was only two miles away down a few quiet, curving roads. No freeways to navigate. No busy boulevards to cross.

He had driven home drunk from parties before. All our friends, including me, had been intoxicated behind the wheel at one time or another, and so far, none of us had been busted. But our buddy Mike MacDonald, who had played football with us at Douglas, had lost his little brother to a drunk driver a few years ago, and then there was that accident our senior year when a bunch of kids were driving out to the Glades to party and crashed into a canal. Five of them drowned. So we were aware of the consequences.

Igoe was convinced that if he concentrated, kept a watchful eye on the speedometer and his hands at ten and two, he should be able to make it home without too much trouble. The dorm wasn't far. He pushed a cassette into the stereo and turned up the volume. He was playing *The Doors' Greatest Hits*, which I had recorded for him. The tape spooled and the atmospheric ride cymbal and drum intro from "Break on Through" pulsed through the speakers in his truck, followed by the fuzzy, slightly sinister guitar riff.

Pulling out of the parking lot, Igoe drove down the stretch of road fronting the strip mall and stopped at a traffic light, as the church organ kicked in and Jim Morrison's elegiac voice soared above the other sounds:

You know the day destroys the night
Night divides the day
Tried to run
Tried to hide
Break on through to the other side

Igoe sang along absentmindedly as the light changed from red to green. Even though he was relatively close to campus, he didn't know this area very well, and instead of turning left down a street that would have taken him back to FAU, he went right, deeper into the wilds of unincorporated West Palm. Soon, he was lost in the Bible-black swampland, driving in circles on lumpy asphalt, the cypress trees, palmettos, and waist-high saw grass on the sides of the road illuminated by his headlights.

He continued to sing, looking for any landmark that would point him home.

> We chased our pleasures here
> Dug our treasures there
> But you can still recall the time we cried
> Break on through to the other side
> Break on through to the other side

Igoe saw an on-ramp for I-95, the freeway that ran through Boca and down to Coral Springs. He knew that if he got on, he would know how to get back to campus. His speedometer crept up to sixty as he merged into streaming lights of the late-night traffic. Rain beat on the roof, and the tires made whooshing noises as they sprayed pools of water that had collected on the interstate.

It must have been absolutely arctic in the back of the truck, and the music was blasting from the open windows, but I was so blitzed, I never woke up.

Igoe rewound the tape so he could hear "Break on Through" again, playing the drums on his steering wheel. As he screwed with his stereo, the truck drifted across two lanes of traffic. Horns honked. If he had looked in his rearview mirror, he might have noticed the pair of headlights that had been tailing him for the past few minutes, keeping a close but safe distance.

> Made the scene
> Week to week
> Day to day

Hour to hour
The gate is straight
Deep and wide
Break on through to the other side

The freeway split into a series of arteries. As his windshield wipers moved back and forth like a metronome, Igoe glanced up at the large green signs over the interstate that listed miles and destinations. He realized that he had somehow missed the exit for campus. He was nearing Pompano Beach, where he had grown up as a kid. He decided to get off, circle back around, and then head north toward campus.

On the Cypress Creek Road exit a few seconds later, Igoe realized he was going too fast, about seventy-five miles per hour. He eased up on the accelerator, clutched, and downshifted into third gear as the slick pavement snaked around in a gentle curve. He misjudged the turn and took it too wide. The truck began to bounce over the uneven ground on the grassy shoulder to his left.

Igoe overcompensated by torquing the steering wheel in the opposite direction and slamming on the brakes. The truck's back end whipped around clockwise, and the centrifugal force pinned me against one side of the truck's bed as the wheels hydroplaned across the road and onto the right shoulder. In an instant, the world shifted on its axis as Igoe's front bumper barely missed the square concrete base of a large light structure and then slammed sideways into a sturdy-looking fence. The momentum catapulted me out of the back. My rag-doll body, still unconscious, flew through the air, first sailing over the six-foot fence, then barreling through a dense thicket of trees and shrubs like a cannonball, laying waste to limbs and branches. I splashed down headfirst into a wide drainage canal, which was littered with partially submerged pieces of craggy broken concrete and other algae-covered debris.

Fireworks—big, beautiful sparking skyrockets in the most magnificent shades of orange, red, blue, green—exploded behind my eyes as I hit the frigid water, and I regained consciousness for a brief moment. I was surrounded by complete blackness, and I had no idea where I was. My thoughts were confused and cloudy. Choking on a lungful of brackish water, I looked down at my legs, which were lying on a slab of rock. They were twisted back and around at an odd angle. The toe of one of my shoes was sticking out of the water.

I felt frightened and nauseous, but no pins and needles of sharp pain; no dull ache from the trauma of bruises or broken bones.

Nothing.

No feeling at all, except for fear.

This is really bad, I said to myself, panicking. I tried to stand up or swim, but my legs wouldn't move. My body was like a big house with a blown fuse. Some parts of me were full of juice, pumping electricity, others weren't. I kept flipping switches in my mind, telling different parts of my lower body—feet, toes, legs—to move, but nothing happened. *This is really fucking bad.* My head momentarily dipped beneath the surface, and I thrashed around until I managed to hook my arm over a low-hanging branch to keep my nose and mouth above water. Blood beat loudly in my ears and I tried to scream for help, but for some reason, my voice wouldn't work, and all I could make was a small, scratching noise.

"Help," I rasped, my mouth filling with water. "Help me!"

Back in the truck, Igoe was checking his head in the mirror to make sure he wasn't bleeding. He wasn't. He had been wearing his seat belt, and it took him a few moments to unhook it because his hands were shaking so badly. He slowly climbed out of the cab and surveyed the damage. At first, he didn't think the accident had been too traumatic. But then he saw the truck's front end, which looked like an accordion with steam hissing from the twisted, dented metal. Igoe reached back in, twisted the key, and turned the truck off so Jim Morrison would shut the fuck up. He tried to collect himself.

A car pulled off the highway and onto the shoulder of the road. Igoe shielded his eyes from the glare of the headlights and saw a shadow get out of the vehicle.

"Hey, buddy," a man's voice said. "You all right?"

"Yeah," Igoe said, still trembling. "I think so."

"Is there anyone else in the vehicle that needs medical assistance?"

"No, I was the only one in the truck," Igoe said, looking around nervously. "But I need to get out of here. If I don't leave soon, I'm probably going to get a DUI."

The man was backlit by his headlights. He moved out of the glare and approached Igoe. "Actually," he said, "you're not going anywhere. I am an off-duty police officer."

He flashed his badge and identification.

"I've been following you for a couple of miles," he continued. "You were swerving all over the freeway. I've already alerted the Broward County Sheriff's office about a possible intoxicated driver and the accident. They should be here any minute."

"You've got to cut me a break," Igoe said, licking his lips. "Nobody saw any of this. It was just an accident. No harm, no foul. Just let me go. I promise, I'll walk home."

"Let him go," an unconcerned female voice said from the car. It was apparently the cop's girlfriend. "It's okay," she said. "The kid's scared. Just give him a warning. He learned his lesson. He won't do it again."

The cop seemed to mull it over in his mind.

"Can't," he said, almost regretfully. "I already called it in."

It wasn't long before the Broward County Sheriff arrived, the red and blue gumballs flashing on top of his cruiser. Fear had made Igoe more lucid, but he knew he wouldn't be passing the field sobriety test anytime soon. There was no way he could walk the line, recite the alphabet backward, or close his eyes, balance on one foot, and touch his nose with either index finger. And the way he was drinking earlier, he knew he'd blow pure ethanol into the Breathalyzer.

"Who are we kidding here, officer?" Igoe said wearily, holding his wrists up in front of him. "I can't pass any of your tests. You caught me. Now take me to jail."

By this time, a tow truck driver had pulled up and was hooking chains to the Isuzu's undercarriage and preparing to load the wrecked truck onto a metal sled.

"Quiet!" the driver suddenly said, cocking his head sideways like a hunting dog. It was difficult to hear anything above the din from the freeway. For a moment, no one said anything. The driver stood up and walked over to the fence, peering into the dark wooded area.

"Hey, officer," he said, walking back, his steps crunching in the gravel on the side of the road, worry and curiosity registering in his voice. "I swear I heard something over there. It sounded just like a kid whimpering. It was coming from just beyond those bushes there."

He pointed a gloved finger toward the canal.

"It's probably just a raccoon," the officer said, handcuffing Igoe and easing him into the backseat of his vehicle. "There's no one else out here tonight."

They climbed into their cars and left. Thirty feet away, my broken body slowly started to sink below the greasy black water.

pay for what you get

No matter what you do, you can't escape your past.

What you should know about me is that I was born from a great love story. Both my parents are from Cleveland, Ohio. My dad, Tom, comes from a Slovenian family, and went to a strict Catholic school where the priests wanted the students to spend all their time praying and studying and thought that sports were a complete waste of time. To help his family make ends meet, he worked after school at a grocery store called Kroger.

During his senior year, he met my mom, Linda, who is 100 percent pure Italian, at a high school party. She was dating a guy named Jack who had recently joined the military. This was during Vietnam, and a lot of guys in Ohio were signing up for the armed forces or being drafted. Because Jack was away at boot camp, my mom didn't have a date for her prom, which was coming up in a week or two.

"Well, you know, shit, Linda, I'll go to the prom with you," my dad nervously said to her when he learned she was dateless (as you can see, my pops has got a real way with words).

"That would be wonderful, Tom," my mom said.

And then she never called him.

A few weeks later my dad was back at Kroger, stocking shelves, talking to his buddy Dale Lasco, who also worked there.

"What did you do last weekend?" my dad asked.

"Went to the prom at Beaumont," Dale said.

"With who?" my dad said.

"Linda Rainone," he said.

"Get the fuck out of here!" my dad said. "I was supposed to take her to the prom."

After that, he made it his mission in life to win my mom's heart.

They went on their first date a few weeks later, and fell in love that summer while watching fireflies flicker during the warm, still nights. Autumn came quickly and my mom was going away to school at the University of Detroit, while my dad was set to attend Xavier in Cincinnati. They wanted to keep dating, but thought that the long distance would be the end of their relationship. My father didn't have enough spare cash to buy a bus ticket to visit her up in Michigan, but he hung in there. In the winter months, he would hitchhike up I–75 to Motor City, sometimes standing on the shoulder of the road for hours, shivering in the snow with his thumb out, just to spend the weekend with my mom.

They hit some rough patches and broke up a few times, but they always worked out their problems and got back together. During his junior year at Xavier, my dad ran out of money and had to drop out and get a full-time job. Later, my mom decided to come back to Cleveland. Through a family friend, she helped my dad get a spot unloading boxes at a company called Fisher Foods, and they've been together ever since.

As I was growing up, my parents' commitment to each other made me feel safe and secure. It was always clear to me how much they loved each other and our family. It was often a noisy, combative kind of love, one that might have sounded like arguing or bickering to an outsider, but that was how my family has always communicated: by expressing opinions and speaking their minds—loudly. Neither Jeff nor I are afraid of conflict or standing up and fighting for what we believe in, and that comes from my parents. They were always supportive of our decisions, and I knew I could count on them no matter what.

I was born a few years after they were married and feel like I got the best from both of them; my mom's sharp mind and tongue and my father's steel will and inability to take shit from anyone. My mom will tell you that I showed my independence from an early age. When I was two years old, we were still living in Cleveland, across the street from my dad's parents. At six-thirty one winter morning, our next-door neighbor called.

"Linda, do you know where Mark is?" she asked.

"Sleeping, I'm sure," my mom said, irritated that this woman was calling so early in the morning.

"He is," the neighbor answered curtly. "But not in his bed. He's at my house."

I apparently had woken up at three a.m. and gotten a bit of wanderlust. I let myself out the front door in my pajamas and bare feet without waking up our black lab that slept in the hall downstairs. I walked out into the snow and did some exploring around our front yard. Eventually, I started to freeze my ass off. Instead of returning home when I got cold, I went down the driveway to our neighbor's house and rang her side doorbell.

My dad's favorite story from this time in my life is how we used to go "swimming" together. My dad is a stout man, well over two hundred pounds, and he used to have this wispy mustache that he would jokingly say made him look like a Puerto Rican drug dealer. He would come home from work at the warehouse and we would play in the TV room. I would lie flat with my stomach against the floor and he would climb on my back, putting all his body weight on me, and we would pretend that we were doing the breaststroke by spreading our arms out in front of us and kicking our legs. My dad would ask if he was hurting me, but I would just giggle and tell him to keep swimming. He couldn't believe how strong I was or how much weight I could carry on my back.

"Linda," he would say, "you've got to come and check this out!"

"Tom," she'd say, "you're going to crush him. Please, get off the baby."

When I was four years old, my dad got a job managing a frozen food warehouse in Buffalo, New York, and the family packed up, leaving their extended families in the Midwest and moved to the Northeast. My parents didn't know anyone in town and wanted me to meet some kids my own age and make new friends. Soccer was big in Buffalo, so they signed me up for a team in the local recreational league.

I immediately took to the sport. While most kids would play what my mom called "swarm ball" at that age, I would stay in my position instead of chasing the ball around the pitch with the rest of the herd, putting myself in the best place possible to score goals.

"You've always had a very analytical and strategic mind," my mom says. "You could get the big picture of the game before any of the other kids."

Believe it or not, I was a little pudgy at this age and couldn't run as fast as some of the other boys, so I learned to anticipate the ball as a way to beat them. It was just pure logic to me: if you could figure out where the ball was going to be, you wouldn't always have to sprint to get there. It was weird. I can remember envisioning the field as a grid, and seeing how the different players should simultaneously slide in and out of different squares.

"Sports are all about angles," I once told my dad when he was driving me home from one of my games. "If you want to win, all you have to do is figure out the angles."

When I was six years old, I was invited to try out for a competitive soccer team called the Harriers, part of the Amherst Soccer Association. As I learned, there are some big differences between recreational soccer and competitive soccer. Recreational soccer is played for just a few months in the fall. Competitive ball runs year-round, and you travel on weekends to play in tournaments in other towns and states a couple times each month. In recreational soccer, everyone, regardless of their skill level, gets to play at least half the game. On the Harriers, there would be no guarantees. Even if you made the roster, you weren't promised any playing time. It was a merciless meritocracy, and it was pretty intense and demanding for a kid who had just started the second grade. My parents thought it would be a good way for me to channel my endless energy and competitive drive. They were right.

My coaches on the Harriers were two men named Steve Wu and Bill Smith. They taught me the fundamentals of the game, how to pass with your instep, how to shoot accurately with the laces of your shoe instead of punting with your toe, how to head the ball, how to trap it with your feet or chest, how to make off-the-ball runs, how to stay between your man and the goal on defense and channel him to his off foot when he dribbles at you by shifting your stance.

Like I said, it's all about playing the angles.

Even though we were little kids, the Harriers were a talented squad and we worked hard, practicing three times a week, two hours each night, with games on the weekends. The coaches would make us run laps and do push-ups when we would lose concentration or behave badly, deaf to our complaints that we were tired or bored. This was where I first learned about dedication and discipline. I may not have realized it at the time, but I was beginning to see that winning was equal parts talent and hard work, and I started to understand the sacrifice and commitment that it takes to be a champion.

A few years later, the Harriers won the New York State Cup for the U-10 division, beating a team called Vestal 3–1 in the finals. The state cup is a multimonth single elimination tournament, and winning it is a huge honor. A local paper wrote about our team and our success, singling me out for my "ball handling and accurate passing."

In 1985, when I was ten years old, my dad got another job offer and we moved again, this time to Eden Prairie, Minnesota. I didn't want to leave my friends, my teammates, and the town that had basically been my home for what seemed like my whole life. I remember being really upset when I first received the news. I protested by throwing a rare temper tantrum, punching the air with my fists, and screaming that life was unfair.

My mom did her best to comfort me. "Daddy has a new gig so let's go," she said in her typical blunt but loving manner. I cried, which was unusual for me, because I didn't even shed a tear when Jeff once accidentally split my head wide open with a garden hoe. My mom hugged away my unhappiness and told me that everything would be okay.

She was right. I liked Minnesota, quickly joining another traveling soccer team. We flew across the Atlantic to play an international tournament in West Birmingham, England. Visiting a foreign country and playing soccer there was pure heaven to me, and I remember being enthralled by the cultural differences: the odd-sounding accents, the stuffy TV shows, the strange food covered in brown gravy. In England, they called the field a "pitch" and your cleats were called "boots." If you missed a ball, they said, "Unlucky, mate." I was fascinated.

West Birmingham seemed so far away from Eden Prairie, another planet in a whole separate solar system. But we both loved the same game, and somehow that made the world feel smaller. I was also introduced to the European "football" fanaticism and witnessed the popularity and cultural importance of soccer to people outside the United States. Our team held our own against the Brits, and by the end of the tournament, my future was set in my mind: I was going to be a professional athlete, traveling to foreign countries and playing in packed stadiums around the globe.

After the tournament my dad took us to Scotland so he could shoot a round of golf at St. Andrews. My dad is a golf fanatic and keeps a videotape of Jack Nicklaus winning the Masters in 1986 that he watches at least twice a year while sipping a tumbler of Dewar's. It was too expensive for both of us to play (around $250 for a single round), so I was his caddie on the immaculate green grounds. When he lined up at the first fairway, his hands were trembling so much that he couldn't hold his club. He had to settle his nerves before he could tee off.

"This is like church," he whispered to me. "You have to show your respect." He hit the ball and I watched it sail into the early-morning mist, feeling like a choirboy among cardinals.

In Eden Prairie, I expanded my interests, playing organized basketball and football for the first time. I also started skateboarding, and became obsessed with a then-young skater named Tony Hawk, who rode for a company called Powell-Peralta. I got my first job delivering newspapers at 5:30 a.m., pulling a yellow cart through the dark, snow-covered streets, wrapped up in about fourteen parkas and scarves to combat the cold.

Around that time, I was really getting into music, mostly popular bands that I saw on MTV. I used the money I made delivering papers to start my CD collection, which is now in the thousands. The first album I bought for myself was Van Halen's *1984*, which was the last one with Diamond Dave. The keyboard riff in "Jump" made my hair stand up. And Eddie's guitar solo in "Hot for Teacher" was fucking amazing.

The second album I bought was Tears for Fears' *Songs from the Big Chair*.

Give me a break. I was eleven years old. And I still think that "Shout" rocks.

Then, in the summer before eighth grade, we moved again, this time to Fort Wayne, Indiana. I arrived too late in the summer to join any sports teams, so I spent hours alone, hitting tennis balls against our garage door with an old wooden racket because I wanted to be like Andre Agassi, who I had seen hammering his opponents on TV. I told my mom I wanted to grow my hair like his: long and scraggly in the back, short up top. Back in the day, we called that rebellious hairstyle "cool." Now, it's known as the mullet.

In Fort Wayne, I played basketball, because that's all anyone does in Indiana, and also football. The varsity football team from the local high school asked me to kick field goals for them even though I was only in the eighth grade. Then six months later, the movers were back, loading boxes into a truck. This time off to a place called Pewaukee, Wisconsin, a suburb of Milwaukee. My dad has never really explained why he changed jobs so often; only that managing warehouses can be an itinerant business, especially if you are trying to climb the corporate ladder and earn more money for your family. You have to follow the opportunities.

Running a warehouse is a stressful, thankless job, and my dad worked really hard, leaving early in the mornings and coming home exhausted late at night. He had made the move from blue to white collar. He was upper management now, overseeing the guys with the forklifts from his office with the other suits upstairs. But my dad never lost touch with the regular guys on the floor, and that was why he was so good at his job. Now that I am an adult, I can fully appreciate everything he did to provide for us.

But moving around took its toll on Jeff and me. I started to have a tough time sleeping at night, and I can remember the tight knots I would get in my stomach on the first day at a new school. "Kids, meet Mark Zupan," the teacher would say, calling me up to the front of the class. I would never know what to do or how to act, so I would stare at the ground and wring my hands behind my back so they couldn't see. I felt like the constant outsider, my face pressed against the glass, looking in at a world that I didn't quite understand. My way of dealing with my new surroundings was to become quiet, distanced, and removed. It took me a long time to open up and trust people. It still does.

I always dreaded lunch on that first day because I wouldn't have anyone to sit with, except for Jeff. Changing schools so often brought us closer together, and we learned to rely on each other, even though we would constantly fight at home. We were very competitive with each other from an early age. Jeff idolized me and always wanted to follow me around, which drove me nuts, but also made me feel very protective of him.

At recess, the kids would select teams for baseball or basketball or football. I would always get picked last on the first day. They would ask me if I was any good, but I wouldn't say anything, preferring to keep to myself until the game began. But as soon as I had the ball in my hands, the knots in my stomach would untie themselves, and I knew exactly what to do. The rules were in black and white, and the variables were all easily controlled. Touchdowns counted for seven points (after the extra point). After three strikes, you're out. There were no double dribbles. You couldn't use your hands in soccer unless you were playing goalie or throwing the ball in. Any anxiety I was feeling would disappear once I was on the field playing sports. The next day, I would be one of the first kids picked, and that made me feel pretty good.

I always made new friends quickly because of athletics. Sports were my coping mechanism, my constant companion, my secret security blanket, my guidebook to all social interaction. When we moved, I would flip through the channels, looking for familiar faces on TV. Walter Payton was still there, dancing through defenders and finding a reason to celebrate in the end zone, and Michael Jordan was still floating through the air, tongue out, dunking over opponents.

My home address and teammates may have changed over the years, but sports were always there for me, making me feel appreciated and accepted.

When we moved to Pewaukee, I joined the basketball team and became buddies with an ox of a kid named Bernard Louis Domecki III, but we called him "Bean." He was probably a foot and a half taller than me, outweighed me by at least a hundred pounds, and wore his dark brown hair in a crew cut. We looked about as antithetical as two young men could. Bean's parents were grooming him to play college football, and the kid ate like a truck driver with a tapeworm. He got me into lifting weights, but was so goddamn big that when we first started, I had to struggle to put up even half what he could lift. But he showed me where to place my hands on the bar, how to balance the weight evenly, how to breathe, and after a few months of hanging out with him, I could bench more than my body weight.

The first time I ever got drunk was with Bean. He had a college-age sister who I thought was superfine. One night she had a party and her friends introduced Bean and me to a drinking game called quarters. We thought we were hot shit because we could bounce the quarter off the table and into the cup on a regular basis. We started with beer and then moved on to straight shots of Seagram's Seven. We wanted to show the older kids that we could handle our liquor. We couldn't. The next morning I woke up with puke in my mullet while Bean's dad was calling us from downstairs, letting us know he had made omelets for us. He laughed at us from behind his newspaper as we struggled to swallow even a forkful of the fluffy eggs.

Bean and I started high school together at Pewaukee High in 1989, the same year that the Red Hot Chili Peppers released their *Mother's Milk* album. I liked the ninth grade because everyone in my class was new and I wasn't the only outsider. Plus, I already had someone to eat lunch with. Bean wanted me to try out for varsity football with him, but both football and soccer were at the same time in the fall. I decided to play soccer, and made the varsity squad, which was highly unusual for a freshman and increased my status at school, as did my beautiful blond mullet, which was in full bloom.

My dad used to bust our chops when we would hang out at my house and call us the BMOC, or Big Men on Campus. And we were, to a certain extent, but that was only because Pewaukee was such a small town, the kind of place where everyone seems to know everyone else's business, and sadly, none of that business is even remotely interesting.

There was nothing to do in Pewaukee except play sports, cruise, and hang out in the Burger King parking lot on Friday nights, trying to convince girls to give us their phone numbers. Bean and I were kicking it there with some friends during Homecoming weekend when an egg came flying through the air and splattered against my buddy's windshield. Tires screeched from the street, and the kids who threw the eggs shouted some stupid bullshit at us. It was like the Pewaukee equivalent of a drive-by shooting, and being the ninth-grade BMOC that we were, we weren't about to be disrespected like that.

"Let's get these motherfuckers," Bean said.

Five of us crammed into my friend's tiny Ford Escort hatchback, probably looking like the clown act at the circus. When Bean climbed in, the bottom of the car sagged an extra couple of inches and the undercarriage scraped as we exited the parking lot. We immediately drove to the only supermarket in Pewaukee and bought several cartons of eggs. We spent the next few hours tearing around the quiet, tree-lined streets, looking for the guys who had dissed us. We eventually found them in their Ford Bronco back by the Burger King and pelted their vehicle. They hit us back and started to chase our yolk-covered car all around town, flying around corners and flooring it dangerously down the boulevards. Someone splattered an egg on a black Trans Am, and it started to follow us at high speed as well.

After a while, we heard the wail of the police siren. The other two cars quickly veered off in different directions, but the cop stayed on our tail and we knew we were screwed. He took all five of us downtown to jail, where he called our parents. The only ray of light on that awful evening was that he got my mom on the phone instead of my father, who was sleeping. They gave her the details about why I had been detained and then told her that she needed to come down to the station so I could be released into her custody.

"I'm not coming to pick him up," she told the police. "He can stay in jail tonight or you can bring him here."

They brought me home in the back of the cop car.

"You really made some interesting choices tonight," my mom said sternly as we sat in the kitchen.

"I know," I said. To be totally honest, I was a little freaked out. I wasn't the kind of kid who got into trouble very often. I mean, I had to stay after school a few times for talking back to teachers and had certainly been on punishment at home for kicking the crap out of Jeff and staying out too late, but I sure had never been in trouble with the law before.

"You know also that you are going to be grounded for a very long time," she said, giving me that tired look of supreme disappointment that mothers tend to give their wayward sons after they get arrested. "A very, very, very long time."

"Yes," I said, not wanting to hear what my father would have to say about my interesting choices. Let's just say he wasn't amused.

I thought that would be the end of it, but later, each one of us received a fine of several hundred dollars for disturbing the peace and destruction of private property.

"What are you going to do?" my mom asked, holding the letter from the police in her hand. "How do you plan on paying these fines?"

"I don't know," I said. I wasn't about to ask my parents for help.

"You made the mistake," she said. "You have to figure out how you are going to deal with this on your own." She gave me an impersonal pat on the back. "You'll be able to handle it. I have confidence in you."

As a parent, my mom was strict but understanding. When I was younger, she would smack me on the ass with wooden spoons and metal spatulas when I did wrong. When that didn't get my attention, she brought out the rolling pin. "Ouch" is all I would say. My parents learned that I had a high threshold for pain and thankfully changed their parenting techniques.

By the time I was a teenager, my mom rarely reacted in anger when I got in trouble. Instead, she chose to communicate. She would listen to my side of the story and even be empathetic to my plight.

However, if I screwed up and knowingly chose wrong over right or acted ignobly, she would calmly make sure that I was aware of what I had done and that I was accountable for my actions and understood all the consequences.

In my family, there was no taking the easy way out. You lived up to your obligations.

"I'll take care of it myself," I said to my mom.

I had to get some money to pay the fine, and that meant finding a job. They happened to be hiring at a nice family-owned restaurant that my parents frequented called Jake's. I went in and filled out an application and talked to one of the managers. He said that if I wanted to work on the floor in front of the customers and bus tables, I would have to chop off my mullet, which now draped down to my shoulders.

"No way," I said, and took a lower-paying job washing dishes and prepping food.

Jake's specialized in onion rings—baskets and baskets of battered, fried onion rings—and each night, I would sit in front of a big pot in the kitchen and have to peel the yellowish brown paper off hundreds of pounds of onions. I could smell the onions on my hands the next day at school, or when I would sweat at soccer practice. The job sucked, but I never missed a day of work and I always showed up on time and did what I was told without any complaint. Three paychecks paid off the fines. And I still hate peeling onions to this day.

After the egging fiasco, the rest of the year was pretty uneventful. Later that spring, my dad and I were alone in the car, driving to a soccer tournament in Denver, Colorado.

"Guess what?" he said nervously. I knew what was coming. "I got another job opportunity. We're leaving Wisconsin and moving to a place called Coral Springs in south Florida. It's down south, near Fort Lauderdale."

I just shook my head.

"Forget it," I said. "I'm not going."

the next weekend, my parents flew us down to the Gold Coast so we could see where we were going to live. We got off the plane, rented a car, and drove up I-95 from Fort Lauderdale to Coral Springs. I stared blankly out the window at the coconut and palm trees, at the one-story houses with the screened-in porches, and at the sun that never stopped shining and looked like a giant rotting orange.

"This place blows," I mumbled.

We were staying in a hotel thirty minutes from Eagle Trace, and my dad wanted to take us out to look at a house that he might buy, but I refused to leave the room.

"I'm boycotting you," I told my dad. "This is total bullshit."

My mom was prepared for my resistance to the concept of moving yet again. She had already done some research on soccer teams in south Florida, and called ahead to introduce herself to the coach of an elite traveling team called the Boca Lions. She explained our situation and then told him about me and where I had played and asked if I could come practice with their team when we were in town.

Sure, he said, but told her that he had already selected the roster for the season.

A week later, they drove me up to Boca Raton, to a field near the Florida Atlantic University campus, where the team was practicing. I was grumpy and exhausted and didn't want to get out of the car. I couldn't believe that I had to be the new guy all over again. I was tired of this routine, tired of proving myself, tired of fighting my way into a circle of friends that had formed years ago when everyone else met in the first grade. I didn't want to put out the effort because there was a high probability that we'd be leaving again in a few months anyway.

"Just give it a try," my mom said gently.

I walked to the field, put on my shin guards and socks, and laced up my Adidas Copas. The kids in Florida looked different from the kids in Minnesota. They were a lot tanner, and from the way they touched the ball, I could tell they were more skilled. The coach's name was Steve Pete. Everyone called him "Grubby," I'm not sure why. The name didn't seem to inspire much confidence or respect. He took one look at me and called me "Hollywood." That was the nickname of a famous English striker who had similar long hair.

But the kids had another name for me.

"Nice mullet," one of them said. "What's your real name? Michael Bolton?"

His buddies sniggered. The coach pretended not to hear them.

That pissed me off. No one talked shit about my mullet.

Seriously, though, I flew into a blind rage after that. This kid had hit me in my soft spot, zeroing in on where I was the weakest. He had insulted my pride, and I wasn't going to take it lying down. I always play better when I think I've suffered some kind of personal injustice, making the game a battle between the rest of the world and me.

We set up for a half-field scrimmage. Usually during practice, you don't play as physically as you would during an actual game, but I didn't hold back at all, not one single bit. I realize now that I was venting all the aggression and insecurity I was feeling at the time on these poor suckers. I kept it clean and didn't cheap-shot anyone, but I was playing with an undeniable fury. I dumped dudes on their asses with slide tackles and banged them off the ball with my shoulder. If someone got in my way, I went through him. If those kids were going to kick me out of their little club, I was going to kick my way back in. I refused to back down an inch when they would step up and bump chests with me and try to talk shit.

"Shut your fucking mouth," I said as I shoved an opponent back on his heels, totally out of my mind. "If you don't, I guarantee you'll get punched right in your fucking head."

We played for more than an hour, and I don't think I stopped running once. By the end of the game, I had scored some goals and stopped even more. I had outplayed everyone on the field. My team had won, and the other guys weren't calling me "Hollywood" or "Michael Bolton" anymore. My new name was "Beast," because I played like an animal, and that was fine with me, as long as they said it with respect.

My parents, anxious to hear how I did, were watching me from the car as the coach and I walked back to the parking lot after practice.

"You played well today, Mark," the coach said.

"Thanks," I said.

"We weren't looking to add any more players to the roster," he said, "but you really impressed me today, especially with your defensive skills and your tenacity. We're going to Bremen, Germany, next month to play some friendlies and train with a professional team from the Bundes league. Are you interesting in coming along?"

I thought of how much fun I had in West Birmingham back when I was ten and playing on the Harriers.

"Count me in," I said, and suddenly, Florida didn't seem so bad.

I went to Bremen, which is located on the Weser River in northern Germany, and had a blast with the team both on and off the field. On the flight over, I made friends with a kid named Jason O'Brien, whom everyone called "J.O.B." We stayed up the entire flight while everyone else was sleeping, trying to flirt with the stewardesses, who thought we were cute. They gave us dozens of sodas to slam, letting us get totally zonked out on caffeine. We kicked all the cans under the seat in front of us, making a mess.

There was one coach, one assistant coach, and one dad on the trip to supervise an entire team of fifteen-year-old knuckleheads. We ran wild, chasing German girls and drinking all the beer we could get our hands on. The tournament reaffirmed my love for traveling and playing ball.

I started my sophomore year of high school that fall in Coral Springs. My school was called Marjory Stoneman Douglas, named after the famous environmentalist and author who was known as "the mother of the Everglades." Douglas had fought tirelessly for decades to protect the Florida wetlands and its wildlife from urban encroachment. Coral Springs was once a bedroom community that had grown and was morphing into an actual city, and Douglas High was the third high school built in town. It was brand-new the year I started. I always thought it was a little ironic that they drained swampland to build the school and then named it after a woman who tried to save the swamp from being drained, but hey, that just seems to be how they do business down in Florida.

Douglas was a big school, built to service around 3,000 students, and much more racially diverse than Pewaukee High. There were only three classes when I first arrived—freshmen, sophomores, and juniors—mostly transfers from the other two schools. No seniors that year. We totally sucked. We were a brand-new team, and the oldest guys on our squad were only juniors. However, by my junior year, we would end up making it to the district finals.

I met Steve Nelson playing that first year. The coach was new and relied heavily on the more experienced players to lead the team. Nelson will tell you the story about when we played this school called Boyd Anderson. The game was getting pretty heated, and I went up against this guy for a header. We both missed the ball entirely and our coconuts collided with a hollow knock. The other guy was out cold before he hit the ground, but I kept playing. I had a nice gash on my head but refused to come off the field for stitches. I wanted to set an example for my team.

One day Steve and I were hanging out in my garage after school with some friends from the soccer team when I decided that I was ready for a new haircut. I wanted to get the attention of this cute freshman named Kati Hanson, whom I had seen swimming laps in the pool. Some of the other guys had told me that she was a little standoffish and self-centered, but she seemed nice, smart, and sweet to me. I went to my room and got my poster of the Air Jordan symbol, which is a silhouette of Michael holding the ball high above his head in his left hand, about to dunk, with his legs spread wide apart. I loved Jordan, and the Chicago Bulls were my favorite basketball team. M.J. was totally indomitable at that time in his career.

"Hey, do you guys think you can copy this?" I said.

We traced a template and then I sat down in the chair. Clippers buzzed and hair flew as they carefully carved the emblem into my dome. My dad just shook his head in disgust when he saw me that night at dinner. He already hated the fact that Jeff and I had pierced our ears.

"What's next," he said. "Tattoos?"

The following day, everyone at Douglas was talking about my "fresh" hairstyle.

"What the hell did you do to yourself?" said this dark-haired kid who sat directly behind me. His name was Jeff Nickell, and he was built like a praying mantis—long, strong, and skinny. He played defensive end on the junior varsity football team. Even though he was a jock, he was also the smartest person in our algebra 2 class.

"Come on, man," I said, laughing. "Give me a break. It's Jordan."

Nickell introduced me to his best friend, a barrel-chested guy with a warm laugh, named Frank Cava, who had grown up around the block from Steve. They took me over to the stairs by the back parking lot, near the breezeway with the weight and locker rooms, where all the football players would kick it. Florida is second only to Texas when it comes to high school football, and at Douglas, the football players were definitely the cool kids. I was stoked to be around them.

"You should come out and play with us next season," Nickell said, after I told him that I had played football back in Minnesota and Indiana.

"With your speed, you'd probably make a pretty good running back," Cava said.

I was nodding my head in agreement when I heard: "Who's the fucking douche bag with Jordan shaved into his head?"

I turned around and saw this red-haired kid come down the stairs behind us, wearing a Nike sweatsuit, a baseball hat cocked sideways, and a fucking alarm clock around his neck.

"Hi," he said, grinning and extending his hand as if I had been waiting for years to make his acquaintance. "I'm Chris Igoe."

chapterfive

let me drown

I was floating, back in Buffalo, in the community pool that was in the center of our planned community. All the other kids from the neighborhood were there. My five-year-old body felt small and light as I splashed around in the water, and the rectangular pool looked so big and blue that it might as well have been the Atlantic Ocean.

From where I was, I could see my mom's shoes and legs. She was near the side of the pool, talking to another lady, who I recognized as someone else's mother. They were keeping an eye on us to make sure we were all getting along. A group of us were playing "Ring around the Rosie" in the shallow end, and I was holding hands with two older girls, one on either side of me. They both had wheat-colored hair and crystal blue eyes. They were at least eight or nine years old, and a couple heads taller than me. I didn't know their names, and I liked them a lot but was shy about telling them how I felt.

I was too short to stand up on my own, even on my tippytoes. I had to bounce up and down, just to keep my ahead above the surface, which flared and rippled with hundreds of tiny rainbows in the late afternoon sun. I was excited to be included when we started the game, singing a nursery rhyme and slowly rotating in a counterclockwise circle:

Ring around the rosy
Pocket full of posies
Ashes, ashes,
We all fall down!

As we finished the song, we dropped underwater and sat down cross-legged on the tile bottom, still holding hands. We held our breath as the chlorine stung our eyes and made silly faces and pretended to talk, listening to our distorted voices as chains of bubbles streamed from our mouths. When everyone was out of air, we would shoot up through the water like a human geyser, laughing and gasping for breath.

I was so much younger than the other kids, it was difficult for me to hold my breath for as long as they could. We were down at the bottom of the pool and I needed to go up early for air, which embarrassed me. My lungs were burning as if they had been sprayed with sulfuric acid. But the girls refused to let go of my hands, making me their underwater captive. I yelled at them to stop it, but all I heard was an unsettling gurgle. I needed oxygen. My eyes felt like they were bulging out of my head, and my vision tunneled as if I were looking down into a dark drain.

I stared at their expressionless faces, pleading, wildly jerking my arms to get free, trying to tell them that I wasn't joking around, that I was drowning for real. They just giggled as the water became cloudy and cold. The other kids had disappeared some time ago, and now it was just the girls and me. I looked up at the surface, which was a pure white ceiling, and I knew my mom was up there waiting for me with a towel and a warm hug.

Then their innocent faces contorted and ballooned, becoming heavy, bulbous, and wide. Suddenly, they were the lesbian chicks from Dirty Moe's, with thick red lipstick caked to their cruel lips. Their hair drifted slowly in the water like seaweed, dancing and waving in the current. *Don't look at our fat ankles*, they said. They mashed their mouths together and tongue-kissed, and their noses grew into long snouts with jagged teeth. Scales appeared on their pretty painted faces, and they were alligators.

They nipped at my face with tiny love bites that pinched and were more annoying than they were painful. Since they wouldn't let go of me, I asked them to bite off my hands so I could swim to the surface. They promised to make it quick and painless. With two chomps, I was free, shooting upward through a dark canal and breaching the water, belly up, helpless as a newborn baby.

The dream was over and I was awake. I pulled as much oxygen as I could into my lungs, which for some reason wasn't much at all, and looked around, blinking in dazzling midmorning light. The water was at least a couple feet deep, and I was lying on a partially submerged piece of concrete with my limp arm making an upside-down *L* over a low tree branch. It was freezing. My teeth were chattering so much that I was chewing my tongue bloody and I was shivering uncontrollably.

I was in a mental fog, thinking half-complete thoughts. I had the primal recognition that I was severely injured, but there wasn't any specific pain to speak of, just some pricks of discomfort on my face and arm. As my eyes adjusted to the harsh light, I noticed that a line of red ants was parading down my elbow, across my neck, and up my chin. Every few seconds, they would bite my face, which felt like a match being extinguished on my flesh.

I tried to stand up and climb out of the canal, but my legs were totally disconnected from the rest of me, just logs of meat that I couldn't move. I could still sort of move my arms, but my right hand felt numb and the fingers seemed to be frozen, as if I were holding a grapefruit in the palm of my hand.

Where the fuck am I? I thought to myself. *What happened to me?* I tried to drag my legs through the water and onto the nearby muddy bank, but I couldn't bend at the waist. I was stuck. There was no way I could get out of the canal on my own. I needed help.

It's tough to explain the panic you feel when your body won't respond to your brain. It hits you in choking gasps, in strangled sobs, in a sodden haze of fear and disbelief, and I really couldn't process all of it at once. I was definitely in shock.

"Help," I screamed. It sounded like I was trying to yell in a whisper. No volume at all. I concentrated on making myself as loud as I could, thinking about what it would take to get some reverberation. Loud voices start in your belly with a large gulp of air, forced out through your mouth by contracting your diaphragm. I realized my breath was so shallow earlier because my stomach muscles weren't working correctly. I couldn't force the air out of my lungs to make any noise loud enough even to startle a bird from a tree. I tried again, but no luck.

I looked around, struggling to get my bearings. I was very close to the bank on one side of the canal, and to my right, I could see a thick screen of holly trees, vines, and shrubs. Beyond it, I assumed, was a freeway, because I could hear the steady drone of cars.

To my left, water extended for about fifty feet and then met a shoreline where green grass sloped upward, dotted with several neatly trimmed, evenly spaced trees and bushes. Behind the grass was a small private road that serviced a tall gleaming office building off in the distance. To the right of the building, and closer to me, was a square multistory open-air parking garage that looked empty.

The water was flowing, and the slow current was carrying sticks and other debris downstream, where the canal curved right and continued on its way. The morning was still and sultry, and the canal had the sweet, ripe stink of decaying vegetation. The air hummed electric with insects as if ten million bugs were telling me at once that it was going to be a humid day. There was no movement nearby at all, not on the service road, not in the parking garage, nothing at all except for the ants that were slowly trudging down my arm to my face.

I dove down into my memory, trying to figure out what the hell had happened to me, but I came up with only a fistful of vague recollections. I had played soccer in the evening. My dad was at the game. Then I went to Dirty Moe's with Igoe and the rest of the team, and I still had a plastic band around my wrist. But after that, I came up empty-handed.

After a while, my mind and twisted form went limp from the severe trauma and exhaustion, and I had to use everything I had just to keep my arm over the branch and my head above water. I scanned the other side of the canal for help, but it didn't seem like anyone ever used the service road or noticed the canal.

Even though I was only dimly aware of what was happening, I knew that death was a distinct possibility. I wish I could tell you that I had some deep, solemn thoughts about my mortality at this point, but I didn't. There were no epiphanies for me. No memories of my family or friends or unfinished business that would keep me tied to this world, no bright light at the end of the tunnel with warm, reassuring words from ancestors guiding me forward. I had only one question for myself: *How the hell are you going to get out of here?*

Survival is a very strong and selfish instinct, and while my cognitive functions were shorting out, my physical being wasn't ready to call it quits. When I realized that fight or flight wasn't an option, all the twitchy fear faded, and I felt a strange, distanced calm pass over me. Suddenly I was floating above myself, watching events unfold. It wasn't one of those near-death out-of-body experiences that make you feel like you're on your way to Heaven to be closer to God. I am not a person of that kind of faith. What I felt was much more simplistic, yet, for me, profound, because it was a kind of strength and spirit that, in retrospect, I never knew I had. I think I was aware that death was so close and inescapable that some primal part of me grabbed the reins, so all my consciousness could do was sit back and watch.

What ruled me in those hours was a deep animal need to survive, a desire that's been bred into our cells since the days that guys with spears made of sticks and rocks were running from saber-toothed tigers. It's a small, dusty corner in the attic of our genetic memory that you can access only when your body knows that it's literally do-or-die time. Once it takes over, it's an icy cold, almost peaceful determination that focuses every one of your physical resources on the basics: Air in. Air out. Keep arm over branch. Hold on.

The afternoon dissolved into nothingness. Clouds covered the sun, and silver rain started to fall, hitting me on my head and face. I slid in and out of consciousness and would awake with a start as soon as I choked on a mouthful of muddy water. I knew that if I passed out completely, my arm would eventually slip off the branch, and I would drown.

"Heeelp. Heeelp. Heeelp. Heeelp. Heeelp. Heeelp. Heeelp." I repeated the word over and over again, like I was chanting a mantra.

But there was no one around to hear me.

My eyes fluttered and finally closed as my head drooped, my nose and mouth inching closer to the water.

party's over

Igoe didn't like jail. After he was cuffed near his totaled truck on the side of I-95, the sheriff had driven him over to the parking lot of a nearby bowling alley where he could administer a sobriety test on level ground. As promised, Igoe failed it miserably and was taken back to the station house, where he blew a blood alcohol of .27, more than twice the legal limit. He was read his rights, booked, and then put into a holding cell with around ten other tough-looking guys. One of them was announcing belligerently that he had emptied a clip into a police officer, a woman, and her kid earlier that night. He quickly zeroed in on Igoe, who was the youngest guy there and doing his best not to look scared shitless.

"What did you do to get in here, white boy?" the shooter asked Igoe.

"Uh, the same type of stuff," Igoe mumbled.

Sometime in the middle of the night, as Igoe stretched out on a plastic bench and tried to sleep, a few cops came in and started to drag the self-proclaimed killer out of the cell. He resisted, kicking and cursing at them, so they beat him like a piñata with their nightsticks.

Freaked out by what was happening just a few feet away from him, Igoe turned his head toward the wall and closed his eyes as tightly as he could, pretending not to see a thing. But he could still hear the guy screaming in pain, begging them to stop.

The next day, he was still scared, not to mention hung over as hell and pissed that he had destroyed his brand-new truck. His mom came in the afternoon to post bail and pick him up. His dad was in the Virgin Islands on business and was flying home early to deal with the situation.

"How could you do this?" his mom asked him, hysterical with anger, as they walked to her car. "How could you have been so stupid?"

Igoe kept his mouth shut. He knew he was in serious trouble.

"Just wait until your father gets home," she said.

"heeelp. heeelp. heeelp. heeelp."

My voice was barely louder than a whisper. Since the last time I was conscious, my body had slid a few more inches into the water. I was too weak to pull myself up by the branch, and I had to tilt my head back just to breathe.

I couldn't see the other side of the bank anymore, but at some point a car had driven down the small service road and parked on the side. Martin Story worked at the office building. It was around one-thirty on a Thursday afternoon and he was grabbing a late lunch by himself. Story liked to eat in this quiet spot by the canal and watch the ducks float around. The sky was still pissing rain, so he had his windows rolled up as he munched his sandwich and listened to the radio.

He started to sweat from the humidity, and his car was all fogged up, so he cracked the windows to let in some fresh air.

That was when he heard a weird noise outside. At first, it sounded like a frog croaking, or a kitten meowing, but the tenor was too low. He strained his ears. There was something distinctly human about the sound. He got out of his car and walked down to the grassy area near the water. The bleating noise kept repeating itself, like an alarm clock with low batteries.

"Heeelp. Heeeelp. Heeeelp. Heeeelp."

Story scanned the shadows near the bank on the far side of the canal, guided more by sonar than sight. It was hard to see anything through the steady drizzle. But then a round, blurry object in the shallows grabbed his attention.

"Oh my God!" he said.

It looked like the crown of a human head peeking out of the murky water and an arm extended into the braches. Story walked over to the canal, trying to get a better look. There was definitely a body in the water. He raced back to the office building and called 911.

"There's a man in the canal and he's yelling for help," Story said. "I think he's hurt and he might be drowning. Hurry!"

Minutes later, a fire engine rumbled down the service road, and guys in thick tan and yellow coats and helmets crowded the bank. They called to me, but I was unconscious by that time. They didn't know the best way to get to me. The canal looked deep and muddy. They started to strip down so they could swim the distance, but they didn't know how they were going to get me back across safely, especially if I was injured.

They wanted to take the truck and drive it around to the freeway where they could cut through the fence and get to me from the other side. But they didn't know how long it would take them to find the right location, and they could see that I was sinking in the water. There wasn't much time left before I was completely submerged.

While they were discussing their options, a maintenance man from the office building walked up and pulled on a coat sleeve. "I've seen a guy fishing for bass here," he told the fireman. "I think I know where his boat is."

"Show me," said Lieutenant Jim Ferranti, whose engine answered the alarm.

They ran downstream to where a scraped and dented aluminum skiff was hidden in a patch of high weeds. The craft was full of rainwater, and it took the strength of several firemen to turn it on its side and dump it all out.

"Hold on!" one of them yelled to me. "We're coming!"

Once the boat was floating, the firemen realized that they didn't have any oars. One of them sprinted back to the truck and grabbed some flat shovels and rope, which he tied to the front of the boat. Ferranti and another firefighter named Paul Schultz then hopped in the skiff and slowly made their way upstream, using the shovels as paddles. When they reached me on the other side, all they could see was my mouth and nose above the surface. Ferranti would later tell my father that he could have set a small round saucer on my face and completely covered the entire area that was out of the water. I was extremely pale and obviously in shock.

They pulled the boat next to me in the shallow water and I came to in a fit, throwing my arm off the branch and grabbing the side of the boat with all my might. The force almost tipped them over, and they had to quickly counterbalance my weight.

"My legs are stuck," I rasped. "I can't get out."

"Don't move," they said. "We'll do all the work."

They had to partially sink the boat so they could slide me in instead of lifting me out of the water. They pulled me in as gently as they could, laying me down in the belly of the craft. One of the firemen held my head securely between the palms of his hands, doing his best to keep my neck and spine as straight as possible. The shock of the move made me pass out, but I woke up again as they paddled back to shore, while a group of firemen pulled the rope hand over hand to make the skiff move faster.

"Where am I?" I said, staring at the clouds. "How did I get here?"

"We don't know that," Ferranti said. "Were you riding a motorcycle? Did you crash? Were you swimming in the canal? Did you dive in and hurt yourself?"

"I don't know," I said, crying. "I can't feel my legs."

The firemen jumped into the water and dragged the boat up onto the shore.

"He says he can't feel his legs," Ferranti said.

The paramedics carefully lifted me out of the boat and placed me on a backboard, a long, thin plank with nylon straps that they drew across my body to keep me from moving. They fitted me with a tight neck collar. Then they covered my shivering body with blankets, and with a count of three to synchronize, they hoisted me up and into the ambulance waiting at the edge of the bank. I know they kept asking me questions, probably as much to assess my condition as to get information. But it was lost on me, their voices barely registering, like a radio that was on in another room of the house.

"What's your name?" asked one of the medics.

"Mark," I replied, my eyes rolling back into my head.

"Stay with us, Mark."

"My mom's phone number is 384-3586," I said, and after that, I was dead to the world. They took my vitals while the ambulance drove me to the North Broward Medical Center in Pompano Beach. At first, they couldn't find my pulse, no matter where they pressed their fingers. But then they located a ghostly thump, an almost non-existent thirty beats per minute. Under normal conditions, for an athlete like me, my resting pulse would have been around fifty-five.

I had been in the freezing water for fourteen hours. My body temperature was 88.8 degrees and I was hypothermic, too cold for my organs to do their work. My systems were completely shutting down.

"I don't know if he's going to make it," one paramedic said.

dr. jose nabut was the physician on duty when they wheeled me into the emergency room. Attendants cut off my clothes with scissors and Dr. Nabut did a quick examination and wrote in his preliminary report that "the patient has been emersed [sic] for several hours or more in a canal and [was] brought in with an inability to move his lower extremities and with gross sensory deficit in his lower extremities. He is also shivering. There is no history of any near-by motor vehicle or motorcycle accident. The patient has no significant past medical history and is not complaining of any significant pain."

His initial impressions were that I had both severe hypothermia and a spinal cord injury. He knew that if the vertebrae in my neck or back were fractured or seemed unstable in any way, then they would have to operate on me immediately.

With my head still immobilized by the collar, I was strapped down to a bed so I couldn't move at all and hurt myself, and then they placed me in this metallic bag that looked like a hot dog wrapper to help the circulation in my legs. They also put heat lamps all around the bed. When you are hypothermic, they have to increase your body temperature slowly, only a few degrees at a time, or else your system won't be able to adjust and you can die.

Dr. Nabut ordered a workup, which included an assessment of my muscle strength, X-rays and MRIs, and a variety of blood tests. X-rays pick up the bone damage, and MRIs show what's going on with the soft tissue, including your spinal cord. They gave me a cocktail of steroids to limit any swelling that could further compress my spinal cord and cause more damage. They also hooked me up with an IV drip of antibiotics to fight any infection.

They immediately contacted the on-call neurosurgeon, a physician named Jaime Gomez. While it was a bad sign that I couldn't move my legs, it was too early to assess any paralysis. Sometimes when you break your neck, you only bruise your spinal cord, and movement and feeling will return after the bones are stabilized and the trauma starts to heal. So there was hope for me, if they could get my body temperature and pulse back to normal.

While Dr. Gomez was rushing to the hospital, a woman named Pat Healy notified my parents. Pat was actually my mom's good friend. They played bridge or tennis together each week. She worked in the hospital as a patient advocate and had recognized my face when they wheeled me in on the gurney.

She called my mom, who was working at American Express at the time.

"Linda," she said.

"Hi, Pat," my mom said.

"Linda, sit down. I have some bad news. Steel yourself. Mark has been seriously injured. We're not sure how. But you need to have someone else drive you to the North Broward Medical Center in Pompano Beach right away."

My mom couldn't formulate any questions. She hung up and crawled under the desk in her cubicle and started to sob uncontrollably. The people in her office stared at her and wondered if she was having some kind of nervous breakdown. Her friend crawled under the desk with her and asked what was wrong.

"My son is hurt," my mom said quietly.

The next call went to my father, who was in a budget meeting at Southeast Frozen Food. This meeting was the reason why he didn't go out with us for a beer the night before. An assistant interrupted the presentation and asked my father to pick up the receiver and push the flashing button.

"Can't this wait until we're finished?" my dad said.

"It's someone from North Broward Medical Center," she said.

He picked up the phone.

"Hello."

"Tom. This is Linda's friend Pat Healy. I need to tell you that your son has been severely injured."

"Which son?" my father said, his voice tightening. He walked to the corner of the conference room and sat down on a stack of cardboard boxes.

"Mark," she said. "You need to come to North Broward in Pompano as quickly as you can. Have someone else drive you."

Jeff received a similar phone call at home. He had just gotten back from football practice at Douglas and was having a snack in the kitchen. He immediately called his buddy Carl Chiello and asked for a ride.

My dad's friend Dick Newcomb drove him to the hospital. It was close to five p.m., and they hit the commuter-hour traffic. Dick impatiently honked his horn. My dad dragged furiously on his cigarette, and thought about jumping out and running the rest of the way.

"Just go around them," he said to Dick. "Drive down the fucking sidewalk. I don't give a shit. I've got to get to my son."

Dick cranked the wheel right and popped two tires up on the curb and kept going. My brother and his friend Carl were having similar problems, stuck in bumper-to-bumper traffic. Carl ended up running a yellow light, skidding on the wet pavement, and smashing into the back of another car. He quickly reversed and then drove around the car and continued to the hospital, with the other driver yelling at him, middle finger extended.

My dad and brother arrived at North Broward at the same time. My mom wasn't there yet. Pat met them at the front desk and gave them the limited details about where I was found and the rescue. At that point, no one knew exactly how I had ended up in the canal.

"Mark's in really bad shape," she told my dad. "He may have spinal injuries."

"I need to see him now," he said, pulling my brother along with him.

"He's in the Intensive Care Unit," she said. She pointed at Jeff. "I'm sorry but he can't come with us. He's a minor and it's against hospital policy."

"I don't care about hospital policy," my dad said. "He's coming with me. Let's go."

Jeff remembers crying when he first saw me. My head was sandwiched between two sandbags to keep my neck absolutely straight, and I was still wearing the white plastic collar with blue padding. My face was covered in angry red welts from the ant bites, and the rest of me was whiter than the hospital sheets. I was shivering violently even though glowing heat lamps surrounded me—not exactly the big brother Jeff saw as indestructible.

I weakly raised my hand to acknowledge them.

My mom ran in moments later and stood by my side. When she saw how bad I looked, her face twisted in shock, fear, and pain. I started to cry and she touched my cheek.

"It's bad," I croaked.

Then I closed my eyes.

"I thought I was going to lose you," my mom says now. "Your skin was so cold and you were trembling. There are no words in the world to explain what it's like to see your child so hurt. But you maintained consciousness until you saw me. You knew your father and I were there and you were in our hands. We were going to keep you safe."

when my parents met with them, Dr. Nabut and Dr. Gomez explained that when the paramedics brought me into the hospital, I couldn't feel or move my legs and had limited movement in my arms, hands, and fingers. I also had hypothermia and pneumonia from spending hours in the cold water. Then Dr. Gomez took them through the test results and his prognosis. The X-rays of the cervical spine showed a fracture of the C7 and several floating bone fragments. The MRI revealed an acute disc herniation between C6 and C7. There was a contusion of the spinal cord, but the extent of the damage was still unclear.

Basically, he was saying that I had somehow slammed different segments of my spine together, causing the bones to chip. Between each pair of cervical vertebrae, there's this hollow disc shaped like a jelly doughnut that connects and pads the two bones. In my case, that disc was flattened during the accident and pushed backward, where it hit my spinal cord.

Dr. Gomez wanted to operate immediately so he could remove the herniated disc, stabilize my vertebrae, and hopefully limit any more damage. His plan was to get a piece of bone from the bone bank and use it to reconstruct and fuse my spine back together at C6 and C7. While he was in there, he would extract all the bone fragments.

But he had some concerns. If the bone chips started circulating with my cerebral spinal fluid, they could enter my skull and cause brain damage or even death, so they had to be removed carefully and quickly. My deep hypothermia also needed to be taken into account. It's extremely dangerous to operate on someone who is hypothermic, because their organs have already slowed. For the heart, that means it's not pumping enough blood and oxygen to the rest of the body. Add in the effects of anesthesia and couple that with the inherent trauma of surgery, and it can all lead to cardiac arrest on the operating table.

But not everything was total gloom and doom. In certain ways, my hypothermia may have saved my life, slowing my system down so much that my body burned less energy and didn't have to work as hard to keep me alive during all those hours in the canal. Being in such good shape from soccer also helped me to survive, and floating in the water may have kept some of the pressure off my back and spine, possibly making the injuries less severe. The cold water probably limited the swelling, which often does the most damage to the spinal cord. I could still move my arms a little, and that was a promising sign.

Dr. Gomez was a well-respected neurosurgeon, but neck operations are a tricky business, especially when you're dealing with spinal cord injuries, so my mom asked Pat Healy what she thought of him as a doctor. Pat said he was very good at what he did, but as the patient advocate, she advised that we explore all the options available to us and figure out if we wanted to talk to any other specialists for a second opinion.

My parents discussed it briefly but agreed that time was of the essence. Every second that I wasn't in surgery could potentially mean more damage to my spinal cord, and that could cause more paralysis in the long run.

"Look," Dr. Gomez said to my parents, "I don't want to pressure you in any way, but you have to make a decision. The first thing that we are going to do is try to save his life. The next thing we're going to try to do is limit the damage."

"Fine," my dad said, signing the release form. In the spot where it asks you to write the patient's name, he didn't write "Mark Zupan." Instead, he wrote "my son."

if i was going to survive surgery, they first had to raise my body temperature. While I slept under the heat lamps, and the doctors prepared for the operation, my mom called the police from a pay phone. She was trying to solve the mystery of how I ended up half dead with a broken neck in a random canal between an office building and the freeway in Pompano Beach, miles away from FAU.

"Was there an accident near that area last night?" she asked the officer who answered her call. "Anything involving a black 1991 Mustang? No? Do you have any record of anyone else injured around there? Were there any other 911 calls?"

The police knew nothing about the situation. Zip. Zero. Nada. She told them where the canal was and gave them the location of the office building. She also told them to call the fire department and the paramedics who answered the 911 call for specific information.

They said they would follow up with the other agencies and investigate.

She suggested that they might want to send some officers over to search the canal. "For all we know," she said, "someone else could still be in there. I don't think my son was alone last night. He was with a group of friends from his soccer team."

That's my mom. Telling the police how to do their job.

Good idea, they said. We'll take care of it. They promised to contact her at the hospital if and when they had any new information.

"Thank you," she said.

She hung up and then dumped more dimes down the slot,

punched numbers with her finger, and made call after call, trying to piece my night together.

My dad went and got her from the waiting room when they were ready to take me up for surgery. They walked next to the gurney as they wheeled me into the operating room. The surgery would be long and complicated and was scheduled to take several hours. Dr. Gomez would be performing a microdiscectomy and partial vertebrectomies on me, using a bone graft that came from a dead woman's hip. They could have taken some bone out of my own body, but that would have meant another surgery and more risk.

The herniated disc would be removed through an incision in the front of my neck: this is called the anterior approach. When they go in through the back, that's the posterior approach. I had injured the front of my spine and that's why they went in through the neck. A small piece of bone would be inserted in place of my disc, and the fusing would take place slowly over the next several months as my body healed the fracture.

My dad stood over me as I was lying on my back, lost in the sluggish twilight between life and death. He stared into my eyes, not knowing if he would ever see me alive again. He had been stoic to this point, a real rock of reassurance, telling my mom and brother over and over that somehow everything was going to be all right, but at this moment, his big body began to quake. He started to make a guttural, almost feral noise, and his eyes leaked tears. It was as if my father couldn't express all the anguish he was feeling, and his only articulation was the wounded bellow that began to pour out.

My dad later told me it wasn't just pain he was feeling. He knew it was impossible, but he was using all his strength to try to force his mind and soul into my body.

He desperately wanted to trade places with me.

igoe's mom was driving him back to our dorm room at FAU. His father still wasn't back from his business trip in the Virgin Islands, but was expected to land soon. While they were driving, Igoe picked up the car phone, which, back in 1993, had a regular receiver with a cord attached to a console the size of a shoe box that rested in between the two front seats.

Igoe called our friend Ray Gentile, who had played football with us at Douglas and lived in the same dorm as we did at FAU, but not in our suite. Ray and Igoe used to pretend they were hard-ass gangsters back in high school. The coaches would put together highlight reels of the football team that they would show during pep rallies. In one of them, Ray gave a shout out to his probation officer, kissing his pointer and middle fingers and saying "Peace." Like Igoe, Ray was a nice kid, and about as gangster as a Girl Scout.

"I'm hard, Ray," Igoe said. "I've just been in jail. I'm calling you fresh from Broward County lockup, fool."

"You're an idiot," Ray said. "What the hell did you do?"

"I went 1-8-7 on a muthafucking cop."

"Shut up. Seriously, what did you do?"

"DUI."

"No shit." Ray's sister had been one of the kids who died in that accident during our senior year. He changed the subject. "Hey, have you heard about Mark?"

"No," Igoe said, his mind racing back to Dirty Moe's, trying to recall when I left the bar. "What happened to Mark?"

"He's paralyzed and he's in the hospital."

"Shut the fuck up. Are you serious? Like, paralyzed for real?"

"Yeah. They found him under some bridge out in Broward somewhere. Hey, wasn't he with you last night?"

"We were getting hammered at Dirty Moe's," Igoe said, wondering if he could somehow be involved. "But then Mark took off at some point. I passed out at the bar and when I woke up he was gone. I drove home by myself. They pulled me over at the Cypress Creek exit off I-95 near Coral Springs."

He paused for a moment.

"Are you sure someone told you he's paralyzed?"

Ray had a reputation for exaggerating. He also had a reputation for being completely full of shit at times. Igoe didn't know what to believe.

"That's what I heard," Ray said.

Igoe started to worry, remembering the shoving match that we had gotten into with the frat boys over by the stage. He thought that maybe those guys waited for me outside the club and then jumped me when I was walking home. They could have beaten me, put me in the trunk of a car, and driven me out somewhere and dumped me in the swamp.

His mind was racing when his mom dropped him off in the parking lot in front of the dorm, and he ran upstairs and walked into our room. It was exactly how we had left it the night before. Both beds were made. Clothes were still on the floor.

Shafiei walked in and told Igoe that I hadn't been to soccer practice and the whole team was flipping out, wondering what had happened to me. There were all these rumors flying around that I was dead or crippled. Our friend Jahn Avarillo stopped by the suite, wondering what was going on, and Igoe told Jahn what Ray had told him. They decided to start calling all our friends to try and figure out where I was and if I was okay or not.

Then the phone rang.

"Is Christopher Daniel Igoe there," said a stern, no-nonsense voice.

Igoe's stomach dropped three stories and hit the basement.

"Speaking."

"Christopher Igoe of the 4500 block of Bristol Lane in Parkland?"

"That's me."

The highway patrol officer identified himself and said that he was investigating a case that could be related to Igoe's case.

"Do you know a Mark Zupan?"

"I do," Igoe said.

"He was found injured today in a canal near the Cypress Creek exit of Interstate 95, very near where you had an accident and were subsequently arrested for driving under the influence," the officer said. "We have reason to believe that Mr. Zupan was in the back of your truck when you lost control of the vehicle. I am calling to tell you not to go anywhere. We are sending a trooper over now to talk to you. Mr. Zupan is in intensive care right now at North Broward.

He is undergoing emergency surgery and they do not know if he will survive. If he dies, you will most likely be charged with vehicular manslaughter. If he makes it, you will be charged with criminal negligence. Is that clear?"

"Yes," Igoe said, staring out the large window that looked over the courtyard where the kids were yelling and laughing, playing volleyball and grilling hamburgers. His brain was on overload. Guilt and uncertainty made his heart beat irregularly, and he thought he was going to vomit. He felt dizzy, as if his life were suddenly swirling down the bowl of a toilet. He suddenly had the urge to hurl his body through the glass window and hoped that his head would hit the pavement when he landed.

Could I have done this to Mark? he thought. *Could I have killed my best friend?*

"You've got it wrong," Igoe said. "There was no one else in my truck. Check the report. Why didn't the off-duty cop who was tailing me see anyone fly out the back?"

"Tell it to the trooper when he comes to get you," the officer said.

Igoe hung up the phone and immediately called his parents. His father was back home by then, and Igoe told him everything that had happened. His father said that he would call his lawyer and have him deal with the police, but now they needed to go to the hospital right away to see how I was doing and to give support to my family.

When Igoe walked into North Broward with his parents, the waiting room was full of people. Kati, Steve Nelson and his girlfriend Dana Lewis, and some of the soccer guys, as well as a few of my parents' friends were crowded around my mom and dad, who were sitting in plastic chairs and seemed to be comforting the very people who came to help them.

I had been in surgery for maybe half an hour by then. The mood was somber and everyone spoke in hushed tones. Two troopers had been by earlier to explain to my parents that Igoe had crashed his truck near where I was found, and that he was driving drunk. The skid marks, geography, and physics suggested that I was thrown out of the back when he lost control on the wet curve and crashed into the fence.

My parents told them immediately that they did not want to press any charges against Chris, and if the police decided to pursue the matter, they would not cooperate.

None of our football buddies were there yet, and Igoe felt very alone, exposed, and scared. He remembers the distinct sensation of all the air being sucked out of the room when he entered, and everyone swiveling their heads in slow motion, staring at him for a time longer than it took for the Egyptians to build the pyramids, judging him, seeing all the darkness he now felt in his soul. In Igoe's memory, the scene has a hyper-real quality. People's faces and clothing had sharper outlines and brighter colors. Each tick from the hanging clock sounded like an atomic explosion, and the fluorescent lights were buzzing like a million locusts. But nothing was louder than his own panicked, shallow breathing.

"I'm so sorry," Igoe said to the entire room, overcome with remorse. "Is Mark going to be okay?"

No one knew what to say.

My father stood up and walked over to him and grabbed him by the arm.

"Chris," my dad said. "I need to talk to you outside. Now."

He thought that my dad was going to take him down the hall and beat the shit out of him. As soon as they were alone in the hall, Igoe broke down.

"I'm so sorry," he said, bawling, his tears smearing on my dad's shoulder. "Mr. Zupan, I never meant to hurt anybody. I never meant to hurt Mark."

"It's not your fault, Chris," my dad said, hugging him tightly. "We know that you didn't do this intentionally."

He took a step back and faced Igoe, speaking to him man to man.

"But you share in the responsibility of what has happened to Mark," he said firmly. "You both made big mistakes, ones that will affect your lives forever. Mark might not make it through the night. And you're going to have to figure out how to deal with that."

"I know," Igoe said. "I'm sorry, Mr. Zupan. I'm so sorry."

* * *

as you probably figured out, I didn't die on the operating table.

Hours later, the disc had been successfully removed through my throat and the bone inserted between my vertebrae. I was recovering back in intensive care, in critical condition and not yet completely out of the woods.

My parents and brother were still at the hospital, contorting their bodies uncomfortably in the plastic chairs in the waiting room, staring off into the silence, black circles ringing their sad eyes, their faces made to look sallow and wan by the weak white fluorescent lights that seem to hang from the ceilings in every hospital.

Go home, the nurses finally said to them. You can't see him tonight. Come back first thing tomorrow. There's nothing more that you can do for him now. We've done everything we can. It's up to his body now. Get some rest. You're going to need it.

They drove back home to Coral Springs but still couldn't sleep. At three a.m., my mom was wide awake and restless. There was no one left to call or comfort, no doctors left to query, no insurance companies to contact or forms to fill out, no police to badger. She had been so busy that she had successfully avoided dealing with her grief, which snuck up behind her and knocked her to her knees with a sucker punch in the gut.

While she was down, her emotions climbed all over each other, fighting for her attention. She felt an uncontrollable anger at the unfairness of it all, and wanted to blame someone for what had happened.

How could Mark have been so foolish to drink so much and pass out in the back of a truck? Why was Chris driving drunk? He knows better than that. What the heck is wrong with these kids? How could they put us through this?

Then she felt guilty for thinking that and decided to point the finger at herself.

If I had been stricter, tougher, more vigilant, maybe I could have prevented this. If I had just been a better mother, I could have kept him out of harm's way. If I had just taught him a little more restraint, we wouldn't be in this situation.

Her sorrow then told her to question a higher power. My mom grew up in a Catholic household and her mother attended mass every day, but she isn't a religious person. But at this point, she was willing to give anything a try.

How could you let this happen to my son? He never did anything to hurt anyone. He's really just a boy. How could you? Are you that cruel?

And then came the bargaining that any grief counselor will tell you is normal.

If you let my son survive I will become a better person. I've learned my lesson. Please, God, just give us all a second chance. Please. I'm begging you.

Blame and bargaining weren't getting her anywhere, so she went through a scrapbook in her mind, paging through her memories one by one. She thought of me, her first baby, and how she had loved me with all her being, and watched me grow, and how proud she had been of me for my accomplishments over the years and how just over a month ago, I had entered college, on the verge of manhood, full of hopes and dreams for the future.

But that was all in the past, and now it was clear that nothing would ever be the same again. The doctors had prepared her for the possibility that the paralysis could be permanent and that I might be confined to a wheelchair for the rest of my life. That concept was just too overwhelming, and she began to have what my father described as "a good cry." Her friend Judy Scheuplein was there with her, patting her back and trying to comfort her as she wept on the living room floor. My dad stepped out on the porch to have a smoke. There was a police car with its lights off parked in front of our house.

"You all right, Mr. Zupan?" the cop asked, window down.

"Yeah," my dad said.

"I'm supposed to let you know that I'm here if your family needs anything."

"Thanks." My dad had a lot of friends on the Coral Springs police force.

Then my dad slowly walked through the streets of Eagle Trace, following the route I used to run when I was training for soccer, placing his feet where I had placed mine.

tiny little fractures

Slowly, i opened my eyes. It was like staring through two jars of Vaseline.

I was lying back in a bed, and it felt as if someone had tried to slit my throat while I was sleeping and packed my head full of cotton. Making matters worse, some sadistic son of a bitch had strapped me down and stuffed thin, clear plastic tubes in my mouth, down my throat, up my nose, into my arms, and even inside my penis.

I was surrounded by racks of flashing machines that beeped and huffed and chugged. The large plastic neck brace I was wearing was tighter than a noose. I felt claustrophobic as hell and wanted to rip everything out and run down the hall, screaming. I tried to force the tubes out of my mouth with my tongue. I felt like a lab rat, and I thought of the Metallica video for "One" from the album . . . *And Justice for All*. The song is about this guy who stepped on a land mine. He's trapped in the hospital bed and can't see or move or talk at all to tell the doctors he wants to die. His body has become his prison cell. I knew exactly how he felt now.

My blurry vision cleared and a middle-aged nurse entered the room and gave me a stiff military smile. "Good morning, Mark," she said. She was chipper. I fucking hate chipper people. "Don't try to talk. The tube down your throat goes into your lungs and the machine is helping you breathe. You've been restrained for your own safety. The doctors operated on your spine last night, and the bones are fragile and need time to heal. Your throat is probably very sore. Essentially they had to push your vocal cords to one side to access your spine. You're going to be here awhile. You've been placed in skull traction to keep your neck and spine straight and secure. But if you promise not to move, I can undo your wristbands."

I blinked as if to say yes. For some reason, blinking felt like my eyelids were squatting three hundred pounds. She carefully removed the straps from my arms.

"Good. Now I'll go get your family and let them know that you're awake."

I couldn't turn my head to watch her walk out the door. I still had no idea what had happened to me, but it was becoming obvious that I had jacked myself up pretty badly.

My dad, mom, and brother came in and sat down as if they were sitting in the front row of a funeral. When they saw that I was awake, it was as if the corpse moved in the casket. Waterfalls of tears ran down their cheeks and dripped off their noses. They told me how happy they were to see me alive and conscious and then ran through the events of the last two days, starting with the accident and ending with my operation. Word had spread about what had happened, and Igoe and a bunch of my other friends had come to the hospital early that morning and were outside in the waiting room.

I was still dazed and groggy from the anesthetic, and my memories of this time are fuzzy. I recall hearing their words, but somehow the sounds were disconnected from their meaning. I broke my neck. I almost died. I might be paralyzed. Huh. That's really interesting. Can I go now? It was as though they were talking about someone else named Mark. I remember thinking that I didn't mind being in the hospital. This was the place where the doctors usually just stitched me up or plastered a cast on my arm. In a few days, I would be ready to play again.

But I was beginning to get my mind around the fact that things were different this time. While they were talking to me, I decided to conduct my own experiment. I told the toes on my right foot to wiggle. The sheet at the foot of the bed stayed completely still. I tried it again. And again. And again. Then I just stared dumbly at the spot where my feet were.

Holy fuck, I thought, truly feeling fear for the first time. *I can't move them at all.*

I decided to forget the toe test and pretended that it never happened.

I couldn't talk, so the nurse brought over a small board about the size of a restaurant menu that contained all the letters of the alphabet, numbers zero through nine, and various punctuation marks. I was supposed to point to a letter or number with my finger, and spell out simple sentences. I thought and then picked the letters slowly, my eyes poring over the board. It took me a few minutes to figure out what I wanted to say, my trembling finger pointing at different spots. My mom repeated the letters out loud, one at a time.

I A—M—I—U—C—K—Y—?—?—?

To this day, I'm not completely sure what I meant by that remark. Was I saying that I was lucky to have survived the accident? Maybe. Or was I questioning the luck of my survival now that I couldn't move my legs at all? That also seems possible.

But my dad took it as if I was looking for some kind of confirmation.

"That's an understatement, buddy," he said. "You are lucky. Damn lucky."

A man in a white coat walked into the room and introduced himself as Dr. Jeffrey Samuels. He looked at the charts and said he wanted to have my temperature checked. It had been dipping and then soaring after the surgery, elevating as high as 102 degrees as my body tried to stabilize itself. My blood pressure had been all over the map as well.

My temperature was 99.7 degrees, almost normal. My pulse was back in the 100s and I was breathing regularly, although I had one massive coughing spasm from the water I had in my lungs. Just so you know, it's tough to cough with tubes jammed into your mouth that connect to a machine that's breathing for you and sounds like Darth Vader giving you CPR.

Dr. Samuels gave me a quick physical examination. He asked me to point to the Y on the board if I could feel where he pressed his hands on me.

"Can you feel this?" he said.

He touched my upper arms, first the left, then the right.

Yes to both.

My hands.

Yes.

My fingers.

Yes.

My shoulders.

Yes.

He walked his hands down my spine to the middle of my thoracic vertebrae.

Yes.

Then I saw his hands touch my legs and there was no feeling of pressure. I panicked and almost pointed to the Y, knowing that I should be able to feel his fingertips when they pushed on the soles of my feet, my calves, my thighs, my pelvis. But in truth, he could have hacked my legs off with a dull machete while I sang the national anthem and I wouldn't have missed a note. That's when it finally hit me. A lifetime of running effortlessly on grassy fields, of touchdowns, of goals, free kicks, and friendship flickered behind my closed eyes.

I started to struggle violently in the bed.

"You're going to be all right," my dad said. "Keep still."

My freakout had no effect on Dr. Samuels. He had this curious look on his face. He said that he could feel a slight vibration in some of my leg muscles when I tried to move them, and that was a positive sign that the nerves were starting to work again. Now that I thought about it, maybe I was experiencing a tingling sensation down there at times. It was hard to tell. He then took me through a series of range-of-motion tests. I could shrug my shoulders, and my biceps and triceps were responding, but my hands were very weak, and the fingers on my right hand were frozen into an eagle's claw. My legs were unresponsive when I tried to lift or bend them.

"There is no movement in the legs as yet," he later wrote in his report, "but again this is a very early situation and we can be hopeful [and] cautiously optimistic that there will be some recovery given the fact that the sensation is partially retained."

Dr. Samuels explained to us that there were two types of spinal cord injuries: complete and incomplete. A complete injury means there isn't any function below the level of injury. The spinal cord has been damaged so badly that it can't transmit any signals down to the rest of the body. An incomplete injury means that there is limited feeling and function below the spot where you got hurt. Some impulses from the brain can be sent down the spinal cord, which is now like a frayed electrical cord with a short in it. Certain commands can get through and others can't. Many people with incomplete injuries can move one arm better than the other, or can feel sensations, like heat or cold, on parts of their bodies that they can't actually move. But once your spinal cord is damaged, he said, there is nothing a doctor can do to fix it.

I learned later that the level of the injury on your spine can help you try to predict what parts of the body might be affected by paralysis. Neck injuries generally result in quadriplegia, meaning some impairment in all four limbs, which is what I was exhibiting. Injuries above the C4 level may require the person to wear a ventilator to breathe. With C5 injuries, you can move your shoulders, but you can't move your wrists or hands. C6 injuries, you can move your wrists but have no hand function. Individuals with C7 injuries can usually move their arms but have dexterity problems with their fingers. Below that, down at the thoracic level, injuries usually make you a paraplegic, with impairment in just the legs.

I also found out that there are around 450,000 people living with some kind of spinal cord injury in the United States. There are about 10,000 new injuries each year, and the majority of them, around 82 percent, involve males between sixteen and thirty years old. Most of the injuries are a result of automobile accidents. Quadriplegia is slightly more prevalent than paraplegia.

Winding up the examination, Dr. Samuels told us how hard it was to give an accurate prognosis at this stage and explained the need for rehabilitation and that there would be both early and late phases of recovery. In other words, he had no idea how much function I would get back in my arms and legs or when it might return. Only time would tell. But he felt that I was stable enough to begin a gentle series of exercises as soon as possible.

Dr. Samuels signed off his report by thanking Dr. Nabut and Dr. Gomez for "asking me to see this pleasant and interesting man and allowing me to participate in his care."

hospitals are full of shitty rules but are usually run by pretty decent people. Only family members were supposed to be allowed in to see me while I was in the ICU. You can't imagine how many brothers, sisters, cousins, aunts, and uncles I suddenly had. The nurses just smiled and brought my "relatives" into the room in clusters of two and three.

It's hard for me to explain how ridiculously happy I was to see my friends. Back when I was in high school, I used to talk to Dana about what it would be like if one of us suddenly died. I wondered, would anyone come to my funeral? Would anyone cry? Would they miss me when I was gone? What would they say about me? I finally had my answer. That first full day in the hospital felt like my wake, and when I think about it now, I guess that's because a part of me had actually died. A man loses his innocence when he realizes his own mortality. But it's at that exact moment that he understands the preciousness of his life and the people in it.

I had been in Coral Springs for less than four years, but I had made lifelong friends there. I wanted them to know how much they all meant to me, how important they were in my life, and how I would never forget that they came to help me in my time of need. They had my loyalty for life. The attention and support did a lot to comfort my family and me.

Igoe was one of the first people that I remember coming in, and he had this look like he had just gone through a root canal without novocaine. A lot of people have asked me what I thought about Igoe at that moment. Was I pissed at him? Did I hate his guts? Did I blame him for what happened? No. I don't remember thinking about any of that stuff. I was still pretty out of it at the time, just happy to be breathing, not quite coherent about what was going on. But I did realize at the time that I had gotten drunk and passed out in his truck. I had done that myself, and that was my burden. No doubt, Igoe shouldn't have been driving drunk, but he didn't know I was back there. If he had, I doubt he would have driven anywhere. He apologized to me again and again, and I knew he meant it. In a way, I owed him an apology too. If I hadn't crawled into his truck, we wouldn't have been in the situation we were in now.

Articles about the accident were appearing in the local newspapers. We heard rumors that there would be TV cameras coming at some point, but for now, all the media was concentrated on the murderer Igoe had met in jail. Igoe didn't want to become famous for driving drunk and breaking his best friend's neck. In private, his family was talking to their lawyer, and they were bracing for a possible lawsuit if my family decided to sue. The Isuzu had been registered to his father's banking software company. But the police ultimately decided not to bring him up on any criminal charges beyond the DUI.

I remember thinking that Igoe looked as if he had lost weight and shrunk since I saw him last. The boisterous kid who once wanted to be the center of attention had taken to hiding in the corners of the room and avoiding conversations with others. When he apologized to me yet again for driving drunk and crashing, I pointed to some letters on the board.

I—T—S—C—O—O—L

"I'm here for you, man," Igoe said.

After Igoe, other friends came and went. No one knew quite how to react. They mostly offered me kind words of hope and inspiration with choked voices. "You're going to be okay," they said. "Just hang in there. If anyone can survive this, you can."

Kati hugged me tighter than she ever had before and kissed me on the forehead.

"Mark," she gasped, "you have to get better. I love you so much."

Steve had a hard time keeping the tears out of his eyes. Dana brought me a little Elmo doll that she tucked under the covers by my head. She was big into Sesame Street characters at the time, and she thought this would comfort me. It did. I guess that just shows you how young we all were back then. We were just kids, sampling the cruelties of life for the very first time.

Jeff Sharon walked in sometime that day and grabbed my big toe, which was sticking out from under the bedsheet.

"How are you doing, you little bitch?" he asked. "Where are your cleats? You need to get suited up. We need you back on the soccer field."

The team had a game that weekend against a school called Stetson University. Coach Donev called a team meeting when he learned I was in the hospital and told the guys that if they needed to take some time off, he understood. It might be a good idea. Some of them were pretty freaked out about the accident. Almost everyone on the team had been at Dirty Moe's that night getting wasted. It caused them to take a good, hard look in the mirror and question their own behavior, maybe even glimpse their own mortality.

For a while, partying stopped at the soccer house. Then it resumed.

Years later, Sharon would tell me that he felt he shared in the blame for what had happened. I was shocked to hear this. Sharon had nothing to do with the accident. But the way he saw it, he was the captain and I was a freshman on the team. He should have looked after me better at the bar and made sure I got home safely. That's when I realized that injuries are like giant bombs. I happened to be at ground zero for this explosion, but I wasn't the only one who felt the blast and caught some shrapnel. It hurt everyone in the surrounding areas in varying degrees, depending on their proximity.

The team decided not to take any time off and played the next scheduled game. They knew me well enough to know that's what I wanted them to do. They said a quick prayer for me before the game, and they all wore armbands or tape with #16 written in Sharpie pen.

"Let's win this one for Zupan!" they said together.

It was a hell of a game. They beat Stetson 2–1 in overtime.

Igoe had called Nickell and Cava as soon as he found out that I was in the hospital. They were up at the University of Florida in

Gainesville. They hopped in their trucks and drove down as fast as they could. Nickell had made the trip only a few times and got confused by the signs for I-75. Despite his big brain, he ended up driving down the west coast of Florida, adding an extra six hours and a drive across Alligator Alley to what should have been a four-hour trip.

When he came into my room, he sensed that the atmosphere had become too depressing. He thought that someone had to be upbeat and decided to cheer me up. "You know, Mark," he said, "it's unfortunate about your accident, but I've got bigger fucking problems. I just got lost and drove down the wrong coast of Florida." Everyone in the room laughed and felt better. Nickell has always been good at knowing what other people need.

The hours passed and I dozed between visitors. Kati would crawl into my bed and curl up next to me. The warmth of her body was soothing, and I could still smell her perfume on my pillow after she would get up to go home. When I was awake, my other friends did their best to help me forget about not being able to move. I was equally frustrated by not being able to talk. I wanted to tell them that I was going to be okay, to stop worrying about me. I wasn't going to be paralyzed for the rest of my life. Dr. Samuels just had to give us all the worst-case scenarios when he talked about the possibility of me becoming a quadriplegic. That's what doctors did. Even though he was trying to downplay it, I could tell he was optimistic about my recovery. Surely, my feeling and functions were going to come back soon. My upper body was already improving dramatically, and my legs had started to tingle as if someone had cast a magic spell on them. If they just gave me a little time, I knew I would walk out of the hospital.

those first few days in the ICU, I rode the roller coaster of intense hope and utter despair in a narcotic haze. One moment, I felt lucky just to be alive. Then I would try to move my legs and the lack of response would make rage boil inside me. I would become infuriated with the doctors, the tubes, the neck brace, the awful antiseptic hospital smell, the new stillness of my life, and the lack of any concrete information about my condition. My dread was large and vague.

Why can't anyone tell me if I'm going to be all right again? I wanted to know.

Visiting hours were limited, so my friends and parents would have to leave in the early evening so I could get my rest. I would wear a brave face for them in the day and pretend nothing was wrong with me, which is tough to do when you're in neck traction and strapped into a bed that rotates you so you don't get bedsores. When Igoe would come in and sit next to me, looking sad and pitiful, I would point-write little messages to him:

W—H—A—T—T—H—E—F—U—C—K—I—S—U—P—?

"Nothing," he would say sheepishly, perpetuating the charade that everything was fine. Igoe didn't think he deserved to talk about any of the self-loathing that was beginning to consume him. He felt alienated from everyone and thought that they all secretly blamed him for what had happened to me. He didn't think anyone would want to hear about what he was going through when I couldn't even feel my lower body. Igoe was petrified to ask my parents about my prognosis, so he would try to eavesdrop on other people's conversations to learn more about my condition. No one mentioned paralysis in front of me. There was just hopeful chatter about me walking again soon. But I could hear people talking about me as soon as they left the room. I tried to listen but couldn't quite make out their worried whispers.

My parents and I never had a heart-to-heart about what we were all going through emotionally, never discussed the horrible fear we were all feeling. Suffering was something that the Zupans did alone and in private. My family just wasn't equipped to deal with such a traumatic experience. I thought that if I didn't acknowledge my fears to others, maybe they wouldn't exist. But nights were the worst, because there was nothing to distract me from the worries and doubts.

I used to think that my future would be cut-and-dried. I would graduate from college, get a job, get married, and have a family of my own, basically what most normal people do. Was any of that still possible? I was unable to imagine what my life was going to be like anymore. I could envision getting out of the hospital, but then anything past that point was like watching the gray static on a blank TV. What if I had to live with my family for the rest of my life, confined to a bed or stuck in a wheelchair? I didn't know one person in a chair, and when I saw a crippled person at the movies or in the mall, I'd try to avoid eye contact with them and pretend they didn't exist. They always seemed needy and weak and gross to me.

Unable to move in my bed, I would get so freaked out by these thoughts that I would start to hyperventilate. I would have to gather them into a squirming heap and throw them into a metal box in my brain and lock them up tightly so they couldn't escape again.

I will walk again, I'd tell myself. *I will play soccer again. Everything will go back to normal. It's going to be fine.* It had to be. There were no other options. To me, recovery existed only in black-and-white terms. I would either win or lose.

In the predawn hours, while the nurses would squeak around in their rubber-soled shoes, I would close my eyes and return to Dirty Moe's, trying to figure out what went wrong. I couldn't remember much of what happened, so I would go over what people had told me about the accident, but some of it didn't make sense. Why hadn't I walked home? Why didn't Igoe see me when he opened the back window? How did he get lost so close to campus? Why didn't that off-duty cop pull him over when he had the chance? How did the truck manage to slingshot me over a six-foot fence? Why didn't anyone see me fly out?

This would lead to bigger questions.

Why me? I'd say. *Why did this have to happen to me? What did I do to deserve this?*

The movie projector in my head would roll the silent footage from that night and I would study it like the film of a rival team before a football game, hitting pause, rewind, fast forward, searching for clues in the shadows. But I never discovered any new evidence, just the same old shame for fucking up and letting my parents and myself down. Tormented but exhausted, I would fall asleep and dream that I was able to walk and run again. I would wake up each morning and the first thing I would do was check to see if I could move my legs.

No luck.

Dr. Samuels continued to give me range-of-motion tests every day. I would try to move different muscles one by one while he watched me, talking about improved supination and pronation, and scribbling notes on a clipboard. Within forty-eight hours after the accident, I could lift my arms, but I couldn't extend my fingers. My left side, especially my left arm, seemed stronger than my right. I had insensitivity in my groin, but I was pretty sure that I could feel this prickling sensation in my legs, like warming up after being frostbitten.

Nerves take a long time to regenerate, the doctors would tell me. It can take months or even years, if it happens at all. That's when my competitive nature kicked in. It wasn't going to take me years to recover. I was going to be up and walking one year from now, no matter what it took. I was going to work my ass off to fix this problem myself. If my arms were already improving, then it was only a matter of time before my legs did the same.

Nevertheless, it was clear that my body was still in shock. I hadn't taken a dump since the day before the accident, and my colon was packed like a subway car during rush hour. My bladder had become overactive for some reason, and I would pee like a pregnant woman. The staff at North Broward didn't have much new info about what was going on with my body. The human brain, spine, and neurological system in general seemed like the Bermuda triangle of physiology. It was a mystery. There was just some stuff that you couldn't explain.

Someone should do a study on the acoustics in hospitals. It's funny how you can hear only what you want to hear. I would take any positive comment from the doctors about my progress, no matter how small, and treat it like irrefutable evidence that I was going to be fine. At the same time, I would ignore anything they said that was remotely negative. When you're in a situation like this, it's tough to tell the difference between hope and denial.

Even though I refused to acknowledge my disabilities, I started to adapt to them. When they would wheel me around on a gurney on my back for different tests, I couldn't move my neck side to side to see where I was going, so I figured out that I could count ceiling tiles and use that as a road map. Twenty tiles down and fourteen to the left, I knew I was going to physical therapy to start working on my fine motor skills. Thirty-three tiles down and twenty-eight to the right, I was going to get another X-ray.

But one thing that I could never get used to is the steady erosion of dignity that comes with an injury like mine. The doctors and nurses would constantly poke and prod me and roughly insert various objects into different orifices and veins without so much as asking my permission. They would pull back the sheets and lift up my gown to do their business. Let me tell you, sponge baths aren't all they're cracked up to be. In fact, they suck. I would growl at hospital workers, but they could not have cared less. I know that they were trying to heal me, but still, some of it was pretty fucking humiliating. My skin and bones were communal property now. There is no such thing as privacy when you're in intensive care.

We were all just playing this game of wait and see. As long as I was improving a little each day, there was reason to be hopeful that I would make a full recovery. I would go to bed, listening to the chirping machines, and tell my body to hurry up and fix itself.

the first phone call my dad made when he found out about my accident was to his sister Marcia, who is a nurse. She lives in Atlanta and is married to a man named Howard, who used to be a pilot for Delta and was part of a team that handled crisis control for the airline. In 1990, Marcia and Howard went through a hell on earth similar to what my parents were going through now. My cousin Jason was in a terrible car accident, a head-on collision with a tow truck that shattered his legs and knees, crushed every bone in his face, and left him with brain damage. He was in a coma for three months. He lost his ability to taste or smell and has trouble with simple problem solving and short-term memory. He had been in rehab at Emory University for several years at this point and still lived with Howard and Marcia.

My dad had been talking to them almost every day, asking their advice about what he should do. That weekend they had been with my other cousin, Todd, in Charleston, South Carolina. Todd is a few years younger than Jason, and was playing football at the Citadel.

"Thank God it's not a brain injury," Marcia said to my parents when she and Howard arrived early that Monday morning. "You need to be so thankful for that. Mark is still Mark. We are all going to be able to get through this."

Because of their experience with Jason's injuries, Marcia and Howard knew the importance of being in the right rehabilitation facility from day one. It could make all the difference in my recovery. They said I should be under the care of doctors and staff who specialized in treatment of spinal cord injuries. They would be up to date on the latest innovations and techniques and would offer a more comprehensive level of care.

Marcia and Howard immediately asked my parents about their plans.

"We're not sure," my mom said tentatively. She hadn't had time to give it much thought. "We are thinking about keeping him in Coral Springs, near his friends and family."

You have to keep in mind, this was before the Internet existed, and you could type "Spinal Cord Injury rehab" into Google and get tons of information instantly. My parents had been spending every waking hour with me in the hospital. Their only resource had been my doctors at North Broward, who had recommended that I stay with them for my physical rehabilitation. They would be able to give me one-on-one attention, they said.

My parents felt good about this plan. I was going to need the love and support of my family and friends. And the people at North Broward had saved my life. They had successfully performed the emergency surgery on my neck and put me back together again. My parents felt they owed those doctors a debt of gratitude. I was now able to move my arms again, and there were those promising vibrations in my leg muscles. They believed the old Mark should be running around in no time at all.

As a nurse, Marcia realized that the situation might not be such an easy fix. She had taken the liberty of doing some research before she came to Coral Springs. She told my mom that there was a place in Atlanta called the Shepherd Center, which billed itself "a catastrophic care hospital." It had been around since 1975 and started as the Shepherd Spinal Center, which was a wing in a hospital. It grew and moved into its own 32,000-square-foot facility in 1982. The mission at the Shepherd Center has always been to "return catastrophically injured patients to the highest functioning possible, enabling them to live their lives with hope, dignity and independence." Marcia said it was the best in the nation.

There was nothing wrong with the doctors at North Broward, Marcia explained, but they didn't specialize in spinal cord rehab. They couldn't offer the same level of therapy. They mostly dealt with older patients who were stroke victims. Asking them to heal my neck was like asking a plumber to fix your light socket.

She asked to see the facility where they were going to treat me at North Broward. It was basically a small room with a half-empty bookcase and some blue mats on the floor.

"This isn't going to work," Marcia said.

In addition to physical rehab, she knew I was going to need some kind of psychological therapy to help me deal with my new body and new life. She thought that I would feel isolated at North Broward. It would be better for me to be around other people who had similar injuries, so I didn't feel so alone.

My parents were open to the idea of another treatment facility, but "Atlanta is so far away," my father said. "We'd never get to see him." Marcia and Howard offered to look after me while I was there but realized that my family needed to stay together at this point.

Marcia went to a pay phone, called the Shepherd Center, and asked them to recommend a good treatment facility in Florida. They said that Jackson Memorial Hospital in Miami might be the best alternative for us. It had a large wing dedicated to spinal rehab and offered occupational, mental, and physical therapy. It also had a program called the Miami Project to Cure Paralysis, the world's largest spinal cord injury research center, where a neurosurgeon named Barth Green was using the latest electrostimulation therapy and other techniques in an effort to regenerate and reconnect damaged cells to restore function.

Marcia then called Jackson Memorial, which was connected to the University of Miami School of Medicine, and made an appointment for my dad and Howard to tour the facilities at ten the next morning. My dad had to go to Miami anyway—he had set up a meeting with a well-known lawyer. My parents were contemplating suing Dirty Moe's for serving me alcohol as a minor. My family had no plans to sue Igoe's family or his father's business, but they needed to talk to them and their insurance company to see how much their policy would pay to help cover my growing medical bills.

My parents were having problems with their own insurance company. My mom had recently renewed the family auto insurance and asked the agent to give her the same coverage that we had before, something called stacked coverage. Should there be an accident, all our cars, as well as the drivers of those cars, would be covered under one umbrella amount instead of in smaller individual amounts. Apparently, some box didn't get checked on some form and now the company refused to pay the larger amount and honor the verbal agreement. My dad was going to have to take them to court.

His head was probably spinning from all the emotional and financial pressures that the family was now facing, the uncertainty of everything. But having Howard and Marcia here was a big help. That afternoon, my father was able to leave the hospital by himself. He got in his car and drove down to Fort Lauderdale. It had taken him almost an hour of phone calls, but he finally found out which fire station had responded when I was discovered in the canal. He walked into the garage of Station 88 on Northwest Twenty-first Avenue sometime in the late afternoon. The firemen were standing around, cleaning trucks and organizing gear.

He met Lieutenant Ferranti and Paul Schultz, and they told him about Martin Story miraculously hearing my calls for help when he was eating lunch in his car. They told him about the aluminum boat and using shovels for paddles to cross the canal, and how when they reached me, I had only my nose, mouth, an arm, and the tip of one toe above water.

"He's a very lucky man," Ferranti said. "He didn't have much longer to live. A few more minutes at most. If we didn't find that boat, I don't think he would have made it."

They all wanted to know how I had hurt myself and ended up in the canal.

"My son had been partying with his friends after they won a soccer game," my dad explained. "He plays at FAU. He climbed into the back of his friend's truck and passed out, only the kid driving didn't know it. Then the truck crashed and threw him over a fence and into that canal. We figured out that he spent almost fourteen hours in there."

They asked how I was doing now.

"He's hanging in there," my father said. "He broke his neck but he's a fighter. The first night I saw him in the hospital, he was lying there, shaking like a leaf, white as a ghost . . . an angel must have been watching out for him or something."

The unrelenting stress of the past few days caught up with my father and he started to weep in front of these strangers. At first his tears embarrassed him. He wiped them off. Then the guy who never hugs anyone hugged every fireman he could get his hands on.

"You guys saved my son," he said. "I can't thank you enough."

"Tell the kid we wish him well," Ferranti said. "He's got some kind of constitution."

indifference

A week after the accident, my condition had improved so much that I no longer required intensive care. The nurses called it my graduation day. They could have called it Mark Zupan Is the Biggest Cocksucker in the World Day and I would have been just as pleased. Why? For starters, leaving the ICU meant I was finally getting that damn tube out of my throat once and for all. I would be able to talk and eat solid food again.

"It's doubtful, but we might have to put these tubes back later," the nurse told me as she pulled on rubber gloves.

I frantically pointed to the spell board.

N—O—!

The nurse put one hand on my chin and used the other to pull the plastic, and I gagged and retched and coughed up what felt like a garden hose. Then they removed the feeding tube from my nose that went down into my stomach. As it came out, I could taste the stomach acid.

"I never want to see that thing again," I said in a scratchy voice.

My voice, I thought. It felt good to hear my own voice again. It reminded me that I was still alive.

My old room in the ICU had these big glass windows that faced the hallway, and it felt like living in an aquarium with my injuries and lack of function on display for everyone to see. I was transferred to room 609, which had windows that actually faced outdoors and a TV hanging in the corner that hooked up to a VCR. The bed had the same rotisserie technology as the one in the ICU. Igoe used to play with the controls, flipping the switch back and forth.

"Look, Mark, you're dancing," he'd say, as the bed tilted from side to side.

The bed was also outfitted with a long pole above my head running parallel to the mattress with a sort of trapeze triangle hanging down. When I was ready, I would be able to pull myself up and hold my balance while I sat. But for now, I was still flat on my back.

The change of environment did a lot to improve my spirits. Every available space in the room was soon covered in cards, balloons, stuffed animals, and flowers. I stopped thinking about my injury and being stuck in the hospital every waking moment. Human beings are great at acclimating, and I guess I got used to being there. In the ICU, the proximity to pain and misery was inescapable, which caused people to speak in reverent whispers and walk on eggshells, maybe thinking if they talked too loudly death might notice them and pick a fight. The sunshine and fresh air that came through the window in my new room reminded me that broken bones heal, scars fade, and sometimes even the sickest people get better.

My friends were still coming by the hospital every day, and now they were able to camp out in my room for hours at a time. It was like a Sunday night dorm party back at FAU, minus the kegs. We would hang out, talk, play music, and watch movies. I asked them to rent The Doors. Val Kilmer did a pretty good job re-creating Jim Morrison, but Igoe became noticeably agitated and walked out of the room when certain songs were played.

My appetite was returning, but the food in the hospital was disgusting. That first night, I was pushing mushy peas around my plate when the Styrofoam to-go boxes started to arrive. Around a dozen of them. We opened them up like Christmas presents. Prime rib. Five-pound lobsters. Roasted chicken. Fillets. Chops. If it was an animal that you could kill, cook, and make delicious, you could find it in my new room. I was so hungry that I ate two entrées back to back, taking my time, savoring every bite slowly. I never knew baked potatoes with butter, chives, and sour cream could taste so good. I leaned back from my plate with an absurd, dreamy grin.

"Where is all this food coming from?" I asked my mom, as the deliveries kept coming.

"I'm not sure," she said.

The first few meals came from the chefs at Chowders, where I had worked. But boxes kept arriving night after night. We later learned that my dad's friend Richie Gallione had also been sending food over. My dad knew Richie from hanging out at the bar in Chowders and he's the kind of person I aspire to be—generous, humble, and loyal to his friends. Richie never told us about what he did. We heard about it from a third party. He didn't want the recognition. He just didn't want my family to have to worry about what we were eating while I was so hurt.

We had more grub than we could eat, and we would stuff our faces until nine p.m., drinking bottles of Snapple and Gatorade that my mom would bring me from home.

"All right, guys," the nurses would say, peeking their heads through the door. "Visiting hours are over. It's time to go home."

We would rifle through the white boxes to see what we had left. A lobster dinner, a Caesar salad, and a big slice of cheesecake could usually buy us a couple more hours of screw-around time, as long as we kept the noise down to a quiet roar.

There was only one problem with eating so much rich, delicious food every night. I hadn't moved my bowels in more than a week, and my stomach was stiff and bloated. I had what Igoe used to call a dickie-do. It's when your belly sticks out farther than your dickie do. With a painful pressure in my gut, I told my friends about my situation.

"I haven't dropped a deuce since I got here," I said.

"No shit," they said, shaking their heads in disbelief.

"Exactly," I said.

As you can see, by the time I had escaped the ICU, a certain gallows humor had crept into our conversations. My friends, the sympathetic bastards that they are, decided to start a betting pool. The person who picked the right day and hour of my first post-accident poop would go home with a wad of cash.

They would call my room at all hours of the night.

"Zupe. You drop the kids off at the pool yet?" they'd say.

"Nope."

I'd hang up the phone. Five minutes later, it would ring again.

"Zupe. You lay any cable yet?"

"No, man."

After a number of false alarms it finally happened a couple of days later around two in the afternoon. I felt a fleeting sense of satisfaction and relief until I realized that one of the nurses was going to wipe my gooey ass and change my soiled hospital gown and sheets for me as if I were an infant. Then I just felt pathetic. I was glad Kati wasn't there to see it.

I forgot who won the bet, but as I sat in my own shit waiting for the nurse to fill up a plastic pan with water to clean me, I remember thinking it wasn't so funny anymore. Was someone going to have to do this for me for the rest of my life? The thought made me shudder.

The doctor explained that if the nerves in my bladder and bowels weren't able to communicate with my brain, I would have to change the way I thought about going to the bathroom. My body would void itself whenever it felt full, regardless of whether I was on a toilet or not. He said I was going to have to take certain precautions to limit the accidents. I would continue to wear the catheter that drained my urine out of my bladder and into a plastic bag. It was possible that my bowel control would return soon, but he didn't know for sure. He mentioned that many people with spinal cord injuries have to wear adult diapers.

Sweet, I thought. *Chicks love dudes in diapers.*

coach donev and the entire soccer team came by for a visit. They brought me my old jersey and hung it on the wall to the left side of my bed for me. It was weird to see it there, like I was being retired and my number was now resting up in the rafters. My jersey shouldn't be on the wall. It should be on my back.

"I'll see you guys next year," I said. "Don't give my spot to anyone."

FAU's season ended a few weeks later in November with seven wins and seven losses and one tie.

My football coach from high school also paid his respects. My brother was playing for Coach Mathisen now, and they had just won one of the biggest games in the history of the school by beating St. Thomas Aquinas, the defending Class 4A champions, 14–3. A win like this was important to Coach Mathisen, probably one of the highlights of his career. But instead of keeping the game ball for himself, he gave it to me.

Mathisen was a somber-looking man in his late forties with graying hair and a bushy mustache. When he was my coach, I remember him yelling constantly, slapping the sides of our helmets to get our undivided attention when we screwed up. He had always intimidated me, but I respected him for being firm but fair. It meant a lot for him to come and see me and bring me the ball.

"I don't know what to say," I told him, touched by the gesture. "I wish I could have played football for you all four years."

"There's nothing I'd rather do than give you this," he said. "You're a great kid."

I was feeling better, so the doctors increased my physical therapy. After the surgery, the nurses would stretch my legs and arms for me while I stayed in bed. If joints, muscles, ligaments, and tendons aren't exercised regularly, they will contract and stiffen. We still did the stretching, but now I was ready to go to the hospital's gym for therapy. That first afternoon the nurse helped me sit up, putting her arms around my shoulder and then hinging my body. I hadn't been horizontal in quite some time.

"You're going to feel a rush of blood, and you might feel sick or you could pass . . ."

The words had barely left her lips before my eyes rolled white and I was out cold.

After I came to, they had to transfer me into a high-back wheelchair with a move called a one-person lift. I would have to lean off the side of the bed and put my shoulder into the nurse's hip. Then they would grab me by the back of my pants and lift me off and into the chair. I hated it because I felt I was going to fall forward and face-plant on the floor.

"Is there any way I can do this on my own?" I would ask.

For the time being, there wasn't. It was tough for me to learn to trust the nurses and forfeit all my independence. I've never been very good at giving up control.

You see, when you have an injury like mine, it's like you're suddenly in an infant's body again. You have to relearn how to use your muscles to do the most rudimentary tasks. The muscles you can control have to compensate for the ones that you can't use. I literally spent hours working with the therapists on sitting upright on my own. I know it sounds weird, but take a second and try to sit up without using any of your stomach muscles.

Tough, isn't it?

At first, I was like a deflated balloon and would slump over to the side because my trunk was compromised and I had lost my equilibrium and coordination. But eventually, I learned to balance my torso by positioning my arms at my sides like slanted airplane wings. I also had to learn how to get myself up if I was lying on my back. I would twist to the side and then use my arms to push my body into an upright position.

We also worked with weights. First, I would ask them to pull my neck brace as tight as possible to make sure that my weakened spine was totally secure. I didn't want to re-injure myself. The bones were far from healed. During football season, I was benching well over two hundred pounds. Now I was asked to curl and lift small seven-pound dumbbells.

No sweat, I thought.

I couldn't hold them tightly because I couldn't make fists with my hands, so they used Velcro bands to strap them to me. I struggled to lift that pathetic amount more than a couple of times and had to take a break. I was dispirited about how weak I had become.

Then they put me on the floor and asked me to do push-ups while I was on my knees.

"You mean girl push-ups," I said.

At first, I couldn't do three of them.

You have to start small and build slowly, they said. You need to be patient. Listen to your body. You have to remember, you are basically starting with a zero sum.

After a few sessions, I was knocking out sets of fifteen. I was able to maintain a sitting position for eight minutes. I could lift seven pounds twenty times. Doing this stuff was harder than running a five-minute mile in ankle weights. I pushed myself even though the therapist wanted me to take it easy. I would try to do too much too quickly. Then I would feel so tired that I could barely move. But I would force myself to get back in the gym and rally. In my mind, the only thing standing between my old life and me was hard work.

"The patient is very motivated," one of my therapists wrote in a report. I liked physical therapy because it was an active way for me to achieve my goal of walking again. I felt I was solving my problem instead of waiting around for it to take care of itself.

They would monitor my vital signs when I worked out, or when they put me in this contraption called a tilt table. It was a big flat surface on a hydraulic lift. I would lie back on it and they would secure straps across my chest and legs. Then it would tilt me into a standing position, like I was Frankenstein's monster. This helped my circulation and reduced the spasms.

During one of these sessions, the therapist's hand accidentally brushed one of my legs. I felt spider webs of sensation from the quick contact and even the warmth of her fingers. I couldn't believe it. I asked her to touch my leg again. Then my feet. Then my toes.

"Holy shit," I said softly. "I can feel you touching me."

The sensation wasn't as strong as it used to be, and it wasn't totally consistent all over my legs, but it was there. No doubt about it. I was overjoyed. My recovery was happening so fast, much faster than my doctors predicted. I could pull on my own shirt with the help of the trapeze triangle. I couldn't get my shorts on by myself, but I could put on shoes as long as I didn't have to tie them. I was brushing my teeth and washing my face without any assistance. I could eat with a knife and fork, but couldn't open certain containers of food on my own.

I still couldn't move my legs, but yesterday I couldn't feel anything down there, and now I could.

I was going to beat this thing in record time, I told my parents.

"Mark my words," I said. "In one year, I'm going to be back on the soccer field."

I slept soundly that night for the first time since the accident.

thank god I never broke up with Kati. The thought had crossed my mind when I was back at FAU. The injury had brought us closer, and we didn't talk about the problems we were having before. I had come to rely on her more than I ever could have imagined. She would leave school early each afternoon and would dutifully come spend time with me at the hospital. The doctors showed her how to stretch my legs and arms, and she would go through the routine with me, rotating my legs, hips, and trunk. Quick motions can damage joints, so all stretches were done with a smooth, controlled flow.

"Thank you for this," I'd say to her. "I don't know what I'd do without you."

"You're going to be fine," she would say. "I know it in my heart. Pretty soon you won't need me anymore."

There was an unspoken intimacy in the way that she cared for me. She would help me dress, pulling my shorts over my legs and under my butt, helping me to secure the snap. It was like her mothering instinct had kicked in, although sometimes I would feel like I was a doll that she was dressing. She would hold my hand as we watched TV in silence. She never complained that she was bored or unhappy. She never said that she would rather be somewhere else with her friends. She was just kind, caring, and supportive—the perfect girlfriend.

I told myself that I was falling in love with her all over again. Maybe we would get married. I felt lucky to have her in my life. She was my last shot at a happy relationship. If I didn't get better, no girl was going to want to go out with me. Women as pretty as Kati don't dream about hanging out with crippled guys who can lift only seven pounds and constantly piss themselves. I was going to do everything in my power to hold on to her.

One afternoon my mom came in and sat down next to me on the

bed. For the first time in a while, we were the only two people in the room. The number of friends that were coming to visit me on a regular basis had started to thin out. Nickell and Cava had gone back to school in Gainesville. Igoe had resumed classes at FAU, but he managed to stop at least once a day. He and Steve, Dana and Kati were the last of the regulars.

"Mark," she said. "Your father and I have been having some discussions with Marcia and Howard about what we should do. We all think you should go down to Miami for your rehabilitation. There's a hospital there called Jackson Memorial. We drove down and checked it out this past week. They specialize in spinal cord injuries."

"I'm not leaving North Broward," I said. "I'm getting better here. Every day there is more improvement. My arms are getting stronger. I have more range of motion. I have some feeling in my legs again. And all my friends are close by. I would be all alone at Jackson."

What I was really thinking is that I couldn't stand to be apart from Kati. If I went down to Miami, she wouldn't be able to visit me every day. The drive was too far. She'd go back to hanging out with her friends and going to parties. After a while, she'd probably figure out that dating a guy who can't walk isn't much fun and would hook up with someone else.

"Your father and I will come see you every day," she said.

My mom and I talked about Jackson Memorial for a while and made a list of all the pros and cons. She talked to me about my reservations. I wanted to stay where I was, but my mom's logic was impossible to deny. I had to keep my ultimate goal in mind—I still had a long way to go if I was going to walk within one year and play sports again. I could see why the care at Jackson would be so much better for me, and I reluctantly agreed with her. She had already talked to the doctors at Jackson and they had a bed available.

I told her I was cool with going to Miami, but I had one request.

"Pearl Jam's new album, *Vs.*, just comes out tomorrow," I said. "Can you go to the store and buy it for me?"

"Of course," she said, kissing me on my head. "No problem."

If I had to pick my favorite band of all time, it would be Pearl Jam. I listened to their first album, *Ten*, more times than I can count. It was the soundtrack to my high school years. My friends and I would drive around blasting "Alive" after our football games, singing every word together. I had been looking forward to getting *Vs.* for months. When I was in the ICU, I had counted down the days in my head, waiting for it to come out.

The next day, my mom came back with a portable CD player and the album for me.

"Thanks, Mom," I said.

I tried to unwrap it but couldn't get it open with my hands. She had to take the plastic wrapper and the security seal off for me. I stared at the cover art. There was a fish-eye photo of this sheep or llama or something. The animal's eyes showed both fear and defiance, and the image evoked a feeling of forced isolation. You can see that the beast is trapped in some sort of pen, and it's pushing up against the fence, trying to bite the hand that feeds it.

I know what you're going through, brother, I thought.

The songs conveyed a similar kind of lonely urgency, rallying cries against a herd mentality and an unexamined life of mediocrity. The angst from *Ten* had become primal anger on *Vs.*, and the overall sound was leaner, more compact, sophisticated, and subversive. On my first listen, "Rearviewmirror" rocked my world, especially the drumming at the end of the song.

When you spend most of your days dozing in bed, the nights get pretty long. Time stands up, stretches, and then hunkers down and tries to suffocate you. Hours become ages. Television bored me, and I've never been much of a reader, although I did like *Catcher in the Rye* when it was assigned to us in English class. My dad had given me a folder of research about spinal cord injury and other information about quadriplegia. I read it at night, highlighting sections, making notes in the margins. After I finished, I almost wished for my old blissful ignorance because it allowed for more hope about making a total recovery.

The pessimistic thoughts multiplied in my mind again. I put on my headphones and listened to Pearl Jam. I found comfort in Eddie Vedder's howling cries, which kept me company. Vedder infused each song with this world-weary wisdom, like life had stabbed him in the back but he was still standing, irrepressible and indignant. His songs were all about resistance.

There's a special kind of relationship that people can have with music only when they are young and searching. Rock stars become prophets, and each song is a secret coded message about your destiny. The final track on the CD is called "Indifference." It's the least rocking song on the album, just a slow bass line, a tambourine, and some spacey-sounding guitars and organs under Vedder's plaintive vocals. It's more spiritual than savage. I found myself returning to this song again and again. I would close my eyes and let the words wash over me:

> *I will light a match this morning, so I won't be alone*
> *Watch as she lies silent, for soon light will be gone*
> *I will stand with my arms outstretched, pretend I'm free to roam*
> *I will make my way through one more day in hell*
> *How much difference does it make?*
> *How much difference does it make?*
>
> *I will hold the candle until it burns up my arm*
> *I'll keep taking punches until their will grows tired*
> *I will stare the sun down until my eyes go blind*
> *Hey, I won't change direction and I won't change my mind*
> *How much difference does it make?*
> *How much difference does it make?*
> *How much difference . . .*
>
> *I will swallow poison until I grow immune*
> *I will scream my lungs out until it fills this room*
> *How much difference*
> *How much difference*
> *How much difference does it make?*
> *How much difference does it make . . .*

I'd listen to his testimony about suffering and perseverance on constant repeat and insert my life between the lines. It became my anthem as I grappled with the frustration and uselessness that I was feeling, my armor against the dark thoughts that assailed me. Knowing that someone else felt this way gave me strength. Most of my friends had returned to their regularly scheduled lives and I was still here, in the hospital, alone and paralyzed. I realized that their world had only been on pause for a while. My world had stopped completely. But I knew I had to keep moving, keep pushing forward. Sometimes the fight is all you get. Victory doesn't mean anything if failure isn't a possibility.

If I was going to overcome this injury, I told myself, I was going to have to challenge it with every ounce of strength I could muster.

I hoped that it would make a difference.

i left north broward on Thursday, October 28, at 10:30 a.m. I was in a crap-ass mood that morning because I didn't want to change facilities. I liked the doctors and nurses at North Broward. I felt safe with them. Some orderlies took me down to the ambulance and the EMTs loaded me in the back. The drive down to Miami took over an hour. My parents rode with me.

This was the second time in exactly two weeks that I had been in the back of an ambulance, only this time there were no lights and sirens, no one wondering if I was going to die before we got to where we were going. Jackson is located in downtown Miami, near Liberty City, a great neighborhood if you're into sleeping in cardboard boxes, pushing shopping carts full of cans, and sipping booze out of a brown paper sack. The hospital opened back in 1918 and was named after James M. Jackson, the hospital's first permanent physician. For those of you interested in a little history about the place, Chicago mayor Anton Chermak died at Jackson in 1933 after he was hit by a bullet intended for then president Franklin Roosevelt.

When I arrived early that afternoon, the attendants put me into a high-back hospital wheelchair. Later, I would be measured and fitted for my own chair. It would be eighteen inches wide and sixteen inches deep and as big as an old love seat, with metal armrests, wheelie bars, and plastic handles in the back. Making it move was like pushing a wheelbarrow full of cinder blocks, and it was so wide that it barely fit through the normal doorway. Steering it was like turning an ocean liner.

I was still wearing my neck brace, and I wouldn't be taking it off for many more weeks. While my parents talked to the administrators and filled out the remaining paperwork, an attendant pushed me into the main lounge. The staff was throwing a Halloween party for the patients. I'm using the term *party* here loosely. I remember downcast people of all ages and colors in wheelchairs sitting around drinking red fruit punch in paper cups and eating cookies shaped like cats and witches from the supermarket bakery. Some were playing board games. Others were watching soap operas on TV. Good times.

My dad would later tell me that the place always reminded him of the VA hospital from the Tom Cruise movie *Born on the Fourth of July* or the facility where Jack Nicholson lost his marbles in *One Flew Over the Cuckoo's Nest*. He wasn't sure if he wanted to leave me there, but he couldn't exactly put me in the car and take me back home with him.

I decided to skip the festivities and go check out my new digs. I was going to share one large room with three other people. There were curtains on cross-shaped runners that separated the room into quarters when you needed some privacy. My bed was the first one to the left of the door. I introduced myself to the new roommates, who had passed on the party as well. My right hand was still contorted like a claw, and shaking hands with strangers was really embarrassing for me, but this wasn't an issue at Jackson. My new roommates had recently injured their spines as well, and two of them had less hand function than I did. I wish I could say that the severity of their injuries put mine into perspective, but it didn't.

There was one guy a couple years older than me who had broken his neck wrestling with his buddies. His name was Adam; he was in real bad shape and could barely move. Another guy, Ian, was in his midthirties and had been partying at his house one night and dove into the shallow end of his swimming pool, hitting his head on the bottom and breaking his neck. My third roommate, Kyle, had been there a while and could actually stand up and walk a little. I would watch him with envy and amazement and ask how he did it.

"Practice," he told me.

After Kyle moved out, I got another roommate, this Christian guy who wanted to talk to me about God's master plan. I wasn't big on that conversation. He would put his hands to his ears when I would talk to my parents and drop a few "F" bombs in the conversation. He changed rooms and was replaced by a teenager named Nick Lapira. Nick was a skinny kid with light brown hair and a nervous kind of energy that reminded me of a squirrel. He was from West Palm, Florida, and he had crunched his spine by diving into the ocean's sandy bottom. His injury was higher up on his neck than mine, and he could barely use his arms at all. The way he would look at me reminded me of my little brother, Jeff. When I would talk to him, he would hang on my every word.

My parents helped me unpack my clothes, CDs, and photos. It made me remember that it wasn't too long ago that Igoe and I had been unpacking at FAU and how much my life had changed in the past two weeks. I wondered how Igoe was doing back at school without me, living in our old dorm room all by himself. Was he having fun without me?

"You going to be okay here?" my dad said.

"I'll be fine, Dad," I said. "Don't worry about me."

My parents took off, promising me that they would be back the next day with Kati, Steve, and Dana. We were all going to have lunch. I couldn't wait to see Kati again. It had only been a day since we were last together, but every time I thought about being apart from her for an extended period of time, I would get this sick feeling in my stomach and my insecurity would make me want to put my fist through the wall. I felt like I had turned into a ticking time bomb that only she could defuse.

The nurses took me on a tour of the facility. The wing had several stories, and despite the shabbiness of the lounge, it was a pretty nice place with a friendly staff. They had Ping-Pong tables on the top level and a good-size gym with tons of free weights and other machines. They explained to me that we would be having several hours of both physical and psychological therapy each day. I liked that I was going to be able to cruise around the facility on my own, even if it was in a wheelchair. At North Broward, I spent most of my time in bed staring at the ceiling. My life had always been about movement, and sitting still loosened my already tenuous grip on sanity. I began to think of myself as a shark—if I stopped moving, I would die.

They rolled me back to my room. With four guys in there, it was close quarters and the place didn't exactly have the best vibe. It was like a prison, where people had little to lose, and that made them desperate and unpredictable. It was clear that no one was happy about their current situation. Ian was the most pissed off about his injury and seemed to enjoy taking his anger out on others. He had his pants down and was lying on his side. A nurse was helping him with a bedpan. Staring at naked man crack is not my idea of a nice way to spend an evening. I turned my head toward the wall so I wouldn't have to look at his hairy horizontal smile. I wished I was anywhere else in the world but in that room.

"Angle my ass toward the new guy," Ian said. "I want him to have a nice view of the fun we're having here." The nurse ignored him. She grabbed the curtain and yanked it closed. I couldn't see anything that was going on, but the smell painted quite a mental picture.

"Welcome to rehab," I heard him say from behind the screen.

i woke up early the next morning and was taken down to the cafeteria to have breakfast. Afterward, I was introduced to my team of therapists. I quickly learned that living at Jackson would be like going through quadriplegic boot camp. For the next two and a half months, I would have strength and endurance training, electrostimulation therapy, and classes on grooming, homemaking, fine motor skills, skin care, sexuality, driving, and safety awareness, plus vocational evaluation and training. Their job was to help people like me acclimate to our new bodies and teach us skills that we would need to survive a life with limited function. In addition to the four hours of physical and occupational rehab each day, I was expected to participate in both individual and group psychotherapy on a weekly basis to address the mental and emotional impact of my spinal cord injury. I would be introduced to the group at the next session.

Not going to happen, I said to myself.

I thought back to my childhood and remembered what it felt like to be the new guy, standing in front of the class, nervous as hell. There was no way I was going to sit and listen to a bunch of strangers cry about their problems. And I certainly wasn't going to share anything with them. I had internalized all my emotions, and I wasn't about to let any of my negative feelings see the sunlight. As far as I was concerned, I didn't have any problems. The only issues I had were physical. Once I was walking again, everything else would be cool.

We spent the morning designing a schedule, and by the time we were finished, it was close to noon. My parents were expected to arrive any minute. I went back up to change my clothes. I wanted to look my best because Kati was going to be there. I had difficulty applying deodorant because of my hands. Before the accident, I was right-handed. But now I could move my fingers better on my left, and was forced to do most activities with my off hand.

Still, I felt like I was wearing invisible mittens. I could put deodorant on my right armpit with my left hand, but I couldn't hold the container in my right hand to put it on my left armpit. I had to use my left hand for both sides and ended up smearing it all over my shirt. I had already figured out that teeth are a crippled person's best friend and can be used as a third hand. I tried to put the cap back on with my mouth and I got Degree antiperspirant on my lips and tongue, which made me gag. Note to self: never do that again.

When I came down, my parents, Kati, Steve, and Dana were all waiting for me in the lobby. Igoe was also there, standing apart from the rest of the group. His mom had driven him down and dropped him off at the hospital. It was the first time they had seen me in a wheelchair. They all pretended like it was no big deal, but for me, it was another moment that made me realize my injuries might be permanent.

I noticed that Kati's white teeth were indenting her pink lower lip. Hoping to cheer me up, she had dressed up for Halloween and was wearing a slinky cat costume complete with a tail and makeup whiskers painted on her face.

"Hello, Kitty," I said.

"Hey, babe," she said, kissing me lightly on the corner of my mouth. "I've missed you."

I hoped that she didn't taste the deodorant.

We decided to take the train to Bayside Mall. I had never been outside in a wheelchair. I was already feeling insecure and self-conscious about the way I looked, but I wasn't prepared for the sideways glances I was receiving from complete strangers. People were literally looking down at me now. They would stare at me until I looked back at them and then they would turn their heads or avert their eyes. I felt like they were studying me, picking me apart, trying to figure out how I ended up in a chair so that they could save themselves from whatever horrible thing had happened to me. It made me feel like a total freak show.

We got to the end of the block and had to cross the street to get to the train. They rolled me to the curb and we looked down at the foot drop to the gutter. I might as well have been sitting at the edge of the Grand Canyon. My dad wanted to hold the handles and ease me down, but what if he lost control and I toppled over? I didn't want to take that risk. I was aware that I was being irrational, but still I was worried that I would get hurt again. We were stuck and no one knew what to do.

I looked around and realized that at certain intersections, there were slanted curb cuts built into the sidewalk and designed for people in wheelchairs. The closest one was back near the front of the hospital. We backtracked to the curb cut and crossed the street. This was the first time that I noticed the almost invisible world of handicap accessibility.

We caught the train, exited, and then rode an elevator to the ground floor. It was gray and cold that day, so we stopped by the Gap so I could buy a sweatshirt. Kati was pushing me as we entered the store. It felt so good to be with her again. She seemed to be having fun. Even though I was in the chair, things almost felt back to normal for a second.

As we looked at the clothes, a clerk walked up and studied my wheelchair, my neck brace, my blue hospital booties, and the red constellation of fading ant bites on my face.

"I like your costume," he said to me.

"Look, buddy, I'm not wearing a costume," I said flatly.

He blushed and awkwardly apologized, but he probably didn't feel as bad as I did.

We made our way down the strip of stores to the Hard Rock. The hostess didn't look at me when she asked how many people were in our party, even when I answered her. We followed her across the floor. The tables were spaced only a few feet apart from each other and the restaurant was crowded. My dad was pushing me now and couldn't maneuver my chair through the tight spaces and kept banging into the backs of other sitting patrons.

"Excuse me," I mumbled. "I'm sorry."

When we finally made it to our table my chair was too high to fit under it, so I stuck out in the aisle. I had to go wash my hands before I could eat, because they were dirty from pushing the black rubber wheels, and that meant returning to the maze of tight tables. The trip to the bathroom felt like it took around thirty minutes. Even the smallest task seemed to take the longest time these days, and I couldn't do anything myself. Nothing was easy anymore. When we returned, I was frustrated and cross with myself because I had made everyone wait for me before they could order. If my friends didn't have a good time visiting me, I didn't think they would come back.

When the waitress came, I ordered a pulled pork sandwich. It probably wasn't the best choice for me. The shredded meat was smothered in sauce and made the soggy bun hard to handle. I picked it up awkwardly with my left hand, and when I took a bite, the pork slid out the bottom and ended up all over the front of my new sweatshirt. Kati leaned over and tried to rub the stains out with napkins that she dipped into her water glass.

"Stop it," I said, pushing her hand away. "I can do it. You don't have to baby me."

She gave me a hurt look as I fumbled with my napkin.

I tried to pick the sandwich up again, this time with both hands. There was no way I could get it into my mouth without spilling most of it on my lap. I slammed it back down on the plate so hard that all the silverware rattled and a water glass jumped off the table.

Great, I thought. *I can't eat a sandwich in public without making a fucking mess of myself. This is pathetic. I can't believe that anyone would want to hang out with me.*

The whole table was silent while I seethed with aggravation. Igoe had an anguished look on his face and looked like he wanted to run out of the restaurant.

"Mark," my mom said. "It's okay. Just calm down and take your time."

"Screw that," I said. "Take me back to the hospital. I want to be alone."

things i don't remember

Life at a rehab facility is all about structure. The therapists fill your day with order, routine, and endless activity so you don't have any free time to throw a rope over a rafter. If I wasn't tossing a rubber ball back and forth with a partner to increase my dynamic balance, I was picking small wooden pegs up off the floor, improving my manual dexterity. Or I was hooked up to different electrodes, flexing again and again when I felt the tiny shock stimulating my muscles. Or I was in the gym, working on pelvic tilts or trying to stand on my knees to help strengthen my lower back. I would also do this crawling exercise on all fours that they called quadruped creeping. Relearning how to use your muscles requires monotonous repetition, and I was able to zone out and lose myself completely in the mindless activities.

Physically, I was still getting stronger. Feeling and motion were coming back in bits and pieces. Sitting in a chair, I could lift my legs about half an inch by now, my left better than my right. My bowel control had finally returned, although I was now learning the joys of the special poo-poo chair that quads get to use. It has handles on the sides so you can use your arms to lift yourself on and off the toilet. I had also been introduced to stool softener and suppositories, which I called magic bullets. Stick them up your ass and forty-five minutes later you were doing your business. At least I was able to wipe myself.

In my mind, all problems could still be solved with willpower and hard work. I was going to get back everything I had lost. My recovery had become a game of inches, and fortunately that was a game I knew how to win: you just grind it out, push forward, and roll over the opposition any way you can.

Emotionally, however, I was a total wreck, only I didn't know it. I was still in complete denial about my injury, and I refused to go to group therapy. If I had, I probably would have learned that when you suffer an injury like mine, you go through the same stages of grief that people experience when they are diagnosed with a terminal illness.

You start with denial, telling yourself that there's nothing wrong and everything will be fine. Then you feel anger toward the situation and wonder why you were singled out for such a fucked-up fate. Then you try to bargain with whatever higher power you believe in, saying, "If you fix me, I'll be a better person." After that you get depressed because nothing has changed for all your efforts and then finally, if you're lucky, you end up with acceptance.

I was stuck somewhere between denial and anger. Maybe denial isn't the right word for it. How about nonacceptance? I kept telling myself that I would be back on the soccer field by the one-year anniversary of my accident. I did all my physical therapy with this single goal in mind. In my defense, though, the doctors had not ruled this out as a possibility. In fact, they seemed just as hopeful as I was that I would walk again. After my excursion to the Hard Rock Café, I absolutely hated being in a chair. Even though I had my own chair now and could push myself around the facility, I refused to go on any of the weekly field trips to the bowling alley or to the lake with the rest of the group. They were trying to make us feel comfortable outside the safe hospital bubble. But I didn't want to be seen in public as part of the handicap brigade.

I attended the required classes because I had nothing better to do between sessions at the gym, and I watched patiently as they showed us how to get out of bed and into the chair on our own. We practiced getting in and out of the shower stall and buttoning shirts. Soon, I was able to catheter my own penis, and I could cook pasta on the stove without burning my hands or setting myself on fire. I took a driver's evaluation test, and they recommended that I drive a specially modified car with hand controls, because my lower extremities were "unable to overcome gravity," as they eloquently wrote in my weekly report.

I thought all this training was a waste of time, because I was going to be normal again as soon as I could walk. I wouldn't need to know how to live like a gimp.

I found it much easier to focus on other people and their problems. My roommate Nick would constantly bitch and throw temper tantrums about taking his meds. Every single person in the hospital had to take a handful of pills each morning. I was on at least twenty different medications, with exotic names like ticarcillin, aztreonam, and cefoperazone. I took a cocktail of antibiotics, steroids, antispasm meds, and painkillers. The pills were another lame part of rehab and it sucked to take them all, but compared to all the other shit we had to deal with, it wasn't that big of a deal.

"What the hell is your problem," I finally said to Nick.

"They hurt my throat when I swallow them," he said.

"Well, don't try and take them all at once," I said. "Make sure your mouth isn't dry. Drink some water before. Place them on the back of your tongue. You'll be fine."

I wasn't telling him anything he didn't know. I realized at the time that he was acting out, attempting to exert some sort of control over his life because he felt he didn't have any. I saw other guys doing the same thing. They wouldn't get out of bed in the morning or they wouldn't eat their food. They would yell at their therapists and refuse to exercise, even though they knew it would help them in the long run. These tiny acts of protest were all they had in a world where fate had rendered them powerless. They were aware that they were only hurting themselves, but they didn't care. Sometimes self-destruction can feel pretty satisfying.

It's only in hindsight that I've come to understand I was just as angry as they were. I gave my middle finger to the world by skipping group therapy and going to the gym, which was my sanctuary, the only place I could find peace. I would strap the dumbbells to my hands and work out, trying to burn through the frustration I was feeling.

The 7 pounds that I was benching back at North Broward became 50 pounds. Then 100. My favorite machine in the gym was called "the rickshaw." You would back your chair into it, and it had handles connected to weights that you would push down, working out your chest and arms.

Even if I was too tired to lift, I would park my chair in a corner of the weight room, watching other patients do their physical therapy just to see if there were any recovery techniques I could learn from them. I would compare myself to others as a way to gauge my progress, and I would compete against them in my mind to help my motivation.

"You're in here again?" the therapists would say to me when I would return for my third or fourth time for the day. "Don't you do anything else but lift weights?"

"Sure," I'd say, "I eat. Sometimes I sleep."

I guess you could say I became obsessive about working out, my determination bordering on mania. While I could hide in the gym during group therapy, individual therapy wasn't so easy to blow off. My therapist, a young woman named Francine with long black hair, would track me down, pull me to the side, and try to engage me in conversation. She would force me to talk about things I didn't want to talk about, such as what my future was going to be like once I moved back home, or how my injury was going to affect my relationship with Kati.

I kept telling her that everything was fine.

She didn't believe me.

Her constant questions pissed me off, and I made it my goal to humiliate and embarrass Francine whenever I could. One day she sat me down and gave me what's known as a Rorschach test. She held up different pieces of paper, and I was supposed to tell her what images I saw in the abstract ink splotches. It's a way to judge your mental state and examine the subconscious. The first one looked like a melted chocolate butterfly smashed on a windshield.

"Tell me what you see," she said.

"I don't understand how this is going to help me walk again," I said.

"Come on, Mark. Just describe what you see."

"Fine, Francine," I said, staring at the drawing. I leaned in close to her, so close that I was inches from her face, invading her personal space. My eyes dipped down toward her chest.

"Hmmm. I see a woman with big tits."

She got an uncomfortable look on her face. Flustered, she held up another drawing.

"How about this one?"

"I see a woman with a big hairy pussy and big tits."

I could tell she was mortified by what I said and maybe even a little afraid of me. I knew I was being a total dick to her, but for some reason I couldn't stop myself from creeping her out. I liked seeing her suffer. Instead of facing up to my own insecurities, I tried to scare her away. She became the outlet for my fury. I had become just as hostile as my roommates.

"Are we finished yet, Francine?" I asked sweetly. "Can I go back to the gym?"

my pent-up rage made Jackson Memorial a lonely place. The accident had somehow made me schizophrenic. One moment, I would be clear-headed about my injury and the fact that I was a quadriplegic with an incomplete spinal cord injury. I'd be rational and even outgoing. I'd get along fine with my roommates and my therapists and complete the tasks at hand.

Other times, I would succumb to my anger and go out of my way to antagonize anyone I could with this go-fuck-yourself attitude. I would mask my pain with a gruff exterior and assault others with rudeness. I'd always been pretty good at making new friends. But at Jackson, I often pushed people away and rejected others before they could reject me. I found no relief talking to the other patients about what they were going through, no satisfaction in comparing experiences. The only camaraderie I felt was hanging out with my roommate Nick.

One afternoon, I overheard another patient talking to his family. They were getting ready to leave and go out for some food or something, and I thought they were babying him, making sure he had a sweater and extra catheter bags. I tried to hold my tongue, but the words came out before my brain could stop them.

"I can't believe you all are spoiling a grown fucking man," I said. "He's not a child. You think you're helping him but you're not. He should be doing this shit on his own."

The dude's parents just stared at me like I was a cloven-hoofed creature that had magically appeared out of a puff of black smoke. That outburst earned me a write-up in my weekly evaluation and more talk about how I needed to work on my anger management. Still, I couldn't stop myself from voicing my opinion to these people even though I knew it was none of my business. But underneath all my aggressive behavior, I was scared shitless. I felt ugly and unlikable and I didn't know how to handle it. I would constantly time-travel in my head, going back to the night of the accident, making different decisions.

I told myself I didn't care if people liked me or not anymore. I was at Jackson for the physical therapy, not to make friends. Looking back on it, I realize that I was mostly pissed at myself. The way I saw it, I had managed to ruin my life in one evening, and the remorse I was feeling—the resolute sadness, the self-betrayal—was inescapable. I was going through a period of mourning for my old life. No matter how hard I tried, I couldn't forgive myself for being so careless. I promised myself that when I got out of the hospital, I would never drink alcohol again. Never. I believed I had been given a second chance, and I wasn't about to make the same mistake. That would be the only way to atone for my sins of stupidity.

As I said, back then it was all black or white.

Truth be told, I've blocked out many of my memories about daily life at Jackson. The experience was just too painful. It was one of the hardest chapters in my recovery, and I'm thankful I don't remember every excruciating detail about what I was feeling. If I did, I don't know if I would have been able to push forward with the rest of my life. I've realized that the ability to forget is sometimes much more useful than the ability to remember.

My mother or father would drive down to Miami and visit me each night after work. Their visits meant everything to me. I know those trips weren't easy on them. My dad was back at his company, and my mom was working full time and going to night school to earn her master's in computer science. We would sit in the cafeteria and share the awful pre-made entrée that I was required to eat before I could leave the premises. Then we would go get some Chinese food or pizza down the street. I would tell them about how I was sure I was going to walk again, and they would tell me what was going on back in the real world.

Their news wasn't good. My dad had been to see his lawyer. It didn't look like there was going to be any million-dollar settlement for me. Dirty Moe's didn't have insurance to cover my claims and its well-connected owner knew all the loopholes in the system. They thought about going after the Broward County Sheriff's office for ignoring the tow truck driver when he said he thought he heard something in the bushes, but their lawyer advised against it.

My parents' insurance company still refused to pay the stacked coverage. There was no paperwork backing up my mom in saying she had asked for it, so my parents had no recourse and ultimately received the lesser amount. Igoe's insurance company had paid out a little as well. In the end, we received around $300,000, and that money immediately went to bills not covered by my medical insurance. There would be no financial safety net for me. Like most people, I was going to have to find a well-paying job and learn to support myself.

Most patients lived at Jackson full time, but my mom and dad decided it would be a good idea if I came home on the weekends so I could see my friends and get used to living at my parents' house again. This was a big coup. No patient had ever been allowed a weekend furlough before. The insurance company had forbidden it, saying they wouldn't pay for an empty bed. But my mom was able to argue them around to seeing things her way.

One Friday night as my dad was driving me back up to Coral Springs for the weekend, he told me that we were going to stop off and watch my little brother play football. In his junior year, Jeff was playing cornerback on the varsity squad. Because Douglas was a new school, it didn't have its own stadium, and so the team played football at Coral Springs High. Initially, I told my dad I didn't want to go. I was nervous because I was going to be seeing a lot of friends for the first time since the accident.

What are they going to think of me? I wondered.

Were they going to look at me the way I used to look at people in chairs? Were they going to stare, or worse than that, pretend I didn't exist at all? I felt like I had been away from the real world for so long. Would anyone even remember me?

In those days, I judged myself by other people's standards instead of my own.

But any tentative feelings I had soon passed. I was so excited to be away from Jackson, I didn't care where we were going. When we drove up to the school gate, a parking attendant stopped us and then spoke into a walkie-talkie. For some reason, he recognized my father.

"Mr. Zupan," he said. "Coach Mathisen wants you and Mark to come down to the field."

"Uh, okay," my dad said, looking bewildered.

We parked and my dad got my wheelchair out of the trunk and helped me into it by using a device called a transfer board. Basically he would help me to slide my ass along a smooth wooden plank that bridged the gap between the car seat and my chair. Once I was in, I pushed myself down the track to the Douglas side of the field. Fans were crammed together on the bleachers, watching the teams get ready to play under the stadium lights.

When we got next to Coach Mathisen, he said hello to us and then signaled his team. All the Douglas players stopped what they were doing and ran single file to the five-yard line. They removed their helmets and took a knee. Coach Mathisen told me that the team had planned this with my brother and some of the other guys I had played with last year. They wanted me to know they hadn't forgotten about me. It was a sign of respect given to me at a time in my life when I needed it most. Since the accident, I had lost almost all my self-confidence.

"What's up, Zupe?" my buddy Jon Miller called from the grass.

Miller was like a little brother to me. He had been a sophomore when I was a senior, and the kid was an incredible athlete. Nickell, Cava, Igoe, and I had always looked out for him when we were at Douglas and made sure the other older players didn't pick on him.

We were friends with his sister, who was our age and one of the prettiest girls at Douglas. She used to date our friend Ray Gentile. After my accident, Jon had come to North Broward to visit. He was always upbeat, but my mom later told me that once she found him out in the parking lot crying with his head in his hands. He told her that it hurt him to see me this way.

Somehow, the crowd understood what was going on. They started to chant my name, softly at first, but then it grew louder.

"Zupan! Zupan! Zupan!"

The noise was deafening, and I could feel the weight of thousands of eyes on me. It was a totally surreal feeling, and I wanted to hug them all and hide my face at the same time. I knew in my heart that I didn't deserve their applause. I hadn't accomplished anything. I was in a fucking wheelchair. That's all. Their kindness started to feel like pity instead of compassion.

"What am I supposed to do?" I asked my dad.

"I don't know," he said.

I decided to lift my arm into the air. I could barely get my hand above my shoulder, and I did my best to make a fist. Maybe I was remembering what Igoe would do with his black power glove before each football game. The crowd cheered louder.

I didn't want to lose my shit but I couldn't stop myself. Some of my tears were from the love and support that I felt they were showing me. But there was another reason I was crying that night. As I looked out at the line of guys in their maroon uniforms with white numbers, I realized how much I missed suiting up and feeling the camaraderie and competition.

To put it simply, I missed playing.

I wondered if I had lost that part of my life forever.

in early december, I took four steps.

My physical therapist couldn't believe her eyes when she saw it happen. I had been standing between the parallel bars for more than a month now, supporting myself with my arms, trying to remember how to move, willing my worthless legs to start doing something. Anything.

And then, suddenly, they did.

The steps were slow and unsteady, and I didn't have the most graceful gait. Spasms rippled and rolled through my muscles like wind on a flag, but I pressed forward. Through hours of painful trial and error, I figured out my own technique for ambulation. I would lock my legs the best I could and then lift them slightly by bending to the side and dipping my shoulder. I would then rotate my hips and lurch forward. It took about two minutes to walk a total of three feet, but I was so elated that day that I couldn't stop smiling if I tried. I told Nick about it when I got back to the room. He had no movement in his lower body and very little function in his upper extremities. I didn't want to seem like I was bragging, especially to a guy who was almost totally paralyzed, but I had to tell someone.

"That's amazing," Nick said, genuinely happy for me. "Dude, you're so lucky."

After that, I started to have this recurring dream that I was lying flat on my stomach and doing hamstring curls in the gym. I would wake up and my sheet would be wrapped around my legs. I told Igoe about it when he would drive down for a visit. He had lost his license because of the DUI and wasn't supposed to be driving at all. But in true Igoe fashion, that wasn't going to stop him from doing what he wanted to do. The judge had issued him a "business purpose only" license, and so he would pack his parents' Lincoln Mark VIII with pamphlets and brochures from his father's company and come down to Miami to hang out with me. If a cop ever pulled him over, he would say he was working for his father.

I asked Igoe how school was going. He said it was okay but tough because he had decided to quit drinking because of the accident.

"Me too," I said. "I'm never drinking again."

We shook on it. What Igoe didn't tell me was that he was slowly drowning in the guilt he felt over the accident. He had been to see a therapist but bailed after one session. He was feeling alienated from our old friends, and his behavior was becoming increasingly erratic, even paranoid. Once when he was walking through the cafeteria at FAU, he thought he heard a stranger whisper to a girl: "He's the one who crippled his best friend." Igoe turned around, and slammed his tray of food into the guy's face.

"You got a fucking problem with me?" Igoe yelled. "I didn't mean to do it!"

Igoe fucked that dude up pretty good. The only problem was, the guy swore he had never heard of Igoe before and never said what Igoe thought he had said.

Over the next few weeks, Igoe came down to visit me as often as he could, more often than Kati, whom I would talk with on the phone. We were having a hard time finding things to talk about these days, so we kept the conversations short and sweet.

I asked Igoe to keep my walking a secret from my parents and Kati. I wanted to surprise them by taking a few steps when I moved back home in early January, but I couldn't contain myself. I ended up calling Kati on the phone.

"You're not going to believe this," I said. "I walked today!"

"Omigod!" she said. "You're kidding me. You can walk again!"

There was silence on the line.

"Well, no," I said, "I can't actually walk. But I took four steps. Between the parallel bars. I used my arms to support myself. But still, it's a huge improvement."

I strained my ears and tried to detect any disappointment in her voice, but if there was, I couldn't hear it. Her words just seemed to echo her unbridled happiness.

"That's amazing news, Mark," she said. "I'm so proud of you. I told you. We're going to be fine. Everything is going to be fine. You're going to be back to your old self in no time."

With my physical therapy kicking into high gear, I started to focus on other parts of my body that I had been ignoring. The doctors had removed my neck brace, but I still kept my head as still as possible at all times, and if I moved it, I did it slowly and deliberately, like a robot. The doctors discovered that the bone graft had slipped forward between the two reconstructed vertebrae at some point, and if you pressed on my windpipe a certain way, you could feel the protruding edge. They decided not to operate again. It didn't bother me. I would touch my throat and thank the dead woman who lived in my body.

But one nagging question had been eating away at me for weeks. I had been too scared to ask any of my doctors about it, because a "no" would have been totally unbearable. Would I be able to have sex again?

I started to get some answers in the sexuality class I had at Jackson. I would pretend that I was only half listening to the instructor, but in reality I was hanging on every word he said. I learned that men normally have two types of erections. One is called a psychogenic erection, which starts in your mind as a result of seeing or hearing or imagining something arousing. The brain sends messages down your spinal cord that off-ramp around your waist and go to your penis. Men who have a high-level incomplete injury like mine are less likely to have an erection like this, but it's possible. The second kind of erection is a reflex erection. This occurs when there is direct physical contact to the penis or other parts of the body that are erogenous zones. It's much more common for men with spinal cord injury to have this kind of erection, even if they can't feel sensation.

They talked about various positions for quad sex (no big revelations; the dude is usually on the bottom if he can't thrust his hips, and the woman rides cowgirl-style) and explained that certain drugs can help to attain and sustain an erection long enough for intercourse. But orgasms were another story. I was going to have to wait and see if the nerves would regenerate enough to allow me to climax. The odds weren't very good. I've read that a high percentage of men with spinal cord injury can't ejaculate during sex. This condition is known as anejaculation. Another problem is retrograde ejaculation. This means that you can't shoot the semen out of your urethra, and it travels back up the tube and ends up swimming in your bladder.

I had woken up with a morning stiffy a few times, and I was thankfully still sensitive to touch down there, so I wasn't really worried about being able to get hard. But I wasn't sure I would be able to come. This question started to consume me. All my friends and I used to talk about were playing sports, drinking beer, and getting laid. But what if I could get hard but couldn't bust a nut? I had been sexually active for a couple of years with Kati, and being intimate with her was a big part of my life. I wanted to play a little five-knuckle shuffle at night in my bed to test the waters, so to speak, but I had three roommates and there wasn't any privacy. I would have to wait until I was home alone to see if I could still pop.

This worry in particular was becoming overwhelming. Being able to have sex with a woman was the way I defined my manhood. Without it, what would I be?

The only answer I could think of was "less than a man."

Even though Kati eventually came down to Jackson and attended some sex education classes with me, I ultimately chose to shut my mind down to this kind of stuff, repressing all my doubts and fears instead of acknowledging and dealing with them. I told myself that if I was able to walk again, I would probably be able to have sex too. If not, my life would be over.

As you can see, I wasn't making a lot of mental progress. Here are some highlights from my weekly evaluations:

DEC. 10–"Patient refuses group therapy due to reported discomfort in group settings. Patient continues to deny emotional impact of spinal cord injury, stating that all is well. He is unable to think about plans for the futuro, including a future that is three days away."

DEC. 17–"Patient continues to refuse to go to group therapy. Appeared agitated, easily frustrated and angry when experiencing difficulty with tasks. Frustrated with rehab and states he's ready for discharge."

DEC. 23–"Patient is now able to contemplate plans for the future and would like to return to college but will not do so until he is able to walk. Patient continues to refuse to attend group therapy stating that he is shy in group situations."

DEC. 30–"Patient continues to refuse group therapy but participates in individual psychotherapy. Discussed use of compensatory strategies when patient returns to school. Example: Utilizing a laptop computer and tape recorder instead of handwritten notes. Patient continues to become agitated when asked about plans for the future."

No shit. If you were facing my future, you'd become agitated too.

* * *

on new year's eve, I finally decided to join the group for a field trip. One of my favorite pastimes at Jackson had been tossing a ball back and forth with my therapist. I used to throw with my right arm before the accident, but the right side of my body was much weaker than my left now, so I had to use my left hand to make the long bomb.

My therapist told me that they were going to watch a local team play a game called quad rugby. He said it was like a combination of basketball and hockey but played in wheelchairs. We had played a variation of it in our tiny gym the week before. The recreation therapist had pushed all the mats to the side, and guys in regular and electric wheelchairs rolled around playing a chaotic game of keep-away. It was about as much fun as a parking ticket, but I was desperate to be involved in any kind of organized sport, so I gladly accepted the invitation and even called my dad and asked him to come along with us.

We rode to an armory in Tamiami where a group of older guys in normal street wheelchairs were rolling up and down a basketball court and passing a volleyball around. Once in a while, one of them would break away and cross an end line, where I assumed they scored a point. I watched for a while. The guys would set picks for each other and try to disrupt passes with their arms.

"Why do they call it rugby?" I asked no one in particular. In my mind, rugby was a full-contact sport like football and played by British or Australian guys who liked to drink a lot of beer and wear tight shorts. From what I saw, it didn't seem like this sport had much contact at all. No big hits. No tackles. Then I saw two guys collide at full speed with a play called a crack block. It was like checking someone against the glass in hockey. The chair-on-chair contact made a muffled crunching sound, and one guy went flying out and landed in a twisted heap on the floor. An able-bodied assistant came off the sideline and helped him back into his chair.

"Oh yeah," I said, a smile slowly creeping across my face.

This was definitely a game I could play.

They took a break and the coach, a guy named John Bishop, came over and explained the history of the game to us. Some Canadians from Winnipeg created quad rugby in the 1970s. Back then if you had a spinal cord injury and you wanted to play a sport, you probably played wheelchair basketball. But that sport was difficult for quadriplegics because their limited upper body function affected their shooting, blocking, and rebounding.

Quad rugby was created as an alternative to wheelchair basketball. It was originally called murderball because the blocks and hits can be really violent and aggressive, especially when compared to other sports for disabled people. It's played on a basketball court, with a key area in front of each end line. Players—four on each team—face off in manually powered wheelchairs. To score, the player with the ball, which is advanced downcourt by carrying or passing, must cross the end line with any two wheels of his chair. Obviously, the defense does their best to stop an attack any way they can. The player with the ball must pass or dribble every ten seconds or a turnover is awarded and the ball is given to the other team.

After a goal is scored, the ball is taken out at the goal line. As in basketball, you have a certain amount of time to get the ball over the halfway line or it's a penalty. In quad rugby, you get fifteen seconds. There are also rules pertaining to the key area. Only three defensive players can be in the key at any one time, and if a fourth enters, a penalty is assessed or a goal is awarded. As in hockey, you can get sent to the penalty box for a hard or flagrant foul. Your team then has to play a man down, and that gives the other team the advantage of a power play.

But here's where the rules get tricky. Each player gets a ranking depending on how much function he has in his limbs and trunk, ranging from 0.5 to 3.5. The 0.5 has the most impairment and is comparable to a C5 quadriplegic. The 3.5 player has the most function and is comparable to a C7–C8 quadriplegic. In other words, your handicap in life is literally your handicap in this sport. Teams can have only four players whose rankings equal eight points total on the court at any time. High-pointers, or the players with the most mobility, usually handle the ball and are like quarterbacks. Low-pointers mostly set picks, blocks, and traps. Because my injury was between C6 and C7, I would most likely be classified as a 3.0.

In 1982, quad rugby came to the United States as an exhibition sport at the National Wheelchair Games at Southwest Minnesota State University and after that, it gained traction. The United States Quad Rugby Association (USQRA) was formed six years later to govern and promote the sport at both the national and international levels. Most major cities now have quad rugby teams, and it was, and still is, the fastest-growing wheelchair sport in the world.

The guys separated us into squads and we scrimmaged, playing the official eight-minute quarters. Quad rugby seemed like an amalgamation of other sports that I had played in the past. Defense was either zone or you marked man to man. You had to figure out how to separate yourself from the defender to create space and pass to an open player. The hardest part for me was learning how to keep the chair moving straight while pushing with one arm and handling the ball with the other. But I figured out that you could compensate by articulating your hips, and you could cradle the ball in your lap when you cranked with both arms.

Most guys could throw with only one of their hands. I realized that because of my injury, I was well on my way to becoming ambidextrous. I could throw with both—short passes with my right hand, long tosses with my left—but I felt debilitated, and some passes were pretty feeble. But I was able to work in a few bounce passes to get around the hands of my defender.

The game was pretty fun once it got going, but at times it got bogged down and became a tangle of chairs. There wasn't much competition on the court, and I scored a couple of goals on breakaways. Still, I loved the physical aspect of the game. Some guys out there were timid and would do their best to avoid any contact with other players. I was reserved at first, but that changed pretty quickly. I had learned that hesitation is what gets you hurt in sports. If you don't commit 100 percent when going into a hard tackle, you're usually the one leaving the field on a stretcher. Since the accident, people had treated me like I was made of glass. I was sick of feeling fragile, and I wanted to let off some steam and hit someone.

On the next play, I tried to plow through my opponent and dinged up my chair a bit. I realized just how much I missed the intensity and the contact. It was a total rush. I wasn't worried about getting injured anymore. What was I going to do—break my neck again?

"You're a natural," one of the older players said to me after I blew past my man, caught a pass, and scored. "You should think about coming out and playing with us."

Playing quad rugby was a hell of a workout. I hadn't done any cardio in quite some time, and my lungs felt like lumps of coal in my chest. My arms and shoulders were Jell-O from all the pushing, and sweat stains returned like long-lost friends, which was nice to see, because I had heard that many quads aren't able to sweat or get goose bumps below their level of injury. When we were done playing, I went outside the armory with my father. The fresh air tasted sweet after the exercise. For the first time in a while, I felt calm, mellow, and even content.

"So what did you think?" my dad asked.

"Not bad," I said. "Actually, it was pretty fucking awesome."

"Do you want to join a team?" he asked.

I thought for a moment.

"Nah," I said. "I'm going to be playing soccer back at FAU next year. Why the hell would I want to play a wheelchair sport?"

before I was released from Jackson in mid-January, I had to take a standardized academic achievement test and then meet with a counselor to talk about my career goals. He told me that my scores were outstanding, especially in mathematics.

"What do you want to do for a living?" Mr. Feldsteen asked me.

"I'm not sure," I told him. "When I was going to college, I was premed."

But I knew I didn't want to be a doctor anymore. I had had enough of hurt people and hospitals. Before my accident, I had thought that doctors were these godlike beings who knew everything and could heal anyone. Now I knew that they were just mortals like the rest of us. They make mistakes. They have bad days. Some are smart and good at their jobs and deserve our respect and admiration. Others are total assholes. Sometimes you know more than your doctors do, and it's okay to question their authority, especially if you don't agree with them. It's good to ask questions and trust your own instincts. Press them when you don't understand, and don't take no for an answer. I can't tell you how many times over the years it has happened that doctors who are aware of my condition, and have purportedly read my medical records, have called me a paraplegic because I can still move my hands and arms.

I'm a quadriplegic, you jackass. Do your homework.

Mr. Feldsteen said that because of my high math scores, I might want to pursue a career in engineering. The job seemed to match well with my interests and skill set and paid a good salary. It was mostly a desk job, one I could work in a wheelchair if need be. If I didn't recover complete function in my hands, I could still use a computer for designing and computations. I liked the idea. I had won third place my junior year in high school in a contest to design a new section for the Fort Lauderdale airport. For years, my framed sketches hung on a wall in one of the terminals. When my father was flying for a business trip, he would walk by to check them out.

"Thanks for the advice," I told Mr. Feldsteen. "I'll keep it in mind."

"When do you plan to return to college?" he asked me.

"Next year," I said. "As soon as I'm able to walk again."

i was released from Jackson Memorial on January 15. I could have split earlier, but in the end, I requested to stay a little longer. It used to be that patients like me would live in a rehabilitation facility for as long as eight or nine months. But now the insurance companies want to hustle you out of there as fast as they can. I wasn't sure if I was ready to go back to Coral Springs. As much as I bristled under the structure at Jackson, it was also reassuring. My therapist told me that many quads struggle when they first move home and try to resume their old lives. The first two years are the make-or-break time for anyone with a spinal cord injury like mine. You either adjust to your new body or you don't.

It wasn't going to be easy, they told me. Your life has changed in ways that you are just starting to understand. Just take it one day at a time. If you need help, tell someone.

Easter morning in
Cleveland, Ohio.

Sightseeing in England with my mom, Linda, between soccer games.

Playing forward as a freshman in Pewaukee, Wisconsin.

My mullet and me in Boca Raton, Florida.

Hitting my stride as a
junior at Douglas High.

Graduation Night, 1993. *From left to right:* Frank Cava,
Jeff Nickell, Paul Battista, Ari Levy, Jack Parham, and me.

Steve, Dana, and me, less than a year after the accident.

Eric, Curtis, and me hanging out in Atlanta, 1997.

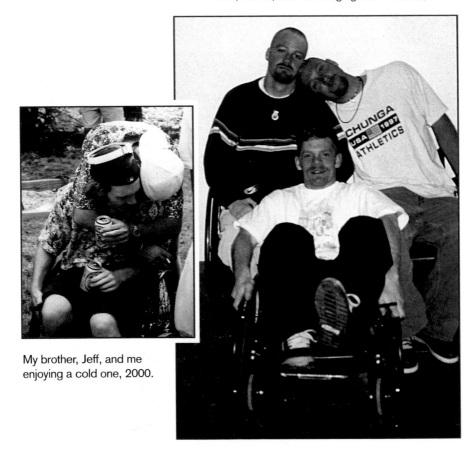

My brother, Jeff, and me
enjoying a cold one, 2000.

At my brother's wedding in
Jacksonville, Florida, 2004.
Igoe brought the helmet for me.

Jeff and me.

Halloween in Atlanta, 1998.
Lieutenant Dan is back in action.

Bungee jumping in Queenstown, New Zealand, 1999.

Skiing in Killington, Vermont.

Golfing at a 2002 quad rugby fund-raiser in Aurora, Ohio, organized by my dad.

Rappelling near the Chattahoochee River with Eric Holden.

Ben Harper and me in Birmingham, Alabama, 1998.

Andy and me celebrating with the Canada Cup, 2004.

U.S. Quad Rugby team in Athens for the Paralympics, 2004.

Chasing down a ball while playing against Germany.

Goal!

Winona Ryder and me at a *Murderball* premiere.

Going for the long bomb in Gothenburg, Sweden.

Paralympics awards ceremony in Athens, 2004.

My Paralympic medal.

After winning the Bronze Medal game against Great Britain. *From left to right:* Chris Igoe, Jessica Wampler, me, Frank Cava, and my brother, Jeff.

Oscar night with Cava, Nickell, and Igoe.

Nickell, Cava, director Dana Shapiro, and me at the L.A. premiere of *Murderball*.

Keith Cavill, Andy Cohn, Scott Hogsett, Bob Lujano,
and me at the New York premiere of *Murderball*.

Scott, Andy, and me filming an MTV special
with *Jackass*'s Steve-O and Johnny Knoxville.

The Potomac River Run marathon in May 2006. *Top, from left:* Cava, Nickell,
John "Dubes" Hughes, and Igoe. *Below:* me and "Big Murph" McCarthy.

In Alaska, July 2006, surrounded by the women in my life: my mom and Jess.

With "Fat Man," aka my dad.

I promised them that I would and thanked them for everything they did for me.

They sent my medical records to an outpatient facility called Palm Lake Physical Therapy Center, near my parents' house. I would be going there five days a week. All in all, I was proud of what I had accomplished at Jackson. I could stand on my own for forty minutes at a time. I was benching more than 150 pounds. I was able to get out of my wheelchair on my own and walk a few feet with the assistance of a rolling walker.

Despite my moodiness and occasional outbursts of bad behavior, I had made some good friends there, especially my roommate Nick. After almost three months together, we had grown close. We had both seen each other at our worst, witnessed the weaknesses that people usually hide, and shared an experience that few other human beings could understand. It felt like we had been on the front lines, and now I was being sent back stateside.

We stayed in touch. When Nick was released from Jackson, he invited me to come and spend the night with him and his family in West Palm. I took him up on his offer. His family lived in a house not far from the beach. Nick and I had some good times together there. But he never recovered much function and grew increasingly depressed about his life. He wasn't able to find anything that made him happy. He believed that because people pitied him, he was pitiful. He dulled the pain by smoking weed and then got into cocaine. He fought his addictions, but a few years later, his father called to let me know that Nick had overdosed on drugs and died.

Breaking your neck can be a real bitch.

He was a good friend.

I still miss him.

the state of florida sent workers to my parents' house to install a metal ramp over the stairs in the garage so I could wheel myself in on my first day back home. They didn't bolt it down properly, and my parents were worried that it would shift and slide when I rolled over it.

"I'll have them come back to fix it," my dad said.

"Don't worry about it," I said. "They're just going to remove it in a couple of months."

My brother, Jeff, was standing in the kitchen. I hadn't seen him in a while. He had been busy with football and school and had made it down to Jackson only twice. Because my parents were in Miami with me almost every night, he had basically been on his own since the accident. It must have been tough on him. He later told me he missed me so much during that time that he would take clothes out of my closet and wear them just to feel closer to me.

I missed my brother too. But I noticed that he was looking at me differently now, staring at my hunched shoulders, my contorted hand, my emaciated figure. It was like he was assessing my weaknesses. He had this patronizing expression on his face that I was seeing more and more these days. People were constantly giving me this thin, forced smile while nodding their heads slightly as if to say, "My condolences for your shitty life."

"It's good to have you home," Jeff said.

Without saying a word, I rolled up next to him. He must have thought I was going to give him a brotherly hug. And yes, that probably would have been a nice gesture at that moment. As he spread his arms and leaned over to embrace me, I socked him squarely in the nuts. He fell over backward into the pantry, knocking cans of food and boxes of cereal off the shelves. I offered him my good hand and helped him up.

"If you think that just because I'm in a wheelchair I'm not going to beat the shit out of you, you're sorely mistaken," I said. "Remember, my punch still hurts the most."

I knew people were going to feel sorry for me. There was nothing I could do about it. But there was no way I was going to let my little brother pity me. Not in this lifetime.

chapterten

home sweet home

If misery loves company, then it absolutely adores solitude. For some stupid reason, I was under the impression that as soon as I returned to Coral Springs, my life would improve dramatically. I could see my family and friends whenever I wanted. I could come and go as I pleased. I could watch what I wanted on TV. I could eat what I wanted to eat when I wanted to eat it. No more cafeteria meals. No more nurses telling me when I had to get up in the morning or turn the lights out at night. I wouldn't have to deal with the strict regulations and schedules that ruled my life at Jackson. I would be in control again.

It's almost comical how wrong I was.

Home wasn't quite the place that I remembered it. It used to be a pit stop between football and soccer practice, an answering service where my friends would leave messages for me while I was out living my life. Now that I was spending almost all my time there, it felt more like solitary confinement, a four-bedroom jail cell where the hands fell off the clocks and the bars were invisible to everyone but me.

Looking back on it, Jackson was tolerable simply because my stay had been for a finite period of time. While I was there, they had done an amazing job of distracting me from my disabilities. The facility had obviously been designed for easy use by quads, so you never fully realized how limited you truly were. The hallways were wide, and hand-rails had been installed practically everywhere. You were surrounded by a staff who made you feel you were the center of the universe. You rolled over on the mat and they cheered. You pulled off your Velcro shoe and they cheered. You combed your hair, they cheered. They took interest in everything you did and helped you with whatever you needed, so much so that you took their assistance for granted. You always had some class or therapy or field trip to attend. I was pissed off and stressed out when I was at Jackson, but I was rarely bored.

At my house, no one cheered for me, and the effects of my injuries became more pronounced. I had difficulty fitting my chair through doorways, especially to the bathroom. When I finally made it in there, I needed help getting in and out of the shower chair. In the kitchen, I couldn't get a glass out of the cabinets and had to ask someone to do it for me. I was just relieved that we lived in a one-story house or else I would have been totally screwed.

My family did their best to make me feel comfortable and help me adjust, but there was little that they could really do. They all had to head off to their jobs or school in the morning.

"You're sure you're okay?" my mom would say as she hurried out the door. "I left lunch for you in the fridge and there's some cash on the kitchen table. Call if you need anything."

"I will," I'd say. "I can take care of myself. Don't worry about me."

And then I would be alone. There was no one to hang out with. All my other friends were away at school. I would roll around through the silent house, looking for something to do before it was time for me to get picked up by a van or call a cab to take me to physical therapy.

Sometimes I would play Sega golf or watch TV or listen to music. Or I would just sit on our back porch, staring at the glassy water in the pool and over the fence at the green golf course where I used to swing clubs. During these moments of solitude, I would indulge in a little self-pity, something I would never do in front of my family. I wouldn't cry, but I would allow myself to feel scared and alone in-stead of trying to repress all my emotions.

Wearing a brave face all the time and telling people I was fine when it was obvious that I wasn't exhausted me, but I didn't know what else to do. I didn't want to be a burden to my family. I had no emotional outlet for my sorrow. I felt trapped by it. I wasn't capable of expressing my fears and anger because I couldn't see how talking about them would help. Words wouldn't change anything. I would tell myself to man up and quit being a crybaby. Rub some dirt on it and get back in the game. I had gotten myself into this situation. I had to figure out how to live with it. No one else could do it for me. I would do it one step at a time. When I would tell my parents about my plans to walk within a year, they would encourage me, but I knew they had their doubts. So did I. But we kept these secrets to ourselves.

In those silent hours, I would poke around the house, searching for the self that I had somehow lost. There were traces of my old life everywhere. I would examine them carefully like some sort of anthropologist who had happened upon the relics of an ancient culture. My parents had cleaned out my dorm room at FAU months ago, and my clothes and shoes were back in my closet. My soccer cleats still had dried mud in between the studs from the night we played Barry. I would run my fingers over the smooth black leather and think about how free and exalted I felt when I scored a goal. My football jersey and my letterman's jacket were hanging in the closet as well. There were pictures on the wall of me playing different sports or hiking in the mountains or swimming in the ocean. I would take down the ones I could reach and stare at my face. I swear I could see sadness in my eyes, as if for years before the accident, I had already started to anticipate what would eventually happen to me.

Then the cab would beep for me and I would roll out front. I would climb into the passenger seat and then ask the driver to put my chair into the trunk. They would usually react to me in one of two ways: they would be overly helpful and talkative, or they would act like being a cripple was a contagious disease. Either way, the interaction was uneasy and awkward. I would imagine the cabbie going home at night and mentioning to his family over dinner, "I met this poor kid in a wheelchair today and took him to physical therapy." Then he would tell his children to be thankful for what they had. I had become a character from a classroom scare film, proof that you should appreciate what you have, because life could be much worse.

Therapy was equally frustrating. I had made the decision to put school and the rest of my life on hold until I could walk on my own. But finally I was forced to examine the different degrees of mobility. It was becoming clear to me that I might be able to walk again one day, but not very well and not very far. I was back on the parallel bars at Palm Lake, lurching forward with my dipping adapted gait. Instead of a rolling walker, they gave me a pair of Canadian crutches—the crutches that have cuffs that fit onto your forearms. I was able to walk for longer distances with these but at the same pokey pace. My biggest problem was that I couldn't quite lift my right leg high enough to take an actual step. And even if I could pick it up, I couldn't move it forward on its own. I had to swing it by pivoting my hips. I told myself to be patient. The doctors had said that function could return for up to two years after the accident.

I'd take a cab back home in the afternoon and wait for someone to come over. I'd hear a car driving by and I'd roll to the front window like a dog impatiently anticipating its owner only to find that it was one of the neighbors pulling into their garage. Usually, one of my friends would show up around four. Igoe would come down from Boca to hang out with me whenever he could. Sometimes he would meet me at therapy and then drive me home. We would play catch for hours with a baseball in the front yard. We didn't know what else to do with ourselves. Grass is the archenemy to anyone in a chair, so I would stay on the sidewalk. He bought a pager so I could get in touch with him immediately if I needed anything. I didn't want to admit it, but I knew Igoe wasn't coming by just because he loved to play catch. He felt like he owed me, and I was starting to agree with him. Guilt and remorse connected us now, a bond that sometimes seemed stronger than our actual friendship.

At times, Igoe seemed to be returning to his old obnoxious self. He'd tell me crazy stories about stuff that had happened to him at school. Because he had stopped drinking, the stories weren't about himself so much as other deranged people that we knew. He was now playing on FAU's club rugby team and doing well at the sport. Igoe had been a decent football player in high school, but he was undisciplined. He was an outside linebacker, and he was always on a one-man mission to kill the quarterback. This would drive Coach Mathisen insane because Igoe would leave his man unmarked if the play reversed. So Coach Matts created a saying for Igoe: "Full flow, I go. Play away, I stay." Igoe rarely stayed. But his aggression and high energy were serving him well on the rugby pitch. I tried to conceal my envy when he told me how much fun he was having with his new teammates.

When my mom and dad came home from work, Igoe would become overly friendly and obsequious. I don't know if my parents ever noticed. He'd stay for dinner, but I could tell he was uncomfortable. I thought he'd get over it after a while.

Steve, Dana, and Kati were all in their senior year at Douglas, and they would come by after school let out. Steve and I would listen to music in my room. Before the accident, I was into anything loud, angry, and aggressive. But now I felt I needed an alternative to all the angst. Steve introduced me to jam bands like Phish and Blues Traveler. Their music was more relaxing, and I would dig on the crazy ten-minute guitar solos. We talked about going to see them in concert that spring.

Kati finally seemed to be tiring of the mothering act, but she stayed pleasant and supportive. We didn't treat each other like boyfriend and girlfriend anymore, but we told people that we were still going out. We rarely had fun together anymore. All our conversations seemed somber and serious and were usually about what we were going to do together once I was able to walk again. Still, I was deeply in love with her—or at least infatuated with the idea of trying to preserve the relationship. I wanted to talk to her about having sex again and what we had learned in class, but I was too insecure about my body. I wanted to know if she still found me attractive, but I couldn't find the courage to ask. She would let me rub her back, and we made out a few times in my bedroom, but she always seemed tentative when kissing me.

I was nervous about being sexually active again too, but not for the same reasons that she probably was. I didn't know if I could, and if I couldn't, well, I didn't know what I would do. I was almost too scared to try. I put it off for the first few weeks that I was back at home. But rolling around the house alone and bored one day, I couldn't help but think that jacking off might be a good way to pass the time before therapy. Sitting in my chair, I unbuttoned my pants and took a deep breath. I had grabbed a bottle of lotion and some porn magazines that I had stashed in my room back when I was in high school. I found a pictorial I liked in the magazine, lubed up, and went to work. It felt good. Not as good as it used to be, but I still had some feeling, which was good enough. It was like the difference between having sex bareback and having sex after double bagging. I used to masturbate with my right hand, but now I had to use my left, and that was odd. I continued to stroke my dick, staring at the naked woman on the page.

I must have yanked myself for an hour before I got close to climaxing. That's when things got a little hectic. Suddenly, I started to sweat profusely and I had goose bumps on my arms. My chest tightened and I had trouble breathing. My skin went cold and someone was banging gongs in my head and my vision blurred. I got worried and wondered if I should quit. Beating off had never felt like this before. I knew something was wrong with me, but I kept going. I had to know if my dick still worked. When I finally ejaculated, my entire body started to spasm. I thought I might be having a heart attack, and I almost grabbed the phone and called 911. It sounds totally comical now, and I'm actually laughing as I'm telling you this, thinking about the paramedics busting into my room and finding me with my cock in one hand and the phone in the other. But let me assure you, it wasn't very funny back then.

I needed to know what the hell had happened to me, so I asked my doctor about it. I dreaded bringing it up, but embarrassment about my body was now as regular as the sun setting and rising each day. The doctor said that it sounded as if I was experiencing something called autonomic dysreflexia, a potentially dangerous reaction to irritating stimulus below the level of injury on my body. Basically, some nerve impulses weren't able to travel up my spinal cord past my injury and on to my brain, and so my autonomic nervous system reacted on its own by narrowing the blood vessels and making my blood pressure rise. High blood pressure, he said, can lead to having a stroke or even death.

The doctor said it was still okay to masturbate. In fact, he recommended it as a safe sexual outlet. But if I felt those symptoms again, I should sit up and stop immediately. He said he would also double-check my meds. Later, it did happen to me again, though not with the same intensity, and this time I knew not to panic. But the initial experience was enough to make me a little gun-shy in the bedroom. When Kati and I finally did the bone dance one night in my bedroom, I was convinced that I was going to start shaking and convulsing underneath her, which added to the overwhelming awkwardness of the moment.

Well, at least I'll die having sex with her, I thought wistfully.

when we got bored with hanging out at my house, Kati and I would go to the mall. It was the one place that I could wheel around comfortably. My bladder functions had more or less returned to normal, but I had to make sure I took a piss before leaving. It seemed to take hours to get me into the car and my chair in the back. Activities that used to take one step now took three or four. I didn't want to be a burden to anyone, but that's exactly what I was, and my lack of independence ate away at me. I hated asking for help but needed it constantly. I was usually the only person at the mall in a chair, and each stare felt like a cut from a tiny knife. I was still a teenager, and other people's opinions, even from kids I didn't know, meant everything to me. All I wanted to do was fit in, but now that was impossible.

One afternoon Steve and I went to the movie theater at the mall to see *Heat*, with Al Pacino and Robert De Niro. I don't know if you've ever noticed, but people in wheelchairs usually have to sit in the very last row and the view totally sucks. I felt bad that Steve had to sit all the way back there with me, but he didn't seem to mind. We got our popcorn and soda and the picture started. Halfway through the movie, I started to feel this weird sensation, like I had to piss and fart at the same time. My face flushed, and I made a mad dash to the restroom and into a handicapped stall, but I wasn't able to get myself out of my chair and up on the toilet in time. Wet shit soaked through my underwear and jeans. I was a mess and didn't know what to do. I heard a quiet knock on the door. Steve had followed me out of the theater.

"Are you all right in there?" he asked.

"I'm fine," I said. "Just leave me alone."

I buried my head in my hands. I couldn't admit to my friend how pathetic I'd become. I could barely admit it to myself. Steve used to know me as the guy who busted skulls on the soccer field. Now I was a fucking invalid hiding in a bathroom stall.

"You don't sound all right," he said. "Do you want to let me in so I can help you?"

"Just get me some paper towels, please," I said meekly.

I unlocked the door, and Steve came into the stall with me. I waited for him to be disgusted, but a look of concern was all he gave me. Steve went above and beyond that day. After handing me a stack of brown paper towels, he took my soiled boxers and threw them in the garbage can. He cleaned my stained jeans in the sink while I sat naked from the waist down, shivering in my chair. They were soaking wet when I pulled them back on.

"This is killing me, Stevieboy," I said, letting my guard down completely in front of one of my friends for the first time. I was tired of pretending that none of this was having any kind of effect on me. "I don't know if I can handle this anymore."

"It's going to be okay," he said. "We're all here to help you."

I felt like my uncontrollable body functions were ruling my life. Months after the accident, I was still in a constant state of physical upheaval. My mom became my nurse. She had taken some classes at Jackson so she would know what to do. At night, she would wake up every four hours to bring me a glass of water and the handful of pills I had to take. This is gross and painful to admit, but sometimes I would become so badly constipated that I would have to ask for her help. She would gently massage my abdomen. If that didn't work, I would lie on my stomach on the bed and she would put on a pair of rubber gloves and smear KY jelly onto her fingers. Then she would spread my butt cheeks apart and insert her fingers into my anus, removing the hardening feces that clogged my bowels, in a procedure the nurses clinically called disimpacting.

Let's just say that those moments weren't the best for rebuilding a young man's self-esteem. I would stare straight ahead and grind my teeth. The act wasn't physically painful, but it made me feel even more pathetic and worthless. Anger mixed with frustration and shame, and the result was this hot, black, claustrophobic feeling, like I was slowly sinking into a pool of freshly poured asphalt.

We wouldn't talk while she was helping me, as if any conversation would somehow make this awful situation even more real for both of us. For years, I've tried to erase those painful memories any way that I could, pretending they never happened. Now that I'm older and have some distance and perspective, I can fully appreciate what my mom did for me. She could have dropped me off at the doctor's office and let me face this humiliation on my own. But she didn't. She helped me to get through it the best she could. I know she didn't want to be doing this sort of stuff for her eighteen-year-old son, but she never complained. She was patient and caring and respectful. She taught me two lessons that I will never forget: family is forever, and love is sacrifice.

I didn't think things could get any worse. And then they did.

i had been trying to get in touch with Kati for about a week. I had left messages at her house, but days would pass before she would call me back. Her mom would tell me she was at the restaurant working, or studying with friends or at swim practice. Just when I would decide to confront her about avoiding me, she would call or come over. Her excuses were always flimsy and halfhearted, but what could I do? I needed her more than she needed me. I didn't want to let her go. I didn't think I would ever get another girlfriend. We would pretend we were still in love, but I could tell whatever we once felt had withered on the vine long ago.

How do you know when someone is cheating on you? I've found that you usually know it in your heart, but your pride just doesn't want to listen. At this point in my life I was the king of denial. My schedule had gotten busier and my mind was more occupied. To help me pass the time, I had gotten two jobs. The first was with my dad's friend Richie, who owned a company that installed security systems. It was a telemarketing gig. He would hand me a list of leads and I would call different companies and try to sell them his services. I would clock in for a couple of hours a day. Richie was more than generous, paying me $500 a week.

My other job was putting together hardware for cabinets for my mom's friend. It was something I could do at home while I was watching TV. Connecting the bolts to the nuts was like occupational therapy for me and helped me to develop my hand dexterity. But it was tedious assembly-line work that told me I needed to go back to college and take academics seriously. I didn't want to be doing this for the rest of my life.

I planned to use the money I was making to buy a new car. Our parents had given my Mustang to Jeff. It was a stick, so I wouldn't have been able to drive it anyway. From now on I would be driving only automatics. I was taking driving classes down in North Miami through Jackson Memorial and learning to operate a hand control for the brakes and accelerator. There was a small lever on the left-hand side of the steering wheel. You pushed it down for gas and away from you for the brake. You steered with your right hand.

For a kid who grew up playing video games, it was no harder than handling a joystick when playing Atari. I picked it up in no time. We would drive through different neighborhoods, and my instructor, Maureen, would evaluate my performance to make sure that I was competent and safe behind the wheel. She told me that I had the best hand-eye coordination she had ever seen. I couldn't wait to get my own car again. To me, driving meant freedom. In physical therapy, I was working on getting out of my wheelchair, standing up on my own and loading it into the trunk. If I used the side of the car for support, I could inch my way along to the driver's side and climb into the driver's seat. I wasn't able to do it every time, but I was getting better. Soon, I wouldn't have to sit around and wait for rides anymore.

I wanted to tell Kati about my progress, but I couldn't get hold of her. Later that night, I asked Jeff if he had seen her at school that day.

"Yeah," he said. His tone made me think he had something else he wanted to share with me.

"Yeah, what?" I said. "Spill it."

"I've just been hearing some stuff about her lately," Jeff said lamely. "I didn't know how to tell you about it."

"What kind of stuff?" I asked.

"That maybe she's seeing some other guy."

It felt like Jeff had just punched me in the nose. I squinted my eyes in pain and disbelief and thought I was going to puke. The bottom dropped out of my world, and I was in a dizzy free fall for a moment, with all the blood draining from my head. I told myself it couldn't be true. Kati would never do that to me. She told me that she loved me. But in the back of my mind, Jeff was just confirming what I had already suspected.

Could she really be cheating on me? I thought. *After everything we've gone through?*

The cold, stabbing feelings of rejection and betrayal were too much to handle and honestly hurt me more than any of the physical pain I had endured in the past few months. I had opened up the best I could to Kati, tried to expose my true self to her, and now I was discovering that she found me repugnant and didn't respect me enough to tell me to my face. Did she think I was so weak and pathetic that I couldn't handle the truth?

And then I heard a quieter, calmer and crueler voice in my head.

You really think a girl like Kati wants to date a guy in a wheelchair? You think she could actually love you now that you're like this? You think she wants to help you get in and out of the car and change the sheets when you piss or shit the bed like a baby? You think she doesn't notice when people stare at you in the mall. You really think that? You used to be an athlete. People used to respect you and look up to you. That's the Mark she loved. Now you are nothing but a doorstop, a fucking gimp in a chair. She only stayed with you this long out of guilt. And the saddest part is that you did this to yourself. You're so delusional, you think that she actually enjoys having sex with you. You know when she closes her eyes she's fantasizing about fucking other guys. Maybe she's right. You are pathetic.

I couldn't shake off what the voice was saying to me. I asked Jeff to drive me to her house. (She lived about five minutes away.) I knew the truth, but I needed to hear it from her. When we got there, we parked down the street and sat in the dark.

"You want me to go with you to the front door?" Jeff asked.

"No," I said. "Let's go to her window."

We snuck down the driveway, over the grass, through the bushes to the window I used to knock on when I would spend the night at her house. We weren't particularly quiet, and I almost hoped she heard us. The lights were on in her room. She was in there alone, lying on the floor, talking on the phone. Her voice was muffled but I could hear her giggling. I couldn't remember the last time we had laughed together. I imagined she was talking to her new boyfriend, and she was telling him about what we did in bed together, and she was cracking up because I thought I was still attractive to her with my gnarled hand and crippled legs. He probably thought that was fucking hilarious as well.

I spied on her for a few minutes like a degenerate peeping tom, trying to decide what to do. Slowly, I hatched a plan. I wanted to catch her in the act of cheating, so her embarrassment would be her own punishment. She would be seen as the stupid, slutty, self-centered bitch who cheated on her poor boyfriend after he broke his neck. All the kids at Douglas would hear about this and punish her accordingly. Then she would beg for my forgiveness. I'd reject her at first, tell her she blew it, and make her think about her shortcomings as a girlfriend and as a human being. But after a while I would accept her apology and take her back to show her what a good guy I was.

Every day for the next week, I had my brother or Igoe drive me over to her house in the afternoon after my therapy. We would park down the street and wait for her to come home to see if she was with anyone. Sometimes we would be out there for hours, sitting in silence. Yes, I'm fully aware that I was stalking her, but I was obviously out of my mind at the time. She had made my worst fears a reality. With my faulty logic, I thought her rejection meant that all the women were ultimately going to reject me because of my perceived inadequacies.

We'd stay in front of her house until late at night, when the light in her window went out. Igoe and my brother never asked why we were there, never questioned my insane plan of retribution, never said, "Hey, Mark, maybe you should just break up with her and go on your way. You guys didn't seem that happy together anyway." They were more than willing to do anything I asked of them. In their minds, anyone who tried to hurt me deserved a beating or worse. It was their job to protect me. Igoe and I were so angry and confused at that time, it was almost nice to finally have someone to hate other than ourselves. For the first time in a very long while, the accident had faded into the background, and there was a bigger, more pressing issue at hand, a problem that we felt we could actually solve together.

"You take care of Kati," Igoe said quietly, staring out the window, pounding his fist into his hand. "You let me handle the boyfriend."

I wished I could kick the boyfriend's teeth down his throat but knew that was physically impossible, and that made me feel even more emasculated. We would sit in the car, stewing, listening to Slayer or Corrosion of Conformity at high decibels, waiting for her to come home with the mystery man so I could pop out of the car and confront them. I wanted to see the sick surprise on her face, followed by remorseful tears and apologies. I wanted to hear her bullshit excuses. I wanted to tell her to go fuck herself. And then I wanted her back.

One night my brother and I pulled up in front of her house and there was a new Chevy Camaro parked in her driveway. Somehow I knew it was the dude's car. This was going to be the moment of truth. But something happened to me. I didn't feel angry anymore. I just felt tired and defeated. This whole plan was ill conceived and fucking futile. None of it mattered. Even if I won her back, she'd eventually leave me again. She was still in high school. She wanted life to be fun and frivolous. She wanted to run on the beach and slow-dance at the prom. I realized that I was a constant downer. She just couldn't handle what had happened to me. All the feckless rage I was feeling slowly poured out of the hole in my heart, and I promised myself I was never going to allow another woman to hurt me like this.

"You want me to come with you?" my brother asked, assuming I was getting out of the car. "Should I get your chair?"

I just stared straight ahead out the windshield.

"No, man," I said, turning away from him to hide my tears. "There's nothing to say. Let's just go home."

My brother looked dumbstruck.

"You're going to let this bitch treat you this way?"

I didn't answer him. I didn't care how she treated me anymore. I felt like my seams were splitting and all the sawdust was pouring out of me. It was over.

"Fuck that," he muttered. He climbed out of the car and walked to her front door and rang the bell. Kati answered. Her eyes were wide, and I could tell she was freaked out by his presence. She was talking to my brother through the crack in the door, so he couldn't see inside.

"Hey, I'm looking for Mark," Jeff said. "Is he here?"

"No," she replied nervously. "I've haven't seen him."

"You sure?" my brother said, roughly pushing the door open and past her into the house. "He told me he would be here. I was supposed to come pick him up."

My brother later told me that he walked into her living room and the guy was sitting on the couch. It was pretty clear that Kati and the dude had been hooking up. The kid was scared. We knew him. He went to another high school in Coral Springs and worked with Kati at this restaurant called Runyons, which was owned by the same people who ran Chowders.

"Don't get up," my brother said to the new boyfriend. "I'll be seeing you later."

He walked back to the door.

"All right, Kati," he said breezily, as if nothing was out of the ordinary. "It was nice knowing you. When you see my brother, tell him that at least one of us still loves him."

She didn't say anything. And then she shut the door.

My brother got back in the car and told me what had happened.

"Fuck that cunt," he said. "She isn't worth it."

Jeff took me home, and I rolled to my room and locked the door. I needed to be alone. I felt like I was the punch line to a joke that everyone knew but me. How could I have been so stupid and naive? All my friends must have known that she had been stepping out on me. Hell, she didn't even try to hide it. But no one had the balls to tell me, because they all felt sorry for me. I had never felt humiliation like this. I just wanted to disappear. I put Pearl Jam on the stereo and turned it up as loud as I could. Meanwhile, Jeff called Igoe in his dorm at FAU.

"Kati has a new boyfriend," Jeff said. "You want to come down and meet him?"

"Yeah," Igoe said. "I certainly do."

He drove down from Boca and came to my house. I didn't come out of my room. He and my brother decided to drive over to Runyons and wait in the parking lot for the guy. They didn't really have a plan, except to beat him unmercifully once he left the restaurant. But the dude was wise to them. He saw them through the front window and refused to come out. Igoe was still on probation at this time. He was willing to assault this kid to defend my honor, but he didn't want to drag him out of the place and do it in front of a bunch of witnesses.

Waiting in the car, Igoe grew impatient. "This guy's a fucking pussy," he said. "He's not going to come out." His body trembled with rage as he clenched his jaw muscle. "This guy thinks he can shit on Mark," he muttered under his breath. "I'm going to shit on him."

He repeated the phrase over and over again, until he was screaming it, pounding his fists on the dashboard. "HE THINKS HE CAN SHIT ON MARK. I'M GOING TO SHIT ON HIM!" Igoe threw the car door open and marched across the parking lot to the guy's Camaro. He climbed on the hood, stomping his feet as hard as he could, leaving round dents where he stepped. He turned around, undid his belt, and pulled down his pants and underwear. Laughing hysterically, he copped a squat and squeezed out a giant messy turd on the windshield.

The dude saw what Igoe was doing to his car and ran out of the restaurant.

"What the fuck?" he yelled.

He obviously didn't know he was waving a red cape at a snorting bull.

"I WILL FUCKING KILL YOU!" Igoe screamed.

He jumped off the car and ran toward the restaurant with his pants and underwear around his ankles. The guy probably realized that Igoe was certifiably insane at this moment and managed to scamper back into the building before Igoe could catch him.

"COME OUT HERE!" Igoe yelled, smacking the palm of his hand on the front window so hard that the glass vibrated. All the patrons turned their heads and stared at Igoe, who still had his pants around his ankles. "YOU FUCKED WITH MY BEST FRIEND," he screamed. "NOW YOU HAVE TO DEAL WITH ME!"

The guy took a smart pill and stayed put. Igoe and my brother eventually came back home and knocked on my door. They told me the tale, which has become legendary in my circle of friends. I chuckled at the appropriate moments and felt a tremendous gratitude to them for sticking up for me. But I couldn't take any pride in what they had done. Actually, it made me feel worse about myself. I realized I reached a point in my life where I was no longer fighting my own battles. In fact, I felt I had completely lost the will to fight.

alone

I spent the next few weeks in my room with the door locked and the shades pulled shut. I turned the stereo up as loud as I could, listening to "Indifference" over and over again.

> I will light a match this morning, so I won't be alone
> Watch as she lies silent, for soon light will be gone
> I will stand with my arms outstretched, pretend I'm free to roam
> I will make my way through one more day in hell
> How much difference will it make?

The "she" in the song became Kati. She had been the bright spot in my life, and now all I had was darkness. After listening to them a thousand times, I no longer thought the song's lyrics were about resistance. Somehow I had misinterpreted the meaning back at North Broward—they were actually about the futility of struggle and the unavoidable nature of loss. Vedder was saying that we were all screwed no matter what, so why even try? It didn't make a difference. The question in the chorus was actually rhetorical. I could see that clearly now.

It was obvious that my efforts to save my relationship with Kati didn't make one bit of difference, because she was with some asshole who drove a Camaro. Weeks later, the pain of losing her was sharper than ever. I would tell myself that I hated her guts for what she did to me. Minutes later, I would pick up the phone and think about calling her and apologizing. I'd dial six numbers and then slam the phone back down in the cradle.

I would stay up all night, restlessly rolling around in my room, staring at old pictures and reading sappy notes that she had passed me in class. I would sleep in the afternoons when the house was empty. I stopped returning phone calls from friends. I blamed them all for being complicit in her infidelity. I stopped showering on a regular basis, stopped grooming myself, and completely lost my appetite. My parents would call me to come to the table at dinnertime, but I would ignore them. I didn't want to see anyone. Nothing and no one could help.

Spring break came around and Nickell and Cava returned home from the University of Florida. You would think most guys would want to spend their week off chasing girls at the beach in Fort Lauderdale, but they wanted to hang out in Coral Springs with me instead. Nickell would later tell me that they had made the conscious decision to come back simply because they thought I needed them. They could sense that both Igoe and I were straining to keep it all together. They'd call me each morning and ask what I was doing.

"What do you think I'm doing?" I'd say. "I'm sitting at home in a fucking wheelchair. It's the same thing I do every fucking day. That's what you do when you're crippled."

"Fuck you and your bad mood," Nickell would say. "We're coming over."

They'd put my chair in the car and take me to Florida Marlins games, to the record store, to the mall, the gym, the movies, anything to get me out of the house. They brought me an article about Mike Utley, the Detroit Lions offensive lineman who had broken his neck in a routine play against the Rams. When they carried him off the field, Utley gave a defiant thumbs-up to the crowd. I liked his style. The article was about Utley coping with his life in a chair. There was a story about him dropping a two-pound bag of M&M's. The pieces of candy spilled and scattered across his kitchen floor. It would have been an inconvenience to most able-bodied folks, but to a quad, it became a test of patience and will. He could have waited and let a nurse clean it up for him, but the article said Utley had too much pride for that. He climbed out of his chair and dragged his body across the floor for three hours, picking up every single tiny round piece of chocolate by himself. I related to him and to his unyielding ambitions to live life on his own terms. Utley's injury was incomplete like mine. He said that his goal in life was to walk off the field where he was injured. I respected his blind determination.

I liked hanging out with Nickell and Cava because they ignored my chair and treated me the way they had always treated me—as a friend. They didn't talk down or indulge me. We would joke around together just like we used to do on the football field. In the gym, they'd ask me what I wanted to lift. "How about starting with some squats?" they'd ask.

"Very funny," I'd say.

One afternoon, we went and saw *Forrest Gump*. Being in the theater reminded me of the day I shat myself with Stevie. We walked in while they were showing the previews, and my friends immediately took seats in the far back where there was room for wheelchairs.

"I'm not sitting back here anymore," I said. "I can't see a goddamn thing."

We moved forward and found good seats in a row closer to the screen. I climbed out of the chair and left it parked in the middle aisle, and took a seat.

"What happens if people walk down and don't see it and trip?" Cava asked.

"Why is that my problem?" I said. I was sick of my injuries making me a second-class citizen. Every day seemed to offer a new set of inconveniences, aggravations, and indignities. My pride couldn't take it anymore. When we were in restaurants, waiters would hand the check to someone else at the table, as if I wasn't capable of paying. It was like I had the social status of a six-year-old. Pushing my chair around, I was constantly bumping into people, having to apologize. It was hard enough for me to get around. "I can't constantly rearrange my life to accommodate everyone else," I said. "If I did that I wouldn't be able to get anywhere."

During the movie, I heard at least two people smash their shins on my chair while they were trying to find seats. I know this sounds mean, but it made me laugh.

"Sorry," I'd whisper, waving from my seat. "My bad."

These people probably had some choice words for me, but it's hard to publicly reprimand a cripple about where he's parked his chair.

I don't know if I bought in to Forrest Gump's "life is like a box of chocolates" philosophy (I remember feeling my life was like a box of turds), and it was tough to watch him lose the love of his life, but there was one scene in that movie that I couldn't get out of my head. When Forrest goes to fight in Vietnam, his platoon leader is Lieutenant Dan Taylor, played by the actor Gary Sinise. Forrest saves Lieutenant Dan's life after a bomb blows off his legs. Years later, they work together on a shrimp boat, and Lieutenant Dan is a real angry son of a bitch in a wheelchair who drinks too much. They get caught in a storm, and Lieutenant Dan climbs up the mast and screams and rages back against the elements that are trying to destroy him. "It's time for a showdown," he yells at the gale-force wind and torrential rain. "You against me." Seeing someone in a chair do that meant so much to me that I went and saw the movie three more times in the theater.

My buddies starting calling me Lieutenant Dan, a nickname I still have to this day.

Even at my lowest, I continued to go to Palm Lake every day for rehab. I was losing my motivation slowly, like air from a leaking tire, but skipping physical therapy would have been too much of a hassle. But it was more of the same dull, tedious sessions of stretching, ranging, balancing, lifting, and then trying to walk on my own. They stuck electrodes on my body, and I would flex when I felt the shock. Any gains I experienced these days were small and required an absurd amount of effort. My right leg didn't seem to be able to win any arguments with gravity. It was time to face the truth. I wasn't going to be playing soccer again within the year. That was total bullshit. I couldn't walk more than ten feet on my own, let alone run. I no longer felt that my recovery was on an upswing. It was flatlining, just like my life.

I was thinking about this one night when the phone rang. It was after eleven on a Friday, too late for anyone to call on the house line unless it was an emergency. I picked up the phone. It was Igoe. He was hysterical. He told me that our friend Jon Miller had accidentally shot himself a few hours earlier. Miller's dad was an FBI agent. Jon had thrown a party at his house and had gotten loaded like a freight train and started acting all crazy. At some point, he pulled out his father's gun and waved it around. Then he put it to his temple and it went off.

Jon had really gone out of his way to still be my friend after my accident and we had grown close in past months, even closer than we had been in high school. I thought about how much it meant to me when he came to visit me at the hospital in my time of need.

"Come pick me up," I said. "We have to go help his family."

There was silence on the other end.

"I can't," Igoe finally said.

"Why not?" I asked.

"Because I've been drinking," he said slowly, as if he wanted to take the words back as soon as he said them. "I was having a party in my dorm room."

"Are you serious?" I asked him. "What the fuck is wrong with you?"

"I'm not driving anywhere," Igoe said defensively. "It's not that big of a deal."

We both knew this wasn't the time to argue about our problems. We needed to be thinking about Jon and his family. Still, I couldn't believe what he was saying. Igoe had made me a promise and he had broken it. Why did my friends feel the need to constantly lie to me? What I didn't say was that I was also jealous. Igoe was out partying, having fun at college while I was at my parents' house alone, stuck in a chair.

A few days later, I went to Jon's funeral with Nickell and Cava. I was inconsolable during the eulogy. I couldn't believe that Jon was really gone, that I was paralyzed, and I blamed it all on the alcohol. I was so pissed at Igoe that I didn't talk to him once.

My relationship with Igoe continued to sour. I would page him constantly, making him drive down from Boca to pick me up from therapy or take me to lift weights at the gym. I knew he didn't want to do it and that he had his own life to live, but I called him anyway. Now that I think about it, calling was my way of punishing him, of exerting control, of sharing my misery. Igoe never said no. But there was now a tension between us that we endured in silence.

Coach Mathisen called me later and asked me to come speak to the students at Douglas. In light of what had happened to Miller, they were putting together an assembly called "Just a Drink—A Deadly Attitude" to address all the recent alcohol-related injuries and deaths. I told him I would, but I had a request. I wanted to walk across the stage in front of the other kids.

"I think that would be very powerful for the students to see," he said.

In hindsight, it was a really bizarre assembly. When the kids came into the auditorium, the first thing they saw was my empty wheelchair sitting ominously in the center of the stage. Principal Kinghorn, looking stern and severe with his thinning hair, balding head, and his conservative gray suit and blue tie, came out and spoke to the noisy students sitting in the bleachers, assuring them that "even though we have suffered some profound tragedies," the school was not "jinxed or cursed or snake-bitten in any way." He said that other state organizations had offered to help with counselors during this time but he refused the outside help, saying, "We need to handle this as a family."

He then introduced Coach Mathisen, who looked like he hadn't slept in a week. Losing another football player to tragedy seemed to add more gray to his salt and pepper beard and a few more pounds to his paunch. "Your speaker is Mark Zupan," Coach Matts said, leaning over the podium. The crowd hushed. "He went to school here last year. Most of you know him. He sat in those seats last year, just like you." He paused from chewing his gum and looked up directly at the students. "He knows exactly how you feel right now. Mark won't be able to speak real loud, so you need to be extra courteous."

The kids clapped and I came out on stage with my rolling walker. Cava's mom, Rhonda, was going to speak after me. Her speech was about how each individual needs to be their own best friend. She was very close with the Miller family and was with them when Jon died.

They had placed my wheelchair in front of a lowered podium for me. It took me about half a minute to get to it. I shuffled behind my walker, like a marionette being controlled by an epileptic puppet master. The way I was straining to pick up my feet, it looked like my shoes were filled with cement. I finally made it to my chair and I was proud of that, but I instantly regretted making a spectacle of myself. I sat down, organized my legs, pulled out the papers for my speech, and scanned the audience, wondering if Kati was there. I saw my brother, Jeff, and that calmed me down. And surprisingly, Igoe was there as well, standing with his back against the wall.

I talked about the night of October 13, about my friendship with Igoe and the accident, about my injury, the lack of concrete prognosis, and the long and arduous recovery process. The kids hung on every word of my survival testimony and watched me with equal parts fascination and revulsion. I was emotionless when I read this speech, just giving them the facts. Still, it felt like my confession. I was doing penance by speaking to this group, and my growing embarrassment was part of the atonement. "Most of you can take walking, writing, going to the bathroom, showering, getting around without having to worry about curbs or grass or other obstacles... just being independent, for granted," I said. I was different, I told them. I couldn't take anything for granted anymore.

I knew I was being used as a scare tactic against underage drinking, but I didn't care. I was doing this for Jon Miller as well as for myself. "How many more times does this have to happen before you understand how dangerous and fragile life is," I asked the crowd, desperate to make my point, to make myself matter.

"I can't tell you guys what to do," I said. "I can't say, 'Stop drinking. Stop being careless. Stop this. Stop that,' because you probably won't listen. When you go out, be careful. Never, never, never drink and drive. If you do go out and happen to have some alcohol, make sure you have a designated driver. If you don't have a designated driver, call somebody, even if it's your parents. Before you leave today, I would ask that the slogan 'Friends don't let friends drive drunk' be changed to 'Friends don't let friends get drunk.' The point is, if you drink, maybe you'll be the one in the canal helpless and not as lucky as me."

As I looked out at the bored faces above the clapping hands, I had an awful epiphany. I had come out on this stage thinking I could make a difference. I thought that I was just like these kids in the audience and that I could speak to them the same way I could have a year ago. But that wasn't true. As I rolled off the stage, I thought I could read their collective minds. Not a single person in that room, besides my brother and Igoe, thought of me as Mark Zupan—friend, athlete, peer. None of them would ever admit this, but they all viewed me as inferior to them. In my mind, every one of them was thinking: *Did you see the way that guy walked? What a freak. I feel sorry for him. He's totally screwed. Thank God I'm not him.*

To them, I was now just some gimp who parroted the words of parents, a cripple whose life had become a cautionary tale.

i didn't necessarily want to die. I just wanted to close my eyes and never wake up again.

The only medication I had in my room was an orange bottle of old acne medicine that I found in a drawer. I read the label, twisted the safety lid, and swallowed the entire container. Then I sat and waited. I didn't really know what would happen.

It was early on Sunday morning. Kati had been on my mind for hours. Steve and Dana had recently thrown me a surprise party at my parents' house for my nineteenth birthday. I was sure Kati had come to her senses and helped them plan it. But she hadn't, nor did she attend the party or even call me to say happy birthday. She didn't seem to miss me at all. I couldn't get her out of my head. I called her over and over again and left a dozen messages on her machine. I couldn't sleep, and that's when I came up with the brilliant idea of downing all the pills. After a while, I started to feel woozy, and my stomach cramped up and ached something awful. Lying in bed and staring at the ceiling light, I had the distinct feeling that I was falling backward down a well, watching the circular opening get smaller and smaller until it disappeared completely.

On the weekends, my dad would usually come into my room after he woke up and lie down in bed next to me, and we would talk sports. He came in that morning with baseball on his mind. He instantly knew that something was off.

"What the hell is wrong with you?" he asked. "You sound goofy."

I started to lie but couldn't find the motivation.

"I took some medication," I admitted and told him about the pills.

My dad ran out and got my mom. They thought about taking me to the emergency room so I could get my stomach pumped. But if the doctors thought I was really suicidal, I would be ruled a 5150, also known as a psych hold. They can commit you to a mental institution for days. My parents didn't want to take that risk. My mom looked at the bottle. It wasn't a very strong medication. My parents recognized that more than trying to hurt myself, I was telling them I needed help. To be on the safe side, my mom called my dermatologist, who said that the only danger was a slight possibility of liver damage. But I should be fine. No need to go to the hospital. But what I did was an act of desperation that couldn't be ignored.

My mom then spent the next few hours on the phone, trying to find a psychologist who would to talk to me about what I was going through and what I had done. Through a friend of a friend, she found someone who was willing to meet with me on a Sunday. I didn't want to talk to him because I was so ashamed, but I was too tired to fight. She drove me to the guy's nondescript office in Coral Springs. I expected him to give me some lame pep talk about how every life is worth living, and that gimps are people too, but he didn't. He just asked me simple, straightforward questions about my intentions and waited patiently for honest answers.

We sat and talked for a while. I decided to put it all on the table, spilling my guts about the isolation, the anger, and the agony I was feeling. Somehow, it was easier to talk to a total stranger. I told him about Kati, Igoe, my family, Steve, Nickell and Cava, and Jon Miller. I told him about the intense pressure I put on myself to walk and play soccer again. I didn't know if that would ever be a reality. Perpetuating this overly optimistic myth with others and myself was exhausting, counterproductive, and I couldn't do it anymore.

We talked about my goals for recovery, and I realized I had been thinking about it in stark black-and-white terms, like passing or failing a test in school. If I was going to push forward, I had to start allowing for some gray in my life. I realized that hard work wasn't going to be enough, and that my dedication to physical therapy would never be able to heal me completely. You have to accept that some things in life are beyond your control.

As soon as I was able to get it all off my chest, I felt a tremendous relief. Now that my problems were out in the open, they seemed to shrink and shrivel. I still had a lot of complicated issues to address, but they weren't as overwhelming as before.

"What do you want to do, Mark?" the psychologist asked me after I had told him my story. "You may not realize it now, but you are in complete control of your future. You are a young man with a strong mind and loving family. Yes, you have some limitations. You're in a wheelchair. That may or may not change. But only you can decide if you want to live or die."

"I want to live," I said without hesitation.

"That's good," he said. "So what's stopping you? Go do it."

chaptertwelve

comeback kid

I decided it was time to redefine my thoughts about recovery. Walking, and later returning to the soccer field, was still the top priority to me, but it wasn't going to happen in a year. I knew I couldn't force my body to obey the artificial deadlines I set for myself, and getting outraged, depressed, or even suicidal over it was about as smart as pissing into the wind. I promised myself I would get out of the house more and try to remember how to have fun again. I planned to get back to school as soon as I could, even if that meant returning while I was still in a wheelchair.

I concentrated on becoming as independent as possible. The first step was getting my own car. From working two jobs, I saved enough money for a sizable down payment. My dad and I drove to a dealership and talked about what kind of car I should buy. We decided that an SUV would be the best bet because my wheelchair could easily fit in the back. I picked out a white Ford Explorer. I wanted to drive it off the lot right away, but it took an extra week to outfit it with the special hand controls.

I can't tell you how much that car changed my life. I was no longer stuck at home alone, literally spinning my wheels, impatiently waiting for a ride. I could drive myself to rehab in the afternoon or even up to Boca to visit Igoe. I was free and independent for the first time in months. I was moving forward, and I realized that movement is what I truly missed. I had been static for too long. Motion meant life to me. Hurtling down the highway, the feeling was fantastically liberating, and my depression started to lift like morning fog off a river.

A week after getting the Explorer, I realized I could go anywhere I wanted. That psychologist was right. Nothing was stopping me but myself. My parents would ask me where I was headed. "North," I'd say, grinning. I'd throw some clothes and a toothbrush in a backpack and I'd drive up to Gainesville and stay in the dorms with Nickell and Cava. Then I would keep driving with no real destination in mind. I'd roll down the windows and feel the warm spring air blow through my hair. I'd look at the cars next to me and I'd wave to them. I would entertain myself by thinking that I looked totally normal behind the wheel. When I was driving, no one could tell I was a quadriplegic. I'd make the trek to Ohio to hang out with my younger cousin Allison, or up to Wisconsin to hang out with Bean. I'd drive for twenty hours straight, blasting my stereo, and then sleep in my backseat at rest stops. I'd be gone for a week at a time, living off Taco Bell and Gatorade. I would call my parents from the road. They would worry about me but seemed to understand that this was something I needed to do. During that first year I put forty thousand miles on the odometer.

The next step was re-enrolling at FAU for summer session. Working as a telemarketer and assembling hardware for drawers had reinforced the importance of academics and my need to build a foundation for a real career. I met with my adviser and got my credits in order. Because I had been in school for only six weeks before my accident, I was pretty much starting over again. I took the advice of the career counselor at Jackson and switched my major from premed to engineering, loading up on the math and science classes.

I finally moved out of my parents' house and into a tan two-bedroom apartment in a complex called the Bocatica Country Club, not far from the FAU campus. The school had a handicap dorm, but I refused to live there. I rented a bottom-level unit with a sliding glass door that opened to a small square patio where we put the barbecue. Some workmen poured a concrete ramp over the stairs to the front door, so I didn't have to check to see if they had bolted it down correctly. I was living with my friend Jason O'Brien, whom I still called J.O.B. We had played soccer together on my old club team, the Boca Lions, and drank all those sodas together on the flight to Germany. He had transferred from the University of Central Florida in Orlando to FAU and was going to play for Coach Donev on the soccer team.

To save money, Jason and I decided to share one of the bedrooms and rent out the other room. We first lived with a guy named Pete, one of Jason's friends, but he moved out after a few months. We needed a roommate, and Igoe was looking for a place to live. I was hesitant about rooming with Igoe again, considering all that had happened to us. We had patched up our relationship since Miller's funeral, but Igoe had returned to his wild ways. He had decided that it was okay to booze and party harder than ever as long as he didn't drive anywhere. But Igoe was still funny and rowdy to hang out with, and I couldn't turn my back on a friend. Jason and I decided to rent him the extra room.

I was living a pretty pious existence back then, using what I had learned at Jackson: that activity, structure, and discipline were the best way to fight depression. I'd wake up at five a.m. and go to the gym to lift weights before class. I had figured out that by strapping myself down to the bench with a wide leather belt, I could get some leverage and lift more weight. I was able to put up about two hundred pounds, which was close to what I was lifting before the accident.

After classes, I'd drive myself down to Palm Lakes for rehab and then go to the library and study for hours. Or I would go to the parking lot behind my apartment complex and practice walking with my Canadian crutches. I did my best to keep my progress to myself so I wouldn't have to live with anyone else's expectations or worry about letting them down. I didn't make any more declarations about when I might walk again, but I remained hopeful. But after a quarter-mile revolution around the track, I was totally spent.

I had mixed feelings about returning to FAU. I was happy to move forward with my life, even if it meant doing it in a wheelchair, but I wasn't able to escape my reputation as the soccer player who had gotten drunk and broken his neck. The baggage I had at FAU was becoming too much to carry. People would come up to me constantly and ask, "How are *you* doing?" their voices dripping with sympathy. A day didn't go by without someone asking me about when I might walk again, or what I thought about Christopher Reeve, who had recently injured his spine while riding a horse. I grew weary explaining that being a quad didn't necessarily mean you were paralyzed from the neck down. I know most people were just expressing their concern and support, but I secretly wished I had some anonymity. I didn't even try to talk to girls anymore, figuring they all felt the same way that Kati did. When I would go to a party, some of my friends would avoid me, especially if they were drinking heavily. And no one wanted to admit they were still going to Dirty Moe's on Wednesday nights.

Truth be told, I had started drinking again as well. When I went to visit my friend Bean in Wisconsin, we went to see Stone Temple Pilots and Candlebox at a concert called Summerfest. We watched the show from the bleachers. I was afraid to try and push to the front of the stage. Bean and I had smuggled in some cans of beer so I had a couple with him. My first sip made me feel like a hypocrite. I had been so hard on Igoe when he had started partying again. But I had decided that I needed to start enjoying life, and drinking a few beers in the sun and going to a concert was fun. But more than wanting to drink, I did it because I wanted to be accepted as a normal nineteen-year-old kid again. I wanted to hang out with my friends and do what they did. I used Igoe's rationalization. I told myself that drinking was all right as long as I didn't get totally blotto and never got behind the wheel drunk. The trick was going to be moderation.

I didn't think I should drink in front of my FAU friends, but my resolve faded after a while, especially when I started hanging out at the soccer house again. I would go to watch J.O.B. and my old teammates play when they had a home game. Jeff Sharon had graduated, but I still knew most of the guys. It was tough to watch them play knowing that I couldn't join them. During their games I'd analyze each play, thinking about what I would have done if I had been on the field. Sometimes being that close to the action would amp me up so much, I could hardly contain myself. Other times, I would become utterly demoralized and fall into a funk. Watching the teams play, I would feel an aching emptiness, an awful void.

I missed how fast and free I used to feel when I would run. I missed the way the ball felt coming off my foot. I missed the hours of practice, the drills, the timed runs, the jokes, the scrimmages. I missed the cuts and bruises, the red badges of courage that you would show off in the locker room. I missed the fights and the shit talking. I missed the beauty of the game, the dribbling, sliding, sprinting, and slamming that is soccer. I missed the strategy, talking to my teammates about lineups and positions and which man to mark. I missed the purpose and fulfillment I felt when I made a good play or scored a goal. I missed the confidence soccer gave me as well as the connection—the oneness—that I felt with my team.

I had spent my entire life on the field, and now I was just another spectator sitting on the sidelines. No matter how hard I tried, I couldn't get used to the fact that I was no longer in the game. I kept myself physically active, constantly searching for that endorphin rush, but lifting weights wasn't enough for me. I longed for competition, the vitality you feel when you pull on your uniform, lace up your boots, and step on the field with an army of friends, ready to go to war against another team. I knew I needed to fill that hole in my life with something. I just couldn't figure out what it would be.

The year anniversary of my accident came and went—Igoe and I barely acknowledged it. I rolled to class on the swaths of concrete that covered the campus, having devised elaborate routes that avoided stairs, tight doorways, or the awful lift elevators for handicapped people that we all call rodeo chutes. I threw myself into studying and rarely missed class. My grade point average began to reflect my commitment.

But the more I focused on academics, the more I realized that FAU might not be the best school for me. While the engineering department was small, I still had hundreds of people in my general education classes, which didn't allow for a lot of personal instruction. One night at the library, I did some research and learned that Georgia Institute of Technology in Atlanta was one of the best engineering schools in the country. I didn't know if I could get in, but I called and requested an application. When it arrived, I filled it out immediately, writing an essay about how I ended up in a chair. I ordered my test scores and transcripts, stuck a stamp on the application, and hoped for the best.

I continued to do my homework, eat my meals, go to the gym and rehab, and watch other people play. The soccer guys were nice to me, but I could tell my presence weirded some of them out. Looking back, it's upsetting to think about how much I wanted to be part of the team again. They had all bonded during the season, and I was clearly just a guest in their world. I would tag along with them whenever I could and sometimes felt more tolerated than accepted. One day a bunch of them decided to go to the tattoo parlor, and they invited me to come along. I had been thinking about getting a tattoo for a while. Staring at the wall full of drawings, I picked out a black panther for my right shoulder. A few of the guys bitched when the needle scratched ink into their skin, but I embraced the pain for reasons they couldn't understand.

On Halloween, the team threw a party at the soccer house. Alcohol sometimes made my already overactive bladder freak out. I suddenly had to pee every fifteen minutes, and I wasn't wearing a catheter. I ended up pissing my pants and having to sneak a shower during the party and borrow a pair of shorts from someone. That kind of embarrassment would cause me to go back to the room I shared with Jason, lock the door, and blast Metallica for hours. J.O.B. would call me Moody Mark, and he and Igoe would eventually coax me out of my room. We'd get some beer and hang out and watch TV or play video games. When we'd drink, they would get Jason's bike helmet out of the closet and strap it on my head "for safety reasons," they'd say, laughing. I'd detach the armrests from my wheelchair and throw the metal bars at them.

We were hanging out one afternoon when J.O.B. and I started talking about skydiving. I had always wanted to try it before my accident because I heard it was a total rush. At this point, my inner adrenaline junkie had been detoxing for too long. I needed a fix.

"We should try it sometime," he said.

"We should," I said, letting the conversation die, thinking there was no way in hell I could skydive, because of my condition. I started to make a mental list of all the activities I couldn't do anymore, and my spirits started to sag. But then I consciously stopped the self-sabotage and thought for a second. Did I really know that it would be impossible? No, I didn't; I was just assuming. I decided to push against my limitations, just give them a little shove to see how strong they really were. I went and grabbed a phone book and found an ad for a skydiving company about an hour away, up near Lake Okeechobee. I called and said that I wanted to make a reservation for two people.

"We have two spots available for tomorrow morning," the guy at the company told me.

"Cool," I said. Then I hit him with the million-dollar question.

"Does it matter that I'm in a wheelchair?" I asked.

"I don't know," he said. "Are you healthy?"

"Yeah," I said. "I'm totally fine. I just caught a little case of paralysis." That made the guy laugh.

"It shouldn't be an issue," he said. "You won't be jumping out of the plane in your chair. You'll be strapped to the front of one of the instructors, so it doesn't matter as long as you feel comfortable giving it a try. We've jumped with people in wheelchairs before."

"Okay," I said excitedly, still not believing how big a difference that single phone call had made. "We'll be there tomorrow."

We got up early the next morning, drove to the airstrip, and went through the training session. We would be jumping at 13,500 feet, they told us, and the fall would last about a minute. The instructor told me that we would be falling at close to 120 miles per hour, which is inching up on terminal velocity for someone falling in a prone position. I couldn't wait to feel the speed. I've never been scared of heights, so my only concern was the landing, because they said we would need to lift up our legs as we hit the ground or else we could break them. My instructor didn't seem concerned when I told him that I couldn't pull my knees to my chest.

"We'll make it work," he said. "I can help you lift them."

They sat us on the vibrating floor of this tiny plane and we took off with the door open. Jason and I were huddling against each other, leaning over and peeking out the door, watching the ground become a green and brown abstract painting accented with blue slashes and circles as the craft climbed into the stratosphere.

"I wish I had brought my chair with me," I yelled in Jason's ear over the roar of the wind and the whirling propeller. "I'd chuck it out the door right now."

As the plane gained altitude, my instructor started to connect my harness to the one on his chest, making sure the clips were good and secure.

"I wasn't going to tell you this," he said. "But I was on a jump yesterday and my parachute bow-tied. I had to cut it loose and use the emergency chute." He laughed in a way that made me think he had recently escaped from a mental institution. "I spent all day looking for it in the rice paddies but couldn't find it," he said. "That thing was worth two grand."

He must have seen the panic spread across my face.

"Don't worry," he said. "The chances of that happening again are slim."

Somehow, I wasn't comforted. My mouth went dry, and my stomach tightened into a nervous ball of dread. We scooted over to the door and let our feet dangle over the edge. We were so high up that we were above the clouds. It was hard to catch your breath in the thin air, and I started to freak out from visions of my body splattering against the hard earth. I had heard that people actually bounce against the ground and fly back several feet into the air if their chutes don't open. I honestly didn't know if I could make myself jump out of a perfectly good airplane.

I wanted to crawl back to safety and tell the pilot to land the damn thing and let me out, but it was too late to turn around. I forced myself to stop thinking about all the things that could go wrong and surrendered to a new experience, embracing my fear instead of trying to run away from it, seeing it for the temporary emotion that it was.

For me, it was literally a leap of faith.

We tumbled belly-first into the sky, and my senses overloaded completely. The wind made the skin on my cheeks ripple and forced my mouth into an awkward teeth-baring, beatific smile that was the perfect expression of the terrified euphoria I was feeling. Skydiving turned out to be an exercise in contradiction, a sensation that seemed to defy physics as I understood it. Instead of feeling like I was falling,

I felt like I was floating up toward the heavens. After a few seconds of free fall, we blew through a white cloud like a bullet through a down pillow, and I was momentarily engulfed in a ghostly world of frigid gossamer.

We exited the cloud, pulling vapor streams with our fingertips, and I could see the ground approaching fast through my goggles. My instructor finally yanked the chute, which shot above us and then bloomed like a giant multicolored mushroom, shading us from the morning sun. We jerked upward as the billowing fabric unfolded and then drifted down effortlessly, like a leaf falling from a tree. The sky became a cathedral, and the silence was immense and overwhelming. It was the quietest, most serene moment I have ever experienced. As I hovered above the earth, I marveled at how one of the most frightening experiences of my life had led me to this place of complete calmness and undiminished elation.

I mused at the paradox and then took it a step further, realizing that without pain, pleasure has less value, that joy is given more meaning by knowing sadness intimately. One cannot exist without the other. I'm not trying to get all Zen here, but that day I came to the conclusion that peace could be found only by accepting these opposing truths simultaneously.

As my feet touched the ground, I was already planning my next jump.

pearl jam was coming to town. I didn't even stop to ask myself if the concert was wheelchair accessible or wonder how I was going to navigate through the thousands of fans. I was going to watch that show from the front row. End of story. Seeing Pearl Jam live meant too much to me. There was no way I was going to miss this opportunity.

As soon as we heard about the concert, Igoe and I went and bought tickets. Our friend Jahn Avarillo was going to come with us. At the time, Pearl Jam was in a dustup with Ticketmaster over outrageous ticket prices, and we loved them for standing up to corporate America so more people could afford tickets and enjoy seeing the band live. It was a real-life David vs. Goliath scenario, and Pearl Jam was sticking it to the man. It made going to the concert seem like more than just seeing music. We were now part of a cause.

For this tour, Pearl Jam was playing non-Ticketmaster venues. They were scheduled to play at Lockhart Stadium, which had been the home field for the Fort Lauderdale Strikers soccer team. The team went belly-up in 1983, so by this time the stadium had fallen into a state of disrepair, which in our opinion only enhanced the counter-culture authenticity of the experience. On the day of the concert, we drove down to Lauderdale and then tailgated in the parking lot. We had brought a case of Corona in a cooler, and I downed six of them before we went in to watch the show. We were definitely D.O.A., as Igoe likes to say—drunk on arrival. It was another humid day, but the wind was blowing, increasing in intensity during the afternoon. There were reports that a small hurricane could possibly hit land later that evening.

The infield of the stadium was a carpet of overgrown grass that turned to mud from the crowds and the scattered showers. Getting around was a real bitch for me, but I didn't let it get me down. Igoe was there to help me when I got stuck. I wheeled into the mass of people and fought back any feelings of claustrophobia, even though all I could see were asses and lower backs. Nothing was going to stop me. I was going to be front and center for this show. I didn't care if I bumped into people or if my wheels were sinking in mud. I actually found that most people let me go in front of them, understanding that I couldn't look over anyone's shoulder or stand on my toes to see the stage.

We finally found a good spot close to the front, just to the left of the stage. Warm-up bands often suck, but at this particular show, a young guy named Ben Harper was one of the opening acts. I liked his sound. He was mellower than Pearl Jam and reminded me a lit-tle of the hippie folk music that Steve liked to listen to, but Harper could rock. As he played a cover of Jimi Hendrix's "Voodoo Child," the crowd went bananas and formed a gigantic mosh pit. I was wor-ried about getting knocked over and trampled, so I tried to keep a safe distance. Igoe and Jahn immediately stripped off their shirts and ran full speed into the swirling mass of sweaty bodies, strutting around like giant spastic roosters gone berserk. I quickly lost sight of them. I figured we would catch up later.

Harper's music was literally transcendent. At some point, I felt my chair rise up into the air. Suddenly, I was almost at eye level with the band. The mosh pit had drifted over my direction and engulfed me. People had picked up my wheelchair and started passing me around above their heads. I couldn't believe it: I was crowd surfing. Me, a fucking quadriplegic, crowd surfing. The happiness I felt—the connection to the music and the crowd—was immeasurable.

I was in a dream state of euphoria, lost in the blaring music, as the sea of hands floated me to the front of the stage. The security guards grabbed my chair and eased me over the six-foot wall that separated the audience and the band. Most surfers would then walk around to an exit that put them back by the bleachers.

"Do not do that again," a guard snarled as I started to wheel down the path between the stage and the wall.

"Tell it to the crowd," I said over my shoulder. "They are the ones who picked me up. It's not like I have the power of levitation."

The bouncer shot me a menacing look. I guess he thought I was being an obnoxious prick. I shrugged it off and pushed back out into the crowd. I was trying to figure out how to get to the front when I met some volunteer firemen from New Jersey, who offered to clear a path for me. But as soon as I got next to the stage, dozens of hands lifted me up and once again passed me over the wall.

"Next time you come over this barrier, you outta here," the bouncer said. "I don't give two shits that you're in a wheelchair. You've been warned."

Just then, another guy walked up and introduced himself as Pearl Jam's manager. "I've got it under control," he told the bouncer. I thought he was going to escort me out of the stadium through a side exit. But he didn't. "Ben Harper is just finishing up his set right now," he said to me. "When Pearl Jam comes out, it's going to get really messy out there. Do you want to come with me and watch the show from backstage?"

"Are you fucking kidding?" I said. "Of course I do."

He wheeled me down the same path I had followed before,

through a door and past some roadies who helped carry me up a flight of stairs. They stationed me in the wings, next to the soundboard and Ben Harper, who had just left the stage. As Pearl Jam set up, Harper introduced himself and we shook hands. I couldn't believe that he would want to talk to me. And then it occurred to me: while my chair made me different, it also made me unique.

"Man, that was amazing to see you crowd surf like that," Harper said. "I almost stopped playing 'Voodoo Child' when I saw you being passed around out there."

"I didn't have to do much," I said.

We watched Pearl Jam together for a while. I could feel my chair pulsate with the beat of the bass drum. Mike McCready was absolutely shredding on his guitar.

"I wish I could play like that," I said.

"Here's something if you ever decide to learn," Harper said, handing me the silver metal slide that he had used while playing his set.

"Wow, man," I said. "Thanks."

I put it in the pocket of my shorts. To this day, I still carry the slide around with me everywhere I go, to remind me of that day and Harper's generosity.

As Pearl Jam played, I noticed that the crowd had separated into three massive swirling pits (Eddie Vedder would later tell *Rolling Stone* magazine that the audience looked "like a Norelco razor"). I listened to all the songs from *Vs.* that had been my solace during those awful nights at North Broward —"Animal," "Daughter," "Dissident," "Rearviewmirror." They didn't play "Indifference" that day, but I still heard the ghostly intro in my head and sang every word to myself. The lyrics once again took on another meaning, which I guess is testament to the power and greatness of that song. As I turned the words over in my head, I realized that any fight, no matter how futile it seems at the time, does make a difference. You never know how things are going to turn out. If I had given up back in the hospital, or killed myself by taking those pills, I wouldn't have made it to this concert and seen Pearl Jam live, something I thought I would never be able to do again.

It seemed as if only seconds had passed, but the show was com-

ing to an ending. I was on the side of the stage closest to Gossard
and the bass player, Jeff Ament, who was wearing long shorts and
was hopping around like a cranked-up grasshopper. The wind started
to really kick and the sky opened up and poured. Vedder climbed
the high scaffolding, long hair blowing everywhere, and continued
to sing. They finished the song and Vedder came down, thanked the
crowd, and left the stage. As the audience yelled for an encore, Gossard took a break next to me.

"If you're tired you can sit in my chair," I said.

He laughed and gave me a high five and a glow-in-the-dark neck-
lace he was wearing before he went back onstage. I had been to previous Pearl Jam concerts and knew that they liked to close the show
with a cover of Neil Young's "Rockin' in the Free World," a political
fight song about the hypocrisy of big business and government. They
would usually invite someone from the audience to come up and
sing with Vedder. McCready picked up his guitar and ripped into
the power chords of the song. The crowd exploded with whistles and
cheers. As he played, I noticed that the other guys in the band were
pointing in my direction. I wheeled my chair around, wondering what
was going on behind me.

"Hey, kid," Gossard finally said. "Come on out here."

It took me a full ten-count to realize he was talking to me.

"Me?" I yelled back. "You want me?"

"Yes, you," he replied. "Get out here and sing."

I pushed my way across the stage. I was more juiced than José
Canseco. For a second, the applause drowned out the music and
the sound became concussive. I was swept up in the swelling energy of the audience. I raised my fist in the air and howled with
them. I have never felt more alive in my life. I almost ate shit on a
big bundle of cables taped to the floor, but somehow I managed to
bunny-hop over them. When I got to the center of the stage, Vedder crouched down and leaned into me as I put my arm around his
shoulder.

"You know the words?" he asked.

"I know the words to every song you guys play," I said.

He smiled. I was out of my mind. I had my arm around Eddie-

Fucking-Vedder. If it hadn't been for his music, I never would have made it through rehab or my breakup with Kati. To say it was a dream come true doesn't come close to covering it. For me, being onstage with Vedder was like meeting Muhammad Ali, Gandhi, and Elvis all rolled into one. We sang two verses together, sharing the microphone. I'm not much of a singer, but that didn't matter. The crowd was singing with us and we became one angry voice, raging against intolerance and apathy.

I will never forget that moment. I grin like an idiot every time I hear that song.

Igoe had been looking for me for a while and couldn't believe his eyes when he saw me come out onstage with the band. He later said that the sight of me up there, singing my guts out, dancing in my chair, having such a good time, gave him the chills.

"That's my boy up there singing with Pearl Jam!" Igoe yelled proudly, eyes brimming with tears. He grabbed complete strangers and pointed. "That's my boy!"

much to my surprise, I was accepted into the aerospace engineering program at Georgia Tech. Receiving admission was an incredible honor for me. I'm not ashamed to admit that being in a wheelchair probably helped me get in there. They were gearing up for the 1996 Olympics and Paralympics in Atlanta, and Georgia Tech was going to serve as the Olympic Village, so the school had recently been overhauled and made more accessible to the disabled.

Before I sent in my acceptance and deposit, I went to Atlanta and checked out the campus with Uncle Howard and Aunt Marcia. The students all seemed more dedicated and studious than at FAU. There were about 8,000 students, 12,000 total if you counted the graduate students. I loved the smaller class sizes. They also took me by the Shepherd Center, the rehab facility that Marcia had originally recommended after my accident. It was in this cool bohemian neighborhood called Buckhead, just a few minutes from downtown.

If Jackson Memorial was the Ramada Inn, then the Shepherd

Center would be a Ritz Carlton. The brick-and-glass building housed about a hundred patients, all with spinal cord injuries. The rooms were bright and airy, and the whole place had a positive vibe that just made you believe anything was possible. The halls were wide and clean and decorated with different kinds of colorful artwork. They had a big, beautiful swimming pool, Ping-Pong and pool tables, and a room full of Nautilus machines and free weights. The gym had this yellow spongy floor and a circular indoor track above it. The staff seemed nice and well informed. So did the doctors. The great thing about Shepherd was that all the specialists were housed under one roof. In Coral Springs, I had to drive all over town to meet with different doctors.

"I wish I would have come here for rehab," I said to Marcia. "This place is great."

"Don't say that," she said. "Wishing you could change the past doesn't do you any good. They did well by you at Jackson, and now you can come here for your rehab."

One of the counselors approached me and asked me how long I had been in a chair and where I had injured my spine. He was in a wheelchair as well. That's how people in chairs tend to introduce themselves to each other. It's like a special handshake to show that you're a member of a secret club. You can usually tell how long someone has been in a chair by how much his or her legs have atrophied. I told him that it had been close to two years since the accident. He asked me if I was going to walk again. I said I was working on it.

"You know, Mark," he said. "From what you have told me, there will probably come a day that you can walk again. But the effort and time it takes you to use your legs to get from here to there won't be worth it. You're going to find that you can get more done in a chair, do more things in life and eventually even feel more confident. John Shepherd, who founded this place, he's a quad and he can walk. But he spends most of his time in a chair."

Could embracing my wheelchair actually improve my life? I had already done things that I never imagined were possible while in a chair, but letting go of my dreams of walking again still felt like admitting defeat. I had given up on myself only once in my life, and I wasn't about to do that again. But if I had learned anything in the past few months, it was that my old ideas about winning and losing didn't always apply to who I was now. As I drove back to Florida, I decided that maybe it was time to reassess life once again and perhaps even plot a new course.

don't give up

It was like déjà vu—or college, the sequel.

My car was once again packed full of clothes and CDs. The only difference this time was that I had to make sure I left some space for my wheelchair. Summer was ending, and I was moving to Atlanta to start school at Georgia Tech. Before I left, I went to see Igoe. I wasn't sure what to say to him. I've never been very good at expressing my emotions to others. But now I realize that I should have tried harder, because there were some things he needed to hear.

I should have told him how much I appreciated everything he had done for me since the accident. I should have told him that despite our recent squabbles and disagreements, I was his friend for life. For all Igoe's flaws, he had shown his strength of will and character. He never tried to run away or shirk what he felt to be his responsibility to me. He understood what it took to be a true friend. He stood by me, stood up for me, always came over when I needed his help, or a ride from rehab, or just a friend. He sucked up whatever discomfort he was feeling around my parents and made my recovery and well-being his priority. He will never know how much it helped me. Without the support of my friends— Igoe, Nickell, Cava, Steve, Dana, J.O.B.— and my family, I probably wouldn't have survived.

Igoe never received any pats on the back for what he did. No one ever talked about the accident or how it affected him. It was just one of those taboo subjects. But I think it was hard for most people to look past the fact that Igoe had initially made a terrible mistake and driven drunk. With some professional help, I had started to address some of the ugly, nasty thoughts I had in my head. Igoe was still trying to deal with his issues on his own, and it wasn't really working that well. He was now experiencing the same kind of alienation, insecurity, and anger that had made me want to kill myself.

I wish I had talked to him about these things. But I didn't.

We gave each other a quick hug and left it at that. I thought he understood how I felt about him. We had been through so much in the past two years. I had learned that tragedy tends to make people closer or it rips them apart. I think we were both proud that we hadn't let the accident destroy our friendship. I was going to miss him, but I also knew it was time for me to move on with my life. As much as we had supported each other through the tough times, we both knew we probably needed to grow up and go our separate ways.

My dad drove with me to Atlanta. When we got to the campus, I realized I had overlooked one very important detail during my previous visit. While the FAU campus was flatter than a white girl's ass, Georgia Tech was covered with all kinds of hills—subtle undulations, gentle knolls, and even slopes that would make nice black diamond ski runs if you just added a chair lift and some snow. In fact, there was one extremely steep hill that led up to the dorm where I was living. Though I told my parents that pushing up the hills would just make my arms stronger, I was secretly thankful for the blue handicap-parking pass that allowed me to park my Explorer directly in front of the building.

My dorm housed sophomores and juniors and was like a giant apartment with seven bedrooms and a communal living room and kitchen. This time around, I had a room to myself. I went in and met my six other roommates: Clint Baggerman, Ken Perignant, Alex Pfiffer, Keith McClausky, Chris Johnson, and Alan Sanderson. They all seemed like regular guys, maybe a little skinnier and nerdier than my friends back home, but that was to be expected at a school like Georgia Tech. They all were in the engineering program as well and knew each other from the previous year. I had to laugh when I heard this. Once again, I was the new guy at school, trying to make friends with an already established group. How many times was this scenario going to replay itself?

I could tell that none of these guys were expecting to have a disabled roommate, and that made our initial introduction awkward. I instantly felt cast as the odd man out, but I had also grown a thicker skin and took it upon myself to show them I was just a normal guy who liked his beer cold and his women hot.

The first couple months at Georgia Tech were no cakewalk. When I was at FAU, I had craved anonymity and wanted a fresh start in a place where I wasn't just Mark, the injured athlete who lost his girlfriend when he broke his neck. So much of my identity had been wrapped up in who I thought I was to other people. I wanted to be unburdened of my past because I felt it was holding me back. Now that I was on my own, I wasn't quite sure who I was anymore. As frightening as that sounds, it was also strangely liberating. I realized I had been relying on the old labels to define myself just as much as other people had.

I decided I had to put myself out there to make new friends. I had done it before. I could do it again, but it would be harder now that I couldn't play sports. I would practice small talk in my head and force myself to strike up conversations with my roommates, but they never seemed to go as planned. I think my intensity made other people nervous. I might have been trying too hard. I ended up spending a lot of time alone in my room studying, which was good, because the classes at Georgia Tech were ten times harder than anything at FAU.

Everyone there was smart. Everyone studied and everyone was extremely competitive. The first day of class, we had to change rooms because it wasn't wheelchair accessible. That made me stand out in a way that I detested. I felt stupid, as if I was going to be the guy who pulled down the curve. I was intimidated at first, scared to raise my hand when a professor asked a complicated question. But ultimately, the competition invigorated me. Not wanting to blow my chance to get a top-shelf education, I became a bookworm, pushing myself to study more than ever. I probably spent more time in the library than in the gym, which was a first for me.

Getting around campus was the real workout. I think I was the only student there in a manual wheelchair, and let me tell you, some of those hills were killers. I had to leave for class much earlier than any of my roommates just to arrive on time and get a seat, so I made the most of my parking pass. My roommates noticed that I could use all the sweet handicapped parking spots, so they started hitching rides with me. A couple of times I had to ask them to help me push up the last part of some hills. My arms would get so sore I could barely lift them. But they had grown bigger and I now had muscle definition, especially in my triceps and upper back, which I had never seen before.

I'd call my mom at night and let her know how I was doing. I stopped trying to hide my feelings from her, but I hated telling her when I was upset because I didn't want her to worry about me. I'd always speak softly so my roommates couldn't hear what I was saying.

"I don't know if I can do this," I said. "Making friends has never been this hard."

"Don't give up," my mom said. "It takes time to get adjusted to a new place. You'll make friends. And if you don't, and you decide that you don't like where you are, you'll come home. So really, there's nothing to worry about."

I was really fortunate that Uncle Howard and Aunt Marcia lived so close to campus. They were my safety net and their house became my home away from home. Whenever I felt low or lonely, I could go hang out with them. They gave me a key so I could come and go as I pleased. The downstairs of their house was set up to be wheelchair accessible, and I would raid their refrigerator and do my laundry. They had this island in their kitchen that I would use to support myself when I climbed out of my chair. The first time my fourteen-year-old cousin, Elizabeth, saw me standing up while I was washing the dishes after dinner, she flipped out.

"I didn't know you could stand," she said.

"Not only can I stand," I said, "I can walk too."

She would come with me when I went to the high school around the block and trudged around the track with my Canadian crutches. While I struggled to make the circuit, I thought about what my doctors had originally told me at North Broward: that my nerves would regenerate for up to two years after the accident. Well, that time was now up and I still couldn't lift my legs like a normal, able-bodied person, despite the hundreds of hours I had spent in therapy. I continued to work on my gait at the Shepherd Center, walking back and forth with my crutches, practicing my balance and weight distribution. They were still strapping electrodes to my legs, trying to jump-start my nerves, but I had long been wondering if all this effort wasn't in vain.

I was starting to get my head around the fact that this was all the recovery I was going to experience. This was as good as it was going to get for me. This realization didn't hit me all at once like a bolt of lightning—it was more a gradual process that took several months. I had made myself stronger, but I hadn't regained any function in quite some time. At this stage in my life, it was obvious to me that I was never going to run again. This made me incredibly sad, but there was also some small relief in finally knowing what my body could and couldn't do. I guess it finally gave me some clarity and closure—the acceptance that other people had talked about but that I hadn't really understood at the time.

Rather than fighting an impossible battle, one that was beyond my ability to win, I chose instead to focus on the life that was within my grasp, and that life happened to be in a chair. You can say I was surrendering to my injury, but I choose to look at it another way. I was surrendering to my desire to live a happy, fulfilling life. I found I could now align my expectations with my abilities. Instead of concentrating on what I couldn't do, I tried to focus on how far I had come. When I had first arrived in the hospital, I was almost fully paralyzed. Two years later, I could bench two hundred pounds. I could walk close to three-quarters of a mile with my crutches. I had skydived. I had crowd surfed. I had realized that most roadblocks existed only in my mind. But my physical limitations were different. They were real.

By accepting them, I wasn't admitting defeat. In fact, I was doing the exact opposite. I was realizing I had done everything in my power to overcome them. And if I related all this back to my old ideas of winning and losing, I guess I was declaring myself a winner once and for all. It had just taken me some time to recognize what victory was going to look like for me.

Spending time with my cousin Jason, who had brain damage from his car accident, helped to put my life into perspective. His head injury had affected his personality. He was still Jason, but he was different from how he was before. He was often confused. He had problems with his memory. I would also see other quads at the Shepherd Center, people less fortunate than me, people who had virtually no function at all and had to get around in those electric sip-and-puff chairs, propelling themselves forward by blowing into a straw. I saw people who had to be on a ventilator to breathe, people who had to rely on nurses to help them with both their bladder and bowels. All this made me appreciate how lucky I was and how much I had actually accomplished in my recovery. I would look at them and think: *There but for the grace of God go I.* I was thankful that I was still myself. I was thankful for my independence.

as usual, my mom was right.

It took a while, but my roommates eventually warmed up to me. One weekend during that fall semester, Nickell and Cava came up from Gainesville and stayed with me, crashing on the floor in my room. Once my roommates saw me horsing around, talking shit, roughhousing and getting loaded with my buddies from Florida, everything changed. They finally saw me instead of the chair. They started to invite me to hang out with them on the weekends. None of us were over twenty-one, so we mostly partied in the dorms or went to see movies or concerts. When we were hung over on Sundays, we would spend the day watching football on TV before we went to the library to study. During that time, I became especially close to Ken and Clint. We liked the same kind of music. We would listen to Sublime, Blind Melon, Alice in Chains. I offered to let them borrow my CDs whenever they wanted.

I learned that Ken played eightman on the rugby team. Eightman is like a linebacker, clearing the path for other players. I told him that I used to play soccer and football, and then about the accident. I could tell he had been wondering how I ended up in a chair. I asked him if he wanted to grab some baseball gloves and play catch in back of the dorm while we talked. I guess I wanted to show him I was still athletic. I would tell him to beam it at me as hard as he could, and I would lean out of my chair to scoop up the short hop. I needed him to see that I still had some skills.

He later invited me to one of his rugby games. I had never seen real rugby played live before, so it was cool to learn about a new sport. Someone at the game told me a funny saying: "Soccer is a gentlemen's sport played by thugs. Rugby is a thugs' sport played by gentlemen." As a man who loved to play the beautiful game like a thug, I wholeheartedly agreed.

I admired the sportsmanship of the rugby players. I also admired how hard they hit each other. After every game, no matter how acrimonious the play, the competing teams would go out to a pub and raise a glass together and sing some rugby songs. I loved hanging out at the bars with these guys and listening to their tales about past games and players. I loved the drama of their stories, loved the slang they used to describe their sport's action, loved the fact that each anecdote seemed to have a hero and a villain and usually ended with the bad guy getting his comeuppance. Watching Ken compete made me realize that my desire to get back on the field was stronger than ever. It also made me realize that I always seemed to bond best with people who loved athletics as much as I did.

by winter, my life had fallen into a comfortable rhythm. I was spending less time at therapy and more time studying and hanging out and just having fun. Getting good grades was something I could actually accomplish through commitment and hard work, and I had been up to the task. There is no finer feeling in life than when you actually achieve the goals you have set for yourself. I had a 3.7 grade point average that first quarter, and I had proved to myself that I could do better academically than I had ever imagined. This gave me confidence, as did making a new group of friends. I was starting to feel like my old self again.

Still, each day seemed to offer a new challenge. One particularly cold and icy morning, I rolled out to my car and got ready to load my chair in the back so I could drive to my aunt and uncle's house. The school had canceled classes that day, so the campus was pretty much empty. I was the only person in the parking lot. My car was parked right at the crest of the hill. The back lock of my SUV was frozen over, so I started to bang on it with my gloved hand.

The force of my pounding made me slide backward. My wheels dipped over the edge of the hill and I lost control, careering down the icy slope like a one-man luge. There was nothing I could do to stop myself, so I rode it out, doing my best to keep the chair upright. I bounced down the hill like a ball on a flight of stairs and crashed into a snowy berm at the bottom. I flew out of my chair and into a hard pile of frozen snow. I was lucky I didn't split my head open or break my arm or leg. I was able to crawl on my belly to my chair and climb back in it, but there was no way I could push myself up the hill with all that ice.

If this had happened to me a year before, I would have been devastated. Sitting at the bottom of the hill, shivering from the cold air and adrenaline, I remembered reading about the myth of Sisyphus back when I was in high school. Sisyphus had run afoul of the gods, and they condemned him to push a heavy rock up a hill for all eternity. As soon as he got it to the top, it would roll down again. I used to empathize with Sisyphus; now, I felt closer to the rock itself. I thought it was the perfect metaphor for my existence. For the past couple of years, I had felt as if I were rolling backward down hills and needing other people to help push me back to the top again. Asking for help had previously embarrassed me and made me feel weak. I realized that needing other people is a fundamental part of life. I couldn't do it alone. In fact, none of us can. Thankfully, I had my cell phone. I dialed my uncle and aunt's number. I hoped they hadn't gone to work yet.

"Uncle Howard," I said when he answered, "you will never believe what just happened to me." I was giggling so much I could barely get the words out. For the first time in a long while, I was able to laugh at myself, laugh at the absurdity of it all. The more I laughed, the better I felt. The cold, bitter, frozen feeling in my heart had finally started to melt.

the shepherd center has a slogan: "Where Life Begins Again."

In addition to physical therapy, Shepherd offers all kinds of sports and extracurricular activities. The list seemed limitless. If I remember correctly, I think they even offered wheelchair hunting and scuba diving. Until now I hadn't really taken advantage of any of the recreational opportunities because I had been focusing on the single goal of walking again.

My therapist, a kind woman in her late twenties named Kathy Herbert, had been on me for months to give quad rugby another shot. Her boyfriend, Bill Furbish, was on a team. She had told me he injured himself when he was about my age. He had finished his final exams to graduate from Georgia Southern College and went out drinking with some friends. He ended up diving headfirst off a bridge above the Ogeechee River where the water was about ten feet deep. His injury paralyzed him from the chest down. Bill was thirty-five years old now and a hell of an athlete. In addition to rugby, he had made a name for himself in Paralympic racing. He had won gold and bronze medals at the 1988 Paralympics in Seoul, Korea, as well as gold and silver medals at the 1987 World Championship games in Aylesbury, England. He was also a world champion water skier. He couldn't stand, so he would sit on a large, wide ski that looked like a wake board with a special cage attached on top. After months of Kathy's asking me to come meet her boyfriend and check out the team, I finally agreed.

Bill had started the club team, called the Atlanta Rolling Thunder, back in 1988 with another quad by the name of Burt Burns, who had been injured by a drunk driver. They were excited for this upcoming season because quad rugby had experienced a successful trial run at the recent 1996 Paralympics in Atlanta and would now be a full-fledged sport for the 2000 games in Sydney, Australia. Team USA had won the gold medal in the exhibition play. Many guys were planning to use club teams—there were a couple dozen in different cities all over the country—to train and prepare for tryouts for the national team and the next Paralympics.

I wasn't aware of any of this as I made my way across the yellow spongy floor at the Shepherd Center. I actually heard them playing before I saw them. My brain registered the familiar noises— whistles, yelling, the ball bouncing on the floor—and then a boom of chairs colliding that sounded like dynamite exploding in a Dumpster. The guys stopped playing when I came on the court. Bill introduced me to Wendy Gumbert, an able-bodied woman who coached the team. I met the other guys as well. Most of the players were a little older than me and they all greeted me warmly, like a long-lost friend.

Among them was a polite dark-haired guy with a sunny disposition, Bobby Lujano. He didn't have any forearms, hands, or lower legs and feet, just rounded, scarred nubs at his elbows and knees. I would later learn that he had contracted meningococcemia, a rare form of meningitis, when he was a boy, and the doctors had to amputate. He lost his arms below the elbow and his legs below his knees. He wasn't a quad like me with a neck injury, but because all four limbs were impaired, he could play on the team. Bob wore special prosthetics made of hard rubber over his arms so he could push his chair and not damage the soft skin. He was new on the team as well. It was crazy how fast he could go and how well he could handle the ball. I was in awe of him.

I noticed the guys weren't playing in regular wheelchairs. Instead, they rode in badass contraptions that reminded me of mini tanks. The chassis were constructed of thick-tubed aluminum and looked like the exoskeleton of a prehistoric insect. Whereas normal wheelchairs weigh about twenty pounds, these things weighed almost twice that. They were low-slung and had plastic shields protecting the spokes on the wheels, which slanted inward toward your hands, ostensibly to give you better maneuverability and balance. Some of them had sturdy-looking metal bumpers in the front near where you put your feet, or pointed grills called cowcatchers. They also had two small wheels in the front and a fifth wheel in the back behind the seat to provide extra stability.

Wendy remembers that when she met me that day, my red hair was long and straggly and partially concealed my face. She thought I was hiding behind it. My wheelchair was too big for me. I would slide down in my seat and end up slouching. To her I seemed unsure of myself and uncomfortable in my chair. "You looked horrible," she says. "But then I saw your arms and I could tell you were a fit person. I could see you had some potential."

She went and got an old quad chair out of a closet and adjusted it to fit my height. Sitting in it for the first time was just an amazing feeling. As soon as I belted in, I felt as if I had gone through a transformation. I felt light again. And fast. The chair seemed to respond to the slightest articulation of my hips. It just felt so sturdy. I couldn't wait to start playing so I could smash into someone. When I was in that chair, I felt indestructible. I felt dangerous.

We didn't do much but scrimmage that day. I already knew the rules of the game from the time I played in the armory back when I was at Jackson Memorial. I was still cocky enough to think I was going to ride herd on these guys, just like the first time I played. What I didn't realize was that back then I was playing with a disorganized bunch of weekend warriors. The guys on Rolling Thunder were dedicated pros who lived and breathed the game.

The way I played that day, you would think I had never touched a ball in my life. The guys just hazed me, trapping me against the sidelines, knocking the ball from my hands, goading me into over-and-back fouls. I was about as green as you could get, but I guess my athleticism impressed them. During a break, Bill pulled me aside and gave me some quick tips. The high pointer on the team, the guy with the most function, controlled the ball and organized offense. He was the playmaker, like point guard in basketball. The low pointers, or the guys with less function, spaced out the court with traps and blocks.

Bill wasn't a very tall guy. Neither am I. This can be a real disadvantage in quad rugby. He showed me how to lean back in my chair and toss the ball over the defender's outstretched hands. He demonstrated how you position your chair on defensive to anticipate an opponent and corral him when he tries to move past you. The trick was wedging the metal grill of your chair into the spot between the wheels and frame of his chair.

Angles, I remembered. *It's all about the angles.*

I wanted to show the guys that I had some talent, so I played as wildly and aggressively as I could, trying to put a big hit on anyone to show I wasn't afraid to mix it up. I was trying to make up for my lack of skill with enthusiasm and intensity. The only problem was that I couldn't catch any of them. They were all in great shape, and I was panting for breath. They would see me out of the corner of their eye and wheel backward or forward out of my path when I would come barreling along. They took me to school, launching their chairs into the side of me like they were human scud missiles. I fell victim to a nasty little technique called "spinning," in which another player rams the front of his chair right behind your back axle. The contact gives you speed wobbles and causes you to lose control, sending you flying ass over teakettle. I found myself sprawled out on the soft, spongy floor more than a few times.

I landed one solid hit that day, catching an opponent on his flank when he was looking the other way and doing his best to handle an errant pass. I had figured out that the trick was to shove your hips forward at the last second to add extra power. I felt like I loaded two and a half years of anger and isolation into that one shot, and pounded him with a bone-rattling metal bang. I felt this incredible surge of strength and purpose, a controlled explosion that somehow detonated everything bad in my life. The release I felt as we slammed together was immediate and satisfying. Yes, I know it sounds like I'm describing something sexual. I'm doing it on purpose. For me, playing sports again was almost as good as having sex. Almost.

By the end of practice, I couldn't imagine that I had made a very good impression on any of these guys. I had been severely outplayed on both offense and defense, but I had kept my composure and didn't lose my temper. Still, I hadn't had this much fun in years. Coach Wendy told me that they were looking to add a high pointer to their roster. After observing the function that I had in my arms and trunk, she thought I would probably classify as a 3.0. She asked me if I was interested in joining the team.

"Oh, hell yes," I said. "Where do I sign up?"

The team went out to dinner together at a local pizza joint. Surprisingly, it was nice to be out with a group of guys in chairs. I was no longer the odd man out. In the parking lot, they all helped each other get out of cars and vans. No one had to ask for assistance. I felt they understood everything I had gone through because they had gone through it too. I felt I could finally let my guard down and just be myself. I felt I belonged.

I wheeled into a spot at the table next to Bob. I was fascinated at how he ate, deftly picking up thin slices of pepperoni pizza between his stumps and eating with a knife and fork. I thought I had it bad because I couldn't close my right hand and here was a dude who didn't even have hands.

"I'm sorry to be staring at you, Bob," I said, "but wow. That's pretty incredible."

"Stare all you want," he said, smiling, "I'm used to it."

That night, as I drove myself back to the dorms, I was so pumped up that I started to swerve my car back and forth across lanes on the freeway, wanting to bump my Explorer into other vehicles, as if I were still on the court. Once I realized what I was doing, I stopped, but the joy of being able to compete again had made me giddy. I pounded the steering wheel with my right hand, hit the throttle with my left, and turned the music up as loud as it would go. I was part of a team again. I knew I had a lot to learn if I was going to get good at quad rugby. And I couldn't wait to get started.

after that day at practice, I lived to play quad rugby. I was still focused at school and continued to clock hours at the library, but I couldn't wait to finish my studies so I could get to the Shepherd Center to play some ball. We would practice twice a week and then travel for games on the weekend. I had never had a female coach before, but I liked Wendy a lot. She was friendly but tough, with a no-nonsense way about her. She knew the game and wanted to win just as badly as we did. She had played basketball in college, where she had decided that she wanted to work with disabled people. Her first job out of school was at the Warm Springs Rehabilitation Hospital in San Antonio, and she had built their disabled sports program from the ground up when she was in her early twenties. That's also when she started coaching quad rugby.

She had coached high school basketball for a couple of years as a student teacher and believed there were many similarities between the two sports. After a while, she moved practice from Shepherd to another complex where able-bodied athletes worked out. She started each practice with dozens of laps around the court to build endurance and then drill work with cones to develop fundamentals of the games—dribbling and passing and defense. Scrimmages would come later. This benefitted me because I was just beginning to develop as a player.

I could see how Wendy associated quad rugby with basketball, especially the dribbling, the setting of picks and blocks, and the transitions from offense to defense. And then there was the fact that we played on a basketball court. But in my mind, it was the perfect amalgamation of soccer and football: a fluid, fast-moving sport where you had to tap into your creativity and improvise combinations on the fly, and it also relied heavily on the spotless execution of set plays and bursts of balls-out, fearless physical contact.

Because I had been using my left hand more than my right for years now, I had become ambidextrous, which instantly gave me a real advantage. I had two weapons instead of one in my arsenal. Most guys were limited to passing and dribbling with only one of their hands, and it was easy for me to anticipate what they were going to do and shut them down.

The best players in quad rugby were the ones who knew what to do when they didn't have the ball. Because of my years on the soccer pitch, I was very effective in my off-the-ball runs and putting myself in the best position to receive a pass and score. In rugby, we call this picking a lane. This is a skill that you can't really teach. It's a decision that's made in a split second, and it was instinctual for me. I would constantly move back and forth, trying to find an opening, exploiting my defender's blind spots, making it impossible for him to keep track of me. Opponents started to respect me for both my power and elusiveness when I was on the court.

While I had no problem picking up the physical aspects of the game and learning the strategy, my chair speed was another story. For a smaller guy, I just wasn't as fast as I should be. I don't know why, because my arms were stronger than most of the other players' and I didn't weigh a lot. I dedicated myself to improving my acceleration by going to the track on my own. I would put on my headphones, set my portable CD player in my lap, and spend hours pushing, working on my timed sprints and my general fitness. My old Canadian crutches grew cobwebs in my aunt and uncle's garage. After I starting playing quad rugby, I rarely used them.

My first season, 1997, we played tournaments all over the South, traveling to Georgia, Alabama, Tennessee, Texas, and Florida. We played in high school gymnasiums and rehab centers with just a handful of supporters watching us from the stands. That was okay; we weren't playing for anyone but ourselves. The Rolling Thunder were going through a transition that year. We weren't one of the top teams, consistently ranking somewhere in the middle of the group in the initial seeding. But we were improving. We would usually play five games each weekend at a tournament. I've always loved pregame rituals when you are gearing up and getting your mind focused on the game. Listening to the steady hum of an air compressor filling up the tires on my newly purchased rugby chair, I would begin by wrapping a bandanna around my head to keep my long hair out of my eyes. I would envision myself outsprinting my opponents and across the goal line as I rolled white athletic tape around my wrists and over the wide-receiver gloves I wore to improve my grip. We would then coat our hands with a special sticky orange resin that helps us catch and handle the ball.

As in hockey, we ran what are called lines or lineups during games. It was Wendy's job to find the right combination of players whose classifications equaled eight points. I had made the starting line simply because I was better than the other high pointer on the team. Atlanta had lost some of their better players to retirement the previous season. Bill and Burt, who were both 2.0s, also started along with another guy named Chad Brewer, who was a 1.0. It took us some time to get used to each other, but after a while, we became like the four limbs of one body.

I had my first breakout game that February at a tournament in Tampa. It was called the Conveen/Action International and at that time it was the largest quad rugby tournament in the world, with sixteen teams playing forty-eight games over the weekend. The lower seeded teams would face off against the higher seeded teams in the first round of pool play. We were ranked eleventh out of the sixteen teams. Our first game was against the sixth-seeded Casa Colina Buccaneers.

Bill and Burt usually called the plays and I would follow their lead. But by this time, I had proven myself as an offensive force and was beginning to take on more of a leadership role. We were down by three going into the fourth period. Instead of losing our composure, we rallied and scored four unanswered goals. As time ran out, the Bucs tied it up and the game went into a three-minute overtime. I had scored fifteen goals in the regulation play, but really became dominant during those final moments in OT. While everyone else on the court was noticeably fatigued, I felt fresh from all the training I had done on my own. I ran circles around my defender and scored three more goals to help Atlanta to pull off the biggest upset of the tournament. We ended up placing seventh overall. I set a personal best record of eighteen goals and succeeded in getting the league's attention as an emerging class 3.0.

At those tournaments, I enjoyed my time off the court just as much as my time on it. For me, playing quad rugby was like joining a support group. I learned so much from just hanging out and observing the more experienced quads. I looked up to Bill and Burt and in a way, they became mentors. They taught me little tricks that made my life infinitely better. They showed me how to get down steps on my own without getting out of my chair or asking for help. If you approach stairs fast and keet your front wheels up by distributing your weight to the back of the chair, you can roll downstairs without falling. Along with Wendy, they also convinced me to buy a new everyday chair. I had been cruising around in the love seat for years. They told me I would probably be much happier in a smaller, lighter stripped-down chair. They were right. After I downsized, my new chair was easier to load into my car, and I never had a problem fitting through doorways or into a bathroom stall again.

But mostly these guys led by example. They just seemed content with their lives and secure with themselves. They had good jobs, and girlfriends. They were men to me. Role models. I aspired to be like them. They had a certain swagger, and they casually referred to each other as gimps, co-opting what had once been a derogatory term for disabled people and defusing it by making it their own, the way blacks had done with the word *nigger* and gays with *fags*. Bill was also about to get married to Kathy. Months later, she would be pregnant with their first child. Don't think I didn't notice that a beautiful able-bodied woman could fall in love with a guy in a chair and that they could start a family together

Our season ended that spring at the national tournament in Spokane, Washington, where we were ranked eighth. We had a decent showing but didn't place in the top four. A team from southern California called Sharp Shadow, coached by a fellow named Reggie Richner, took first place.

when i returned to Georgia Tech, I invited Nickell and Cava to spend a weekend with me at my aunt and uncle's cabin up at Lake Lanier, which is about forty-five minutes outside Atlanta, nestled in the forested foothills of the famous Blue Ridge Mountains. It's postcard pretty up there. You feel totally free and separate from the pressures of the outside world. At night we would roast marshmallows and sleep in bunk beds. We would spend the day lying on the dock, working on our tans or trying to drown each other on tubes towed behind the speedboat. I couldn't get down the path to the lake in my chair because of the rocks, so Nickell or Cava would end up carrying me on their backs.

I hadn't seen my friends in a while. When I asked them later what they remembered from this time, they said they recall sensing a definite change in me but couldn't quite put their finger on it. As Nickell says, it was like I had turned a page in my life.

"How is physical therapy going for you these days?" Nickell asked. "Any idea when you might be back on the soccer field again?"

"Well, guys," I said, "I think the reality is 'probably never.'"

"Are you being serious?" Cava said.

"I am," I said. "I've quit going to therapy. I'm moving on to bigger and better things."

I could see they were thrown by my announcement. I had experienced a similar reaction when I gave my father the news. He had been asking me if I wanted to take a hiatus from school and move back to Florida so I could be closer to Dr. Green and the Miami Project to Cure Paralysis. I was driving with him at the time. I slammed on the hand brake and screeched to a stop in the middle of the lane. The car behind us had a honking fit, as I slowly turned to my father and said: "Has it ever occurred to you that maybe I'm happy with the way I am? I'm tired of constantly trying to become something. Why can't I just be me?"

"I hadn't thought of it that way," my dad said. "But that makes sense to me. If you're happy, then I'm happy. I won't ask you about it again."

Sitting on the dock with Nickell and Cava, I explained my decision to them and how and why I had made it. I talked about my desire to have a full and fulfilling life on my own terms. Nickell likes to call this my *Shawshank Redemption* moment and quotes a line from the movie: "At some point you have to get busy living or get busy dying."

My choice was clear to both of them.

while i continued to thrive at Georgia Tech, Igoe was spiraling out of control back at FAU. He had been drinking heavily for the past year, and his self-medicating had become self-destructive at this point. My friends would tell me his behavior was becoming really bizarre and worrisome. After getting blackout drunk, he'd strip off all his clothes, put on his high school football helmet, and hit himself in the head with an aluminum baseball bat while sitting in the middle of the living room near the spot where he had punched through the wall.

This may sound stupid, but I could never figure out why Igoe would get so drunk. He had so much going for him. He was intelligent, likable, and full of his own easy (if sometimes sleazy) charm. I honestly didn't think it had anything to do with the accident or me. In my mind, I had forgiven him long ago, and we had moved on with our lives. Problem was, Igoe couldn't forgive himself. He told me later that he thought the accident had revealed to others something he had secretly felt for a long time—that he was a despicable human being. He felt awful that he had driven drunk and had walked away from the crash, while I had ended up paralyzed. He wanted to quit drinking and get his life back together, but no matter how hard he tried, he couldn't. Instead he was getting hammered night after night, trying to deaden the psychic pain he was experiencing.

He thought people were silently judging him, and he was probably right. If I had been known around campus as the soccer-player-turned-wheelchair-cripple, then Igoe was known as the belligerent drunk who made me that way. The people who had sympathy for me usually had none for Igoe, who dealt with his depression and insecurity by crawling into the bottle for days at a time. The booze tended to impair his judgment, and he would end up saying cruel or obnoxious things to people, and getting into fistfights. In one particular instance, Igoe kicked in some guy's television set after they got into a row about who was first in line for the keg. Igoe's negative image of himself would be reinforced by his bad behavior and how people reacted to him. Then he would wake up the next morning too hung over for class and even more depressed and insecure. Then he would drink again.

Igoe was still playing rugby, a sport that was just as much about athletics as it was about postgame drinking. He had gotten a fake ID from one of his teammates. The name on it was "Fernando Tomanovich." Fernando was apparently born somewhere in the Eastern Bloc, whereas Igoe just looked Irish. The stats listed him as five inches shorter and fifty pounds lighter than Igoe, but that didn't matter at the bars near campus. They would pretty much accept anything. Igoe used the ID to get into a bar called Club Boca one night that spring. He was tweaking on a drug called mini-thins, which were these stay-awake pills sold mostly at truck stops so that drivers wouldn't doze off during long hauls. Some guys on the soccer team used to pop them before games because they thought the pills would open up their lungs and keep them from getting winded. The pills were made from pseudoephedrine mixed with caffeine, and if you took enough of them, you got all geeked and wired.

Igoe was totally annihilated when he hitched a ride back to school with a guy from the soccer team and two girls. He had a golf-ball-size wad of chewing tobacco crammed in his mouth and was slurring and slobbering all over one of the girls, who was doing her best to fend off his advances. They wanted to get rid of Igoe as soon as possible, so instead of dropping him off at our old apartment, they dumped him at one of the freshman dorms. Igoe stumbled in, fell down, and passed out in the entryway. The resident assistant found him there and tried to wake him up, but Igoe was unconscious. The guy ended up calling 911 and an ambulance rushed to campus. The paramedics couldn't revive him so they took him to the hospital. Igoe had drunk so much that he had alcohol poisoning, and they had to pump his stomach. He came to hours later in a strange bed as one of the nurses was trying to insert a catheter into his penis.

"What the fuck are you doing to me?" Igoe muttered. "Where am I?"

"It's all right, Fernando," the nurse said. "You're in the emergency room."

"Who the hell is Fernando?" Igoe said, forgetting the name on his fake ID. Then he tried to recover. "Oh yeah, that's me," he said dumbly. "I'm Fernando."

"Enough with the acting. We know you're not Fernando," a voice said.

That's when Igoe noticed a police officer standing in the room. The paramedics had called the cops when they found two IDs in Igoe's pocket. He had violated his probation by using a fake ID, and that's a felony in the state of Florida. On his dad's advice, Igoe pleaded guilty, and the charge was reduced to a misdemeanor.

Igoe was sentenced to nine months on house arrest. He dropped out of school, moved back in with his parents, and had to wear an electronic monitoring device on his ankle that would inform the police if he left the premises. Now he was the one stuck in his house, waiting for visitors, searching his soul, wondering how the hell he could have sunk this low.

He didn't know it at the time, but he still had a ways to go before he hit rock bottom.

closer

I didn't plan on making the same mistake twice. No one does.

I was well into my second year at Georgia Tech when my grades started to slide again. By this time, I had set my sights on becoming one of the best quad rugby players in the league. My teammates told me about the upcoming Paralympics in Sydney as well as the World Wheelchair Games, which were held every other summer. There were around five hundred quad rugby players in the United States, and only twelve of them would be selected for the national squad that would travel around the world and play in these different tournaments. I was determined to make the team. I found a new outlet for my obsessive nature and became a student of the game.

Instead of studying, I had been spending all my time lifting, practicing, and playing. I changed my major from aerospace to civil engineering, and I thought I could pass the final exam in electromagnetism with a couple of late-night cramming sessions. I ended up with a big fat F, the first and last failing grade I ever received on a final, thank you very much.

Most of the guys on my team were older and worked regular jobs. They didn't have to study on the weekends the way I did. I would bring my books with me on the road, but it was the same situation I experienced back when I was playing at FAU. I used the same sorry excuses that I had used back then: I had been too busy to study and I wasn't very good at setting boundaries for myself when it came to sports. But I finally realized that excuses were easier to make than changing my old patterns. I started to apply the same discipline I had used in training and physical therapy to my academic pursuits. I knew that if I put my mind to it, I could strike a balance and excel at both school and quad rugby. Unlike other aspects of my life, finding time to study was well within my control. I joined study groups on campus, and when I traveled to play on the weekends, I stayed in my hotel room and cracked books while my teammates were out to dinner. It made me pretty cranky, but in the end, it was worth it.

In the off-season, we had acquired a new player named Curtis Palmer. He was a blond kid from New Zealand and had played on his country's Paralympic rugby team back in 1996. Curtis was classified as a 2.5 and weighed around 140 pounds. He was hummingbird fast. He was also a terrific ball handler. His presence did a lot to improve our team, and the two of us were a formidable combo on offense. We became good friends and later shared a house together. In the pre-season picks for that year, the Rolling Thunder made a giant leap up to become fifth in the nation.

The league itself was also going through changes. As a sport, quad rugby was maturing. Curtis and I were part of a new generation of players who had started their careers playing in state-of-the-art chairs with space-age frames, an anti-tip fifth wheel in the back, and specialized grills that could be used to hook and trap other players. Those chairs had dramatically changed the way the game was played. The young bucks tended to hit harder and play more aggressively than the veterans, who had learned the game playing recreationally in everyday chairs that couldn't take the same kind of punishment.

But that didn't mean that the old guard was going gently into the night. Most of them were fighting tooth and nail to hold on to their starting spots and titles as the league's dominant players. The noisiest of them was a balding guy named Joe Soares, a 3.5 on the Tampa Generals. They were one of the elite teams and had previously won a national championship. They currently ranked second in the league, just behind the Sharp Shadows.

Joe was a real piece of work. Everyone knew he was in the sunset of his career except him. He had been on the USA's Paralympic team and used to be one of the shrewdest and most skilled players in the league, but he had gotten older and slower. Joe thought everyone automatically owed him respect and would scream at the ref and other players and coaches about touch fouls. In my opinion, he was a big fucking crybaby. He had the same low opinion of me, badmouthing and taunting me whenever we squared off.

"I want you to wear Joe like a shirt for the entire thirty-two minutes and try to bait him into calls," Wendy would say before the game. "Hit him whenever you can. I want you to make him feel it." I'd hunt him down and jolt him back to reality with my chair. But I never fouled him with body-to-body contact. At least not on purpose. I would revert back to my soccer days and try to get in his head with some psychological warfare. "You've got nothing, old man," I would whisper in Joe's ear. "You're done. Finished. You might as well retire now."

Joe was a far better player than I was back then. He could see the entire court as few players could, and he had a crablike defense. But my constant chatter would drive him nuts, and he would end up losing his temper and letting his anger take him out of the game. Wendy would tell me that one of her happiest memories from when she coached Atlanta was when we finally beat Tampa to take third place in a tournament. But I would be lying if I said Joe never got the better of me. He would make me lose my cool as well. I was still pretty unseasoned and immature. My big mouth and late hits would win me trips to the penalty box, a place we call the sin bin, where I would usually sulk and complain about the calls.

A few years later, Joe, who was probably in his early forties, would try out for the national team. For the first time in his career, he wouldn't be selected as one of the final twelve players. Instead of accepting that his playing days were over, he would try (and fail) to sue the USQRA for discrimination. The lawsuit didn't make Joe the most popular guy in the league. He'd end up taking all Team USA's plays with him up to rival Canada, where he would become the head coach for their national team and, to me, the biggest Benedict Arnold in the history of the sport.

* * *

while i certainly got into my fair share of squabbles on the court and was earning a reputation as a young and cocky enforcer, I made way more friends than enemies playing quad rugby. And not just with other people in chairs. Coach Wendy and I had become pretty good pals since I joined the team. She was relatively new to Atlanta as well, and we would go out to eat together or check out a movie. She introduced me to her boyfriend, Eric Holden. He was only a couple of years older than me and we immediately hit it off.

To this day, Eric is one of my favorite people in the world. He's just a totally unique individual. He's six feet six and weighs 250 pounds. He looks like a professional wrestler and drinks beer the way most people breathe air, but he has the heart of a Buddha. I've never met a sweeter or more caring person. He's from Connecticut and works in construction, building and remodeling houses. He's one of those guys who can make almost anything with their own hands.

Eric loves music just as much as I do, and we would constantly try to stump each other with obscure trivia questions about long-forgotten metal bands while we shot pool and drained beers at a local sports bar called Scores, which became our clubhouse. He had almost as much arcane knowledge about bands as I did. Eric was also an adrenaline fiend. He had been snowboarding all his life and had even been sponsored for a time, but now he was really into rock climbing. He would secure his rope at the top and literally run down the face of the cliff with his nose pointing at the ground.

"Is it anything like skydiving?" I asked.

"I don't know," he said. "Why don't you come along and find out for yourself."

Early the next morning, he drove me to the Morgan Falls recreational area in Sandy Springs, about twenty miles from downtown Atlanta. To get to the rock face, you had to hike about a mile along a steep ledge overlooking the Chattahoochee River. Eric picked me up like a duffel bag full of feathers and slung me over his shoulder after we hid my chair in some bushes. When we got to the edge of the cliff, the view was incredible, with mist blanketing the banks of the river. I wasn't able to rappel like they could at first because I couldn't grasp the ropes tightly enough to stop myself from falling, so they put me in a harness and lowered me down the seventy-foot drop. But after a while, I got the hang of it and was able to do it on my own by reversing my grip and using my left hand to compensate for my right. Eric went down next to me, keeping my rope from rubbing on the rocks. I can't say it was as exhilarating as jumping from a plane, but still, it was an unforgettable experience and another extreme sport that I could add to my résumé.

Later that afternoon, we met Wendy back at Scores. She and Eric launched into one of their favorite topics of conversation: when was I going to start dating again? It was a good question, but not one I could easily answer. School and rugby had helped me to feel secure about myself again, but I was still a little reserved around women since the whole Kati fiasco. I had noticed some women taking an interest in me, and the chair actually made a great topic of conversation. I would often make up ludicrous stories about how I got injured—anything from being shot from a cannon to losing a fight with a bear—but I wasn't sure if I was ready to open myself up emotionally to be in an actual relationship. However, after a couple of years of making love only to my left hand, I was certainly ready to try to get laid again.

I was doing my best to get myself back into the game. My old soccer buddy Jeff Sharon had come to Atlanta a few weeks before and had given me a call. I hadn't seen him in several years. He was now working for an investment firm. When I saw him wearing a suit and tie, fresh from work, I realized how much time had passed since the accident—more than three years. We were still young but now we were more like men than boys.

We had decided to meet up at a bar in Buckhead. The problem with going out with Sharon was that he was such a good-looking son of a bitch that he made regular guys like me seem about as attractive as the Elephant Man. Add in the wheelchair, and I thought that I would rank just below "herpes outbreak" on the desirability scale.

Spending all your time sitting in a chair, you end up staring at a lot of ass. I'm not trying to sound like a pervert, and I hope you don't think that I'm all about objectifying women. It's just that over the years, I had spent a lot of time at butt level, and as a result I had become kind of an ass expert, a connoisseur, if you will. That night at the bar, I spotted this beautiful blonde in tight white pants. She had the most spectacular heart-shaped ass I have ever seen. It looked thick and firm and ripe. The other great thing about Ms. White Pants's posterior was no panty lines. Not even a thong imprint. This brave woman was going commando. Believe me, it was quite a sight.

She kept staring back over at the table where Jeff and I were sitting. I shot her my best smile, but it looked like she was trying to catch Jeff's eye. A few rounds later, she sauntered over to our table and introduced herself.

"Hi," she said. "My name is Lauren. But you can call me Lori."

"Hey," Jeff said. "I'm Jeff. This is Mark."

"Nice pants," I said.

"Thank you," she said.

Jeff offered her a seat and then started to scoot his chair over next to hers.

She looked at Jeff and said, "Actually, I came over to get to know the guy in the chair."

Jeff and I looked at each other with wide eyes and then started cracking up.

"Yeah, Jeff," I said, laughing, "you presumptuous prick. She wants to know the guy in the chair. Why don't you go to the bar and get us some drinks while we talk."

Jeff gave me a wink, got us some beers, and then left us alone to get acquainted. We actually had a lot in common. Lori also went to Georgia Tech and was one wild, whip-smart girl. Later that night, she ended up coming back with me to Jeff's hotel room, where we made out for a while. I can't tell you how awesome it was to know I could still pick up a hot chick in a bar. We exchanged numbers and planned to go out together a few days later. It was pretty clear she wanted the evening to end the next morning at breakfast.

I wanted to make sure that I was, uh, up for our date. I'd never really had a problem getting an erection, but I wasn't sure if it was as reliable as before the accident. I didn't want any potential for embarrassment. My fragile ego would have been shattered if I couldn't perform on demand. I asked some of the guys on the rugby team about what they used when they were with their girlfriends. This was back in the pre-Viagra days. A few of them used this stuff called prostaglandin. I went and got a supply from my doctor. It came in a syringe, and you actually had to inject it into the shaft of your penis eight hours before you wanted to have sex. (I'm not kidding. I had to stick a needle into my dick. That should tell you how much I wanted to impress this girl. But seriously, could they think of a more fucked-up way to get you hard? It was like curing blindness by sticking glass shards in your eye.) You had to keep it in the refrigerator, and my roommates would call it "Mark's boner medicine."

I thought I should try it out before I was with Lori. My doctor gave me a shot before I went to class in the morning. I had spent months cramming a tube down my dick, so sticking a needle into it really wasn't that big a deal. The good news was that prostaglandin works. Mr. Stiffy was standing up and saluting. The bad news was that I overdosed. My dick was harder than my chemistry final. It was like trying to smuggle a ski pole in my sweatpants. People were staring at me so much in class, I had to roll around with a heavy book balanced on my lap. I ended up having to take a bunch of Sudafed to open up my capillaries and let the blood return to other parts of my body.

On the night of the date, I was ready to go. I picked Lori up at her house where she lived with her parents. I was a little self-conscious about the time it took me to get my chair out of the back of my car, but whatever. It wasn't like she didn't know my situation.

We ate in a nice little restaurant close to campus, and I made sure that the waiter gave me the check when we were done.

"What do you want to do now?" I asked.

"Why don't we go back to your place," she said.

We did. We had some beer and small talk. After a while, we dimmed the lights. I got out of my chair and sat on the bed. She unbuttoned her blouse, removed her bra, shucked her tight pants like a corn husk, and eased back next to me. She helped me out of my clothes. Her lithe body looked absolutely stunning. And because I'm a gentleman and not the type to kiss and tell, I'll just say that we had an exquisite night together.

Oh, fuck that. Of course I'm going to give you all the details. We tore it off that night. A couple of times. Thank you, prostaglandin. But I realized that I was a different kind of lover now. I used to worry only about pleasing myself. Now I was constantly thinking about my partner. I didn't rush the foreplay. I didn't want to. I hadn't been kissed and touched and caressed by a woman in so long. I didn't want it to end. I removed my mouth from hers and inched my way down to her full breasts, her flat stomach, and beyond. Kids, go in the other room for a minute. This part of the book is for the adults. Here's the deal: when you are a quad, you're often a little more appreciative of attention from the females than most other guys. I like to express my gratitude by pleasing the ladies orally whenever I get the chance.

And, yes, chicks dig it.

Lori and I dated for a few months and then went our separate ways. It wasn't true love, but damn, at the time, the loving was good enough for me.

not long after that, Eric introduced me to an old friend of his named Amy Hults who was moving to Atlanta from Connecticut. They had grown up together in a small town called New Milford. She was an athletic woman in her early twenties with luminous brown hair, olive skin, and a smile like a toothpaste commercial. Eric had been talking her up for months, saying that we would make a perfect couple. Apparently, he had been giving her the same hard sell. Her first night in town, Eric invited her to come out with us to the bars.

"Nice to finally meet you, Mark," Amy said, warmly taking my hand in hers. "I was getting sick and tired of constantly hearing about how great you are."

That made me blush.

Amy had a boyfriend at the time, but the instant we met, I felt this incredible physical and mental attraction to her. As Eric said: "Dude, you were totally smitten." When I looked at Amy, I saw a real woman. She had already graduated from college and had gotten a job in TV at PBS as a production assistant. That night, she drove us to Scores so we could hang out and shoot pool. I made an awesome first impression by accidentally leaving my beer on the roof of her car, and the bottle crashed and broke as soon as we pulled out into the street.

Once we got there, I asked her to pick out songs with me on the jukebox and we started talking about our favorite bands. When I looked at the clock, several hours had passed in a heartbeat and it was last call.

The next day, I asked Eric if she had said anything about me.

"She said she thought you were funny," he said.

"Funny?" I said. "What the hell does that mean? Funny ha-ha or funny looking?"

"I would probably say both," Eric said.

"Thanks, man," I said, "for the vote of confidence."

Undeterred, I chased after Amy for about a year, giving her the full-court press, constantly inviting her to come out with us to the bar or to concerts. She usually said yes. At first, I thought it was because she didn't know anyone else in Atlanta. But I could tell I was starting to grow on her. She liked to argue about stuff almost as much as I did and wouldn't give me an inch when I would contradict her. She even made up a nickname for me: "Markass."

An East Coast girl at heart, Amy was having a hard time adjusting to living in the South. She had broken up with her boyfriend and desperately missed her old friends back in Connecticut. "Why is everyone so nice here?" she'd say with an exaggerated look of exasperation on her face. "And talkative? Complete strangers always asking me how I am doing. What am I supposed to say to them?"

"I think that's what they call southern hospitality," I said.

"I think I prefer to live in civilized silence," she said with a grin.

One of the things I liked best about Amy was that she was my intellectual equal. (Shit, who am I trying to fool here? She was more my intellectual superior.) She had an inquisitive mind and was constantly asking me questions about what it was like to be a quad. I always tried to give her the straight dope and was probably honest to a fault. She asked me what I wanted to do with my life. I told her my short-term goals were to make the national quad rugby team, graduate from Georgia Tech, and find a good job. She said her dream was to have a successful career in television and later start a family and live somewhere by the ocean.

Amy was one driven individual. After a few months in Atlanta, she was promoted to associate producer at the PBS station. Later, she became an editor at a local news show, the *Georgia Business Report*. She was also interested in directing documentaries and short films. She had her own video camera, and she started to bring it to my quad rugby games.

"You know," she said to me after we had gotten to know each other, "your life would make an amazing documentary. You should let me follow you around and shoot some footage."

"You're nuts," I said. "Why would anyone want to hear my story?"

By that time, I knew I had her hooked. When I would come to visit her at her second-floor apartment, she would have to carry my chair up the flights of stairs while I pulled myself up slowly using the railing. She never seemed to mind. She was one of those easygoing people who have an inexhaustible supply of kindness and patience. She came with me one holiday weekend to visit my parents. They both totally fell in love with her.

"She's a keeper," my mom whispered to me while Amy was in the living room talking to my dad and we were in the kitchen. "She would make an awfully nice daughter-in-law."

"Slow it down there, Mom," I said. "We're not even officially dating yet."

But I kept up my pursuit. I hope this doesn't sound too selfish, but one of the reasons I liked Amy so much was that when I was around her, she made me feel good about myself. She made me feel interesting and smart and fun. I thought we made a pretty good team.

Our friendship finally turned romantic that spring just as the magnolias were blooming. I kissed her for the first time on Easter Sunday.

"Are you sure you want to do this?" she asked me. "We're such good friends."

"Yes," I said. "I'm sure. I've wanted this for a long time."

We kissed again.

"Does this mean I can call you my girlfriend?" I asked.

"Yes, Markass," she said, sitting on my lap and wrapping her arms around me. "It does."

in may, i was invited to Denver, Colorado, to try out for the U.S. national developmental team, which would be traveling to the coastal town of Adelaide in Southern Australia to compete in an upcoming tournament called the Stoke Mandeville Games, in honor of Stoke Mandeville, England, where the world wheelchair games are usually held. The Americans would be going toe-to-toe against various national and developmental teams from other countries. The developmental team was where the coaches for the national team scouted potential players for the upcoming Paralympics. It was like being asked to try out for a farm team in professional baseball. Making the roster was a big deal, not only because it upped your profile in the league, but also because it exposed you to the elevated competition of playing at the international level.

Wendy had been selected to coach the developmental team along with a man named Ed Suhr. All the prospective players were staying in the same hotel in the Mile High City and riding together on a bus to the practice complex. I was the only player from my Atlanta team invited to Denver, but I knew almost all the other guys by face—if not name—from club play. On that first day, I sat next to a 1.0 named James Gumbert—"Gumbie" for short. He was Wendy's cousin, several years my senior, and loved to give me hell about the white do-rag I wore wrapped around my head.

"What's wrong with you, son?" he'd say in his Texas twang. "Take that thing off. You're scaring me. You look like you're wearing a Klan hood."

I assured him that I wasn't.

There were several other 3.0s, but my main competition was Mike Gilliland, who played for the Arizona Slam. He was big, fast, smart, and more experienced than me. I would have to bring my A-game if I was going to be chosen for the team.

The tryouts started Friday morning with timed sprints and slalom drills through cones, and ended on Sunday with one of the most intense full-court scrimmages I have ever played, with the coaches experimenting with different combinations of lines. In between were twelve-hour practices (with breaks for meals) packed with passing drills and two-on-two games that pitted you against other guys in your classification. All the best young players in the league were there, and everyone was going for broke to impress the coaches, putting extra salt on passes and pepper on hits, bending rims, popping tires, and cracking frames during collisions. We all played past exhaustion, leaving our tire tracks, blood, sweat, and even urine on the hardwood floors (yes, catheter bags do sometimes pop during games).

In my experience the best quad rugby players are usually the ones who were athletes before they were injured. They just understand competition and teamwork. I had been through tryouts like these before, and I didn't let the stress and strain psych me out. I just kept my mouth closed and my head up as I looked for the open man and the goal line. But at the same time, I had been playing the sport for less than two years, so I was still committing plenty of overzealous rookie errors. I've never been very patient and would end up forcing passes or trying to do everything myself. As an emotional player, I had a hard time shaking off mistakes and would waste energy beating myself up over what I should have done.

That Sunday afternoon, we waited near the bleachers for the coaches to finish their meeting and announce the final team. Most of the players were silent, but there were whispers of apprehension. "How many high pointers do you think they will take?" I heard one voice say. "Do you think they will go with the big guns?" another mumbled.

Finally the coaches came out with their list. First they thanked all the players for their efforts, and then they read the twelve-player roster, starting from highest classification to lowest. The first name they called was the guy I wanted to beat: Mike Gilliland.

Motherfucker, I thought. *Oh well. I'll be back to take his spot next year.*

They read my name next. We would be sharing the 3.0 spot. I put my hands in the air to celebrate and caught a few high fives and backslaps from the players around me.

When the coaches finally called Gumbie's name, he started to weep. He'd been playing quad rugby for five years, and this was the first time he'd made the developmental team. A quick vote among the players made him one of our team captains.

Tears on a grown man's face told me how important playing could be.

the first day of the tournament, we were all groggy from the long flight to Australia and the time change. We had jokingly decided to call ourselves the Dynamic Dozen and would be playing against Japan, which was new to the world competition. Wendy and Ed told us the lineup. I wasn't starting, but they assured us that no one would spend much time on the bench.

"I know that you guys are unfamiliar with playing together," Wendy said in her pregame talk, "but I want you to come out quick and find the cohesiveness. Team USA has never been beaten in international play. Ever. Let's make sure we continue that tradition!"

As we rolled onto the court, I stared down at my blue uniform with white and red numbers and realized that I was no longer playing for just any team; I was representing my country. That added a little more pressure, to say the least. Nevertheless, we gelled enough to drub the inexperienced Japanese crew 47–10. We went on to beat the solid South Australian team, which had several players from the Australian national team. Late that afternoon, we rolled over a club team from Queensland with a decisive 48–13 win.

We had three victories under our belt after the first day, and Wendy and Ed cautioned us against becoming overly confident. Tomorrow we would be facing the third best team in the world: New Zealand's national team. My buddy Curtis was on that squad. The whistle blew and the U.S. starters came out listless and flat, but the bench players, including myself, kept us in the game. On a sprint to the goal line, my teammate Willard "The Mountain" Brooks T-boned Curtis so hard that Curtis's chair flipped sideways up and over a goal pylon and his tire blew off the rim. That was the tipping point for us. We came from behind and won 38–35.

We continued to knock off the other squads in quick succession— The Kiwi developmental team, Western Australia, Victoria, New South

Wales. We once again squared off against South Australia in the finals and controlled the game from the opening tipoff. We beat them handily and took home the championship, continuing Team USA's unblemished winning streak. As we passed the champagne bottle around and celebrated, I flashed back to playing soccer in West Birmingham when I was a kid. I wasn't a professional athlete playing in front of cheering crowds in packed stadiums, but I was traveling the world and beginning to compete at the top level of a game that I loved. My life might have changed dramatically since the accident, but my dreams had stayed pretty much the same. And I was still chasing them.

my strong showing with the developmental team in Australia earned me an invite to try out for the actual U.S. national team, which would be traveling to Toronto to compete in the 1998 World Championships. I was among the forty players who flew to West Palm Beach, Florida, on a rainy weekend in December to vie for one of the twelve spots. I wanted to make the team so badly that just thinking about it hurt my brain. This would be a true test of my mettle. I was now competing against the most skilled players in the league, not just the best up-and-coming players.

The tryouts were very similar to Denver, except that the level of ability and play was noticeably higher. I competed in timed sprints and agility drills against other guys at my same point level. All the athletes in the 3.0 class were pretty much equal. We then paired up to do two-on-two in the key and in-bounding pass drills. This gave the coaches an opportunity to evaluate not only our ballhandling abilities but our decision-making skills as well. Before dinner, we ran an eight-minute "pecking order" drill for endurance. We would stagger ourselves and push laps around the gym. If a man behind you passed you up, you had to leave the track and roll around a smaller inner circle, leaving the fastest players sprinting in the outside loop. Endurance was supposed to be my specialty, but I was one of the first 3.0s to be passed.

After dinner, we set up for a scrimmage called the meat grinder. The coaches put three teams on the court—one on offense and two on defense. If the attack could beat the first line of defense in the open court, they had to face another in the key. It was a punishing drill—all chaos and contact— that made your weaknesses transparent. Even though it was just a scrimmage, most players were out for blood, and as a new guy, I had a big target on my back. I caught a few fists and elbows when fighting for loose balls, and after a couple of rotations, my side was killing me, but I kept playing until the coaches called it a night. When the other guys went back to the hotel, I went and saw the team doctor. He pressed his fingers on my side and said I had broken a rib. He taped up my torso and told me to go home and get some rest. My rib would take a couple of weeks to heal.

I was bummed. I thought I had blown my big chance to play on the national team. Looking back on it now, I realize I probably wouldn't have made that squad even if I had stayed totally healthy. While I had the athleticism and strength, I still lacked the poise. But I was getting there. When the other players heard that I had finished out practice even though I had broken a bone, they had a new respect for me—except one guy, I bet. Joe Soares still probably thought I was a disrespectful prick, but this would be his last year playing for the U.S. national team. By the time I would make Team USA, he would have traded allegiances and moved up north, coaching Team Canada.

Good friends are the ones who will come pick you up at the airport. When I flew into Atlanta later that evening, Eric, Curtis, and our friend Dave were waiting for me at the terminal. Because I had come home a day early, they were able to get me a ticket to the Ben Harper Christmas show that night at the Gwinnett Civic Center. After the show, I wanted to see if Ben Harper remembered meeting me at the Pearl Jam show. Using my chair as a beard, I rolled up to the stage and passed a security guard, who just looked at me. I could tell he was scared to ask me what I was doing, fearful that he would offend me. (I swear, if I robbed a bank in a wheelchair, the tellers would help me load the bags of money into the getaway car. Harper was addressing a gaggle of fans. One of his handlers came up to me.

"Are you here to see Mr. Harper?" he asked.

"Why, yes, I am," I said.

I followed him over to the musician.

"Excuse me, Mr. Harper," she said. "One of your handicapped fans is here to see you."

I was overwhelmed by embarrassment. But Harper was totally cool.

"You know how I met this cat?" Harper said, giving me a hug. "It was a couple of years ago. He was crowd surfing at the Pearl Jam show in Florida." He asked me what I was doing in Atlanta. I told him I was a few quarters away from graduating from Georgia Tech, and I thanked him again for the slide he gave me. I still had it with me. We chatted about his music until he had to go. Before he left, he gave me his cell phone number.

"Give me a call whenever you want to come to a show," he said.

I did.

chapterfifteen

glory and consequence

I never thought i'd see my entire life flash across a television screen.

But there it all was, playing as a montage of snapshots set to the melancholy strains of Sarah McLachlan's "I Will Remember You." It was June 12, 1999, the day I graduated from Georgia Tech. Earlier that morning, I had donned a cap and gown and received my diploma while my family and friends clapped and whistled for me. It was a proud moment, but the day was tinged with sadness. Uncle Howard and Aunt Marcia weren't able to be there. My cousin Jason had suffered a grand mal seizure that morning, and they were with him at the hospital.

I had really buckled down my senior year, and the As and Bs I received in my upper division classes pulled my GPA up to an acceptable 2.8. I probably could have done a little bit better if I wasn't spending so much time on the road playing quad rugby, but, hey, that's life. You play with the hand you've been dealt. I was secure in knowing I had done my best under the circumstances and accomplished what I had set out to do.

After the ceremony, we had a party at the house where I was living with Ken and Curtis. Amy had made the video for me as a gift, and we were playing it in the living room. She had put a ton of work into it, calling my mom, my aunt and uncle, Igoe, and Eric and asking them for old photos, which she scanned and set to music with artful edits. It started with some stills of me as a young strawberry-haired toddler with my parents. It showed me standing in a swimsuit in front of the community pool in Buffalo, then growing up, playing soccer on different teams and graduating from high school with Igoe, Nickell, and Cava. There were shots of me sitting in an inner tube at Lake Lanier, skydiving with J.O.B., rock climbing with Eric, blasting past opponents in my quad rugby chair, posing with Ben Harper. I hugged Amy tightly when the screen went black. The video made me realize how blessed I was to have so many incredible friends who had been so selfless in helping me over the years.

Igoe didn't have the same reaction to the video. He looked glassy-eyed and crazed as the tape rolled, pacing around the crowded room like a caged animal. It was early afternoon and he was already three sheets to the wind. He had been on a bender since he arrived in Atlanta. Igoe had become a different person since I left Florida. After his arrest, he never made it back to FAU. Instead, he had found his calling as a salesman and was working as a stockbroker. His aggressive personality, his gregariousness, and love of risk were serving him well at the job. These were the bullish days before the dot-com bubble burst, and Igoe had become a big-money player as a day trader. The previous month, he had cleared more than $20,000. Flush with fast money, he was living in an expensive beachside condo in Fort Lauderdale, driving a Lexus GS 300, and running with an even faster crowd who tended to treat their bodies like garbage disposals for booze, pills, and anything else they came across.

After the morning ceremony, Igoe had convinced my brother to stop off at a strip club, where he tucked bills into G-strings and downed double shots. Now that he was back at the house, Igoe was clearly unraveling in front of everyone. He told me later that watching the video made him feel like he was having a nervous breakdown. He hadn't been around my extended family since the day after the accident, and seeing them all again completely overwhelmed him. He chugged beer after beer and became sloppy and stupid, acting on any idiot impulse: talking loudly, bumping into people, knocking over glasses and plates of food.

It wasn't long before Igor completely took over. At one point he managed to pick up Eric and body-slammed him into my brand-new couch, splintering the wooden frame and destroying the thing. Some of my teammates from the Rolling Thunder had come by to congratulate me, and Igoe head-butted one of them so hard that he almost knocked him unconscious. He was so out of control that my dad had to step in, grabbing Igoe and pulling him outside to the patio.

"Enough," my dad said tonelessly. "Get it together, Igoe. There are children in there."

"I'm trying," Igoe said. "I swear, Mr. Zupan, I'm trying."

I was livid. Ruining my graduation day was the last straw. As far as I was concerned, our friendship was over. Igoe had become too much of a liability. I had gotten my life together, matured, and moved on. I couldn't understand why Igoe was still such an unbelievable fuckup. I thought he resented my academic success because he had dropped out of school. I stopped calling him, and for the first time since we had met each other in high school, we severed ties.

To be honest, it wasn't such a hard thing for me to do. My life back in Florida had started to feel like ancient history, and my friendship with Igoe felt like a relic from my past. He was becoming one of those people you would always call a friend because you grew up together, but you just didn't have so much in common anymore. Florida was a place where I had spent part of my past, a time I obviously didn't always remember fondly. Graduating seemed so much more here and now, and about the future. Igoe had become an annoyance, constantly trying to pull me back into a life with labels I had outgrown.

Things didn't get much better for Igoe when he went back to Florida. One afternoon, he was getting soused at an outdoor bar in Lauderdale with a work colleague when they started to chat up two women. Wanting to impress them, Igoe decided to go get his Lexus so they could check out his fancy ride. As he stumbled across the wide street, he took a break on the median, pulling down his pants and urinating on a shrub. Cars whizzed by on either side as Igoe took his own whiz, enjoying the soft ocean breeze, trying to keep the piss off his pants. The bicycle cop who was riding by wasn't amused. He watched as Igoe zipped up and staggered to the door of his car, where he climbed in, revved it up, and pulled around to the front of the bar.

"What exactly do you think you're doing?" the cop said, riding up to his window.

Igoe, who was coincidentally wearing an NYPD T-shirt, was quick with his reply.

"Officer," he said, hoping the words weren't too slurred, "how about a little professional courtesy for a fellow brother in blue?"

"You're a cop. Really? Where?"

"Up in Suffolk County. I'm here on vacation."

The cop asked for Igoe's driver's license. "If you're from New York, then why do you have a Florida driver's license?"

"That, sir, is a very good question," Igoe said.

The cop pulled down his sunglasses and looked Igoe directly in the eyes. "You know I can arrest you for impersonating an officer," he said.

"Is it too late to take it all back?" Igoe asked

It was. Feeling like a failure and a disgrace, Igoe made the all-too-familiar trek through intake and into jail. He hid his second DUI from his friends and parents. It was just too unbearable. In retrospect, I now understand that Igoe was crying out for help, just as I had done after the accident. His binge drinking and shithead shenanigans were how he showed the world that he was still suffering for what he had done. But for some reason, I couldn't see it back then. In certain ways, an injury like mine can make you myopic after a while. I had been in so much mental pain for so long that I had become almost oblivious to other people's hurt.

This is one of those chapters of my life that I wish I could rewrite. Instead of offering Igoe my hand, I turned away from him, somehow forgetting what he had done for me in my time of need. After the accident, we had been cast in the roles of victim and victimizer, even though I never once thought of myself as a victim, or blamed him for putting me in a chair. But everyone around us did, and maybe I was subconsciously starting to buy into it as well. It wasn't all paranoia on Igoe's part that people were whispering behind his back. In the way of all small towns, everyone around knew the story of how Igoe had crippled his friend, and over the years, it became the event that eclipsed all his other successes and shortcomings.

I had moved away, but Igoe never left Coral Springs. He was never able to distance himself from what had happened, to redefine himself, to start over, to be something more than what he had been when he was young and foolish. If the accident and his subsequent drinking made him believe he was a worthless person, then the second DUI confirmed it. He didn't see any escape at this point. He thought he deserved to feel like shit every day, because the second that he stopped, it would be like saying that what had happened to me meant nothing to him. In his mind, hating himself had become his only redeeming quality.

His court date for his second DUI was set for a Friday. That Wednesday morning, he was at work in his corner office, still drunk from the night before. One of his coworkers stopped by and offered Igoe a sack of Vicodin. Igoe said, Sure, why the hell not. He locked his office door and ate the entire bag. He'd later realize that each pill was an apology in the farewell letter he had been writing in his head for years. However, at the time he told himself his plan was to party until his court date and then let the chips fall as they may. But a bag of pills isn't much of a party. I have to believe that Igoe knew what he was doing. He passed out in his chair and slid to the floor.

His secretary saw him through the window, blue-faced and still. She was scared, but less surprised than you would expect. Even she had noticed Igoe's recent tailspin. She called the paramedics, who had to break down his office door to get to him. He wasn't breathing. They pumped on his heart, hit him with oxygen, and rushed him to the emergency room, where he had his stomach emptied of toxins. This time when he awoke, he pulled the IV from his arm and ran. He went directly to the liquor store and then to his girlfriend's house, where he continued to poison himself. As he vomited uncontrollably into her toilet, she called his parents.

He woke up Thursday morning in his old room back in Coral Springs with his mom and dad sitting beside him. "Chris, this is it," his dad said. "Either you admit you have a problem and address it or you can no longer be part of this family. Your mother and I love you very much, but we cannot tolerate this anymore. You need to get yourself professional help."

Igoe has never been a coward. This was his time to decide if he wanted to live or die. He went to the kitchen, grabbed the yellow pages, and looked up drug and alcohol rehabilitation facilities. He called the first one he saw, and they told him to come in right away. His dad took care of the bill and had Igoe's court date pushed. While in rehab, Igoe was finally able to admit to himself that he was an alcoholic. Group therapy helped to give him some perspective on his disease, his past, and his role in the accident.

"You have created a pattern where you continually punish yourself," the counselor said. "If you had gone to jail for what you had done, you'd be out by now. You've paid your debt. You say that your friend Mark has forgiven you. It's time for you to forgive yourself."

Ten days later, Igoe checked out of rehab, ready to give sobriety a shot. It wouldn't be easy for him, and over the years, he would continue to struggle with his addiction. But with the support of his parents and sister, Danielle, he started to reassemble his life, taking it one day at a time. As the months passed, he kept crossing my mind. I would ask my other friends how he was doing, and this time around, I was the one who was amazed by his determination, his dedication, and his progress. In a way, it was Igoe's turn to learn to walk on his own.

We finally had enough maturity and hard-won wisdom to truly comprehend what we had gone through together and what we meant to each other. He was my best friend. We were both survivors. We had gone through the same ordeal, hit rock bottom and then fought our way back. We both knew we could never forget our shared history, but dwelling on the past had crippled both of us, so we decided to do our best to move our friendship into the future.

there were still many more lessons for me to learn about myself and how I related to others—both off and on the court. After graduation, I flew halfway around the world again, this time to play in the World Wheelchair Games, which for the first time in fifty years was being held not in Stoke Mandeville but in Christchurch, New Zealand. I was part of another developmental team of athletes with limited international experience, and this tournament would set the stage for the Paralympics next fall in Sydney.

From the first day of play, Team USA steamrolled the competition, again taking down Japan, the Swedes (who were the 1999 European champions), and then the Australian "C" team, which we annihilated 52–10. But our match against the Australian "A" squad marked a turning point for both the team and me. The Aussies' coach, an American named Terry Vinyard, instructed his team to slow down the game and waste the clock as a way to counteract our run-and-gun strategy. They put a ceiling on our scoring and kept the game in reach, forcing us to make some uncharacteristic mistakes and turnovers down the final stretch. They ended up beating us 26–25 and handing Team USA one of its first losses in international play.

Vinyard, who coached Joe Soares's team in Tampa, still had a few more tricks up his sleeve. Sometime earlier in the day, he had apparently seen me get out of my chair and take a few steps. He informed the tournament officials and protested my 3.0 classification, saying that I had more function in my legs and trunk than I was letting on. This is a fairly common strategy that some coaches will use to undermine a new player's confidence and screw with another team's main lines. Unfortunately, it worked. I was proving myself to be a dominant class 3.0, and Vinyard wanted to take me out of our usual lineup. He was also probably giving me a little payback for my tough play in the previous game, my shit talking and my cocky attitude on the court.

I didn't take the protest well. The way I saw it, Vinyard was publicly calling me a liar, saying that I had knowingly deceived the physical therapists who award you a classification after an examination in which they watch you play, test your range of motion, and palpitate your muscles. He was saying I had faked some part of the exam as a way to give my team and me an unfair advantage. It probably would have been in my best interest to handle the situation with a little more diplomacy, but I'm not at my best when someone insinuates that I lack honesty and integrity. And let's face it: I'm not a big fan of rules and authority in general. When someone takes a swing at me, it's not my nature to turn the other cheek. My reflex is to hit back. I thought he was calling into question the last five years of my life, and that forced me into a corner. I had invested so much in my rehabilitation and recovery, and now it seemed I was being unfairly penalized by my hard work. Instead of making my case to the panel like an adult, I let my immaturity get the best of me and lashed out during my reclassification exam.

"I'm a 3.0 and you know it," I said to the therapists as they pressed their fingertips into my arms and legs and asked me to lift and flex. "Look at my medical records. I'm missing a muscle in my left shoulder. What I lack in function, I've made up with hours in the gym and athletic ability. Do you know how long it has taken me to get this far?"

They said nothing.

Vinyard's strategy worked. I was reclassified as a 3.5, which jacked up our lines for the rest of the tournament. When I got in the game, I had to match up against other 3.5s, who had a lot more function than I did. We managed to beat New Zealand in the finals and took home the gold, but I felt I had lost my spot on the team.

back in atlanta, I had some big decisions to make. Wendy's cousin Gumbie, whom I had met while playing on the developmental team in Australia, had recently made the transition from player to coach. He had been an assistant coach for the squad that had won the gold in New Zealand and was now building his own team based in Austin; called the Texas Stampede, it would compete with the top club teams in the league. On the flight home from Christchurch, he said he believed in my potential and asked if I wanted to sign up and relocate.

It was a tempting offer. Gumbie was a smart man who knew the game inside out and had already recruited some stellar players, including a gentle giant named Steve Pate, a 3.5 who was one of the most dominant players in the world at the time, and Norm Lyduch, a crafty, bespectacled 1.0 who looked more like an accountant than an expert rugger. My club team in Atlanta was a good squad, and I had learned a lot with them, but we didn't have the depth to compete with the league's best. While joining the Stampede would be a step forward, it also felt like a step backward. I wouldn't be part of the starting lineup as I had been in Atlanta. I would be coming off the bench for Pate and getting less playing time. Still, this would be my opportunity to learn from the best and take my game to the next level. That would hopefully help me make Team USA, which would soon be holding tryouts for the Paralympics.

Then there was Amy to consider. We had been together for a few years by now, and I was still totally taken by her. We had even talked about marriage a few times. Would I lose her if I left? And what about Eric and my other good friends in Atlanta? I didn't want to leave them. Work was another worry. Since graduation, I had sent out my résumé and received a few offers to interview at local engineering firms. At some point, I was going to have to figure out how I would pay the rent on my own. I was slowly starting to convince myself that staying put was the best option. But then I wondered if I was just scared to leave my comfortable surroundings, the same way that I didn't want to leave my family and North Broward after my accident. I looked deep into my heart and asked myself, what was it I really wanted from life? The answer came loud and clear: I wanted to play quad rugby, and I needed to know if I had what it took to compete at the Paralympic level. I had learned over the years that as soon as you stop pushing forward in life, as soon as you become complacent and fearful of new experiences, you stop living. I had been through too much to turn back now. If I wanted to make Team USA, I was going to have to elevate my level of play, and that would take sacrifice.

I decided to take Amy's temperature about it when we were having dinner together one night. We talked about what it was like to have my college soccer career cut short and how it left me with a lot of unanswered questions. I told her I was nervous about leaving her, about moving to Texas for a new team. I asked if she would consider moving to Austin with me. She said she would think about it, but couldn't leave the career she was building in Atlanta just yet. She said she would miss me, but she understood why I had to make the move.

"Go and play for a season and see what you think," she said. "I know you. You'll regret it if you don't. Don't worry about me. I'll be here waiting for you."

i was pretty sure i would like Austin. From what I had read, it seemed like a perfect match for my personality. The city is known as the live music capital of the world, and almost every night of the week thousands of college students from the University of Texas cram the bars that line Sixth Street, mixing with tattooed, pierced, dreadlocked townies, knocking back Lone Star beers and margaritas and checking out bands. I hoped the music scene would help me get over missing Amy and my friends back in Atlanta.

But I didn't get to experience much of the nightlife right away. I was usually too exhausted to hit the town. If I thought Wendy was a demanding coach, it's only because I hadn't spent much time with Gumbie, who was hell-bent on making the Stampede the best team in the league. Gumbie came across as an easygoing southern gentleman with apple cheeks and impeccable manners, but I discovered that he was also a savvy tactician and rugby fanatic who used his aw-shucks charm to disguise an ultracompetitive nature.

A few of his players, including Pate and Norm, were also training for the preliminary Paralympic tryouts, which were going to be held in Pasadena, Texas, outside Houston, so Gumbie worked us harder than ever to be prepared. His strenuous practices took a toll on me, physically and mentally as well. Playing second fiddle to Pate was turning out to be more difficult than I thought it would be. All I had in Austin was quad rugby, and I wasn't getting the minutes I thought I deserved on the floor. Patience has never been my best virtue, and sitting on the sidelines for the Stampede after I had been the go-to guy in Atlanta began to wear on me. I started having regrets about moving to Texas. Maybe I would have been better served staying in Atlanta, where I would be getting more experience in actual games? At least I wouldn't be so goddamn homesick. I didn't even have my own apartment or a job in Austin. I was crashing on a couch in a house that a woman named Kelly, a physical therapist who helped the team, shared with Pate and Norm. I did my best to keep a positive outlook and improve my game, but I found myself becoming increasingly cross and irritable with my teammates and butting heads with Gumbie about how he picked his lines.

Unhappiness plagued me during the Paralympic tryouts that December, and doubt continued to strip away my self-confidence. It wasn't just pregame jitters; it was beyond that. I felt weary, worn down, and out of sorts, partly because I was still classed as a 3.5 and competing for a spot against the highest-functioning players in the league, including Pate and my old nemesis, Joe Soares. I dug deep into my reserves, willing myself to perform above my abilities. But that's when the wheels fell off the wagon for me. Looking for any advantage I could get, I ordered a new quad rugby chair, hoping it would give me the added edge that I badly needed. I had it shipped directly to the tryouts. When I unpacked it from the box, I noticed that the aluminum frame was slightly bent. The chair still worked, but I didn't like the way it handled, and there was no way I could fix it or get a new one. Having to play in that chair psyched me out. I should have known better than to rely on equipment I had never tested, but maybe that shows how desperate I was.

Somehow, I advanced to the second round of tryouts, held at the Olympic Training Facility in Colorado Springs. I did my best to soldier through the day-long practices, struggling for breath in the thin mountain air, enduring the six a.m. wake-up calls, after the sleepless nights, tossing and turning in sheets that smelled like sports cream and scratched like sandpaper. The intensity and level of play was higher than I had ever seen it, and one player actually broke his ankle during tryouts. But by the end of it, I knew I wasn't going to make the cut. When they announced the twelve names that would be traveling to Sydney for the Paralympics, my name wasn't on the roster. I choked back tears and watched with jealousy as the team had their picture taken in front of the five giant interlocking Olympic rings. I felt fate was once again conspiring against me, sending me a message, telling me to hang up my jersey. The next Paralympics were four years away. I didn't think I would ever make it to the big show, and part of me was sick of trying. Depressed and dejected, I boarded the plane back to Austin. It must have looked like my chin was permanently glued to my chest.

we had the game in the bag, but my mood was blacker than a hearse. The Stampede was in Tampa playing an international tournament, and Pate was wiping the floor with the competition and getting all the glory while I petulantly rode pine. Earlier that day, Gumbie had protested the 3.5 classification I received in New Zealand, and the official panel had retested me and ruled that I was in fact a 3.0. The moment was full of irony, because Tampa was Vinyard's town and he had organized this tournament. I should have felt vindicated, but I didn't.

The way I saw it, the classification fiasco had kept me from making the Paralympic team, and I was resentful about it. When a man senses that someone has snatched something that took him years to acquire, he often reacts violently. Misguided as it seems, I was no exception. I wanted to get into the game and rip someone's head off, but I wasn't getting the chance. As long as Gumbie built his offense around Pate, I was about as useful as tits on a bull. With three minutes left in the fourth quarter, I unwrapped the tape on my wrists and removed my gloves. I usually would have waited until the final whistle to do this, but I was feeling unappreciated and discouraged because of my lack of playing time.

On the floor, Pate capsized an opponent like a tidal wave engulfing a small sailboat. The angry slap of metal shattered the plastic casting that housed one of the anti-tip wheels on the front of his chair.

Hobbled, Pate motioned for a sub. Gumbie scanned the bench for me.

"Mark," he called. "Get in there for Pate."

I gave him a nasty look and begrudgingly began to tape back up again, taking my sweet time. Gumbie had made me wait to play, and now I was doing the same to him. Pate rolled awkwardly off the court. The seven remaining players sat silently, wondering what was taking so long. The ref blew his whistle and instructed Gumbie to sub someone in or play a man down.

"What the hell are you doing?" Gumbie said to me. "You're not ready to play?"

I didn't say anything as I carefully ripped the new tape with my teeth.

Gumbie shook his head in disbelief.

"Pate," he said, "can you stay on the floor with a broken wheel?"

"Yeah, I guess," Pate said. "But I won't be able to push very fast. Their offense is going to run circles around me."

"I don't care," Gumbie said. "Just do it."

Pate finished out the game. The other team scored a few times, but there wasn't enough time left for them to gap the wide margin of goals.

Hooray for us, I thought sarcastically at the final buzzer. *Go team.*

As we left the court, Gumbie and I mean-mugged each other. I wanted him to say something to me so I could hit him with both barrels, but he held his tongue. I went outside to help load the bags and equipment onto the bus. I was the only player out there. I was seething, looking for a fight. The way I saw it, I had left my life in Atlanta to play on this team and not only wasn't I getting the proper opportunity to play, I was now being treated like a fucking bellboy, doing all the grunt work for the team. I lost my temper, and I ended up taking it out on Kelly, who was my friend and roommate, when I saw her at the airport. She was supposed to have helped me load the bags, but she hadn't, and now anger was clouding my judgment. I'm not in the habit of yelling at women, but I think I did it because I wanted to engage with Gumbie, and screaming at Kelly would certainly get his goat.

It worked. When Gumbie heard I had cursed at her (they would later get married), he went ballistic. We shouted at each other in front of the airport and made quite a ruckus. After we had told each other to fuck off for a while, Gumbie tried to take the emotional exchange down a notch. He thought for a minute, choosing his words carefully. "Why are you doing this, Mark?" he asked. "You have the potential to be a great player, maybe one of the best in the game. But you have to know that I'm not going to take this shit from you. I am the coach. I've always been straight with you. You knew the deal before you moved to

Austin. But if you don't enjoy playing for me, then you should leave. Go back to Atlanta. But I will not allow you to continue to disrespect the team, the staff, and me this way."

"Fine," I said, too proud to admit I had made a mistake. "I'm gone."

i can be one obstinate son of a bitch when I want to be. As soon as I got back to Texas, I packed up and moved out of Kelly's house and in with another friend of mine, a guy I went to school with at Georgia Tech named Pete. He lived in a tiny one-bedroom apartment in North Austin. I slept under his kitchen table on an air mattress.

I finished out the season playing with Gumbie (even though we had stopped talking to each other) and then left the Lone Star State and went back to Georgia, staying at Howard and Marcia's house. I thought about rejoining my old Atlanta team, but Wendy had quit coaching and the team had folded. Instead of looking for a new team, I told myself that I needed to quit obsessing about sports, grow up, and get a job like a responsible adult. But I think the real reason I didn't talk to other coaches was that part of me was embarrassed about how I had behaved back in Tampa, and I didn't want to have to explain myself to anyone.

I updated my résumé, pulled on a suit and tie, and started interviewing for jobs, ultimately taking a position at a large civil engineering firm called Clough Harbor & Associates. The work was busy if monotonous, and I felt like a drone in the hive with half of my brain turned off, and I settled into the routine. It was nice to get a paycheck every two weeks. At first, I hardly missed my rugby practices and traveling to tournaments on the weekends. Instead, I spent my free time with Amy or playing pool and getting soused on pitchers of beer with Eric.

It was good to be back with Amy, but it wasn't long before I realized that she and I were out of sync. We had started to bicker like an old married couple. I had been passionate about her before I left, but now it wasn't the same. Hanging out together was like the day after Christmas. I think she felt the same way. She had never really acclimated to the South and was talking about moving. If she really

wanted to pursue her dreams of working in the entertainment indus-
try, she was going to have to go out to Los Angeles. I had no interest
in California.

By the end of the summer, it was clear our relationship had run
its course. I still loved Amy, but I think we both would have to admit that the spark had been extinguished by our time apart and our
different life goals. The breakup seemed inevitable. I had become
listless in Atlanta, and I felt unfinished business pulling me back to
Austin. I had left too soon and for all the wrong reasons. I wanted
to give the city another chance and was regretting my decision to
quit quad rugby. I hadn't spoken to Gumbie since our argument at
the airport, but some of my former teammates had called to say that
Pate was leaving the team because he wanted to spend more time
at home with his family. They wanted to know if I was interested in
playing for the Stampede again. If I was, they said they would work
on Gumbie.

With that information somewhere in the back of my mind, I
started to apply for jobs in Austin and got a bite from a small firm
called C. Faulkner Engineering. They wanted me to fly in as soon as I
could for an interview. I made the arrangements and then called Pete.
I told him I was thinking about moving back and asked if I could flop
with him for a while.

"I can blow up the air mattress for you again," he said.

"Sounds perfect," I said.

Early that fall, the Stampede had their preseason meeting, and my
old teammates told Gumbie that they had talked to me about coming
back and rejoining the squad. Gumbie seemed unsure about the idea.
He knew I could be a real asset to the team, but he wasn't sure if my
history of moodiness and disruptive behavior was worth the while.

"We don't need him just because Pate is leaving," Gumbie said.
"We'll be fine."

It's not that we *need* him, they said. We *want* him on the team.

They ended up voting, and the show of hands gave Gumbie his
answer. He called me, and we did our best to work through our differences. As Gumbie likes to say, over the years, we've probably had
more reconciliatory conversations than Dr. Phil. At the end of our

talk, he repeated what he had told the team at the end of their meeting: "From now on, when Mark screws up, when Mark acts out, when Mark goes dark, you guys are the ones who are going to pay for it, because I'm not going to deal with it."

This time, I vowed I wouldn't let my team or myself down, but keeping that promise would be much harder than I ever thought.

be free

It wasn't quite the triumphant return that I expected. I had been back in Austin for only a few weeks when my rugby buddy Mike Gilliland had a birthday. A bunch of us decided to take him out to the bars downtown to celebrate. It was a weeknight, and I had worked all day at C. Faulkner, so I was tired by the time I hooked up with them at an Irish pub called Fado, near Sixth Street. When I got there, I bought a round of Jaeger shots and some pints of Guinness for the table. I had work the next day, so I planned on leaving early, but because I hadn't seen Mike in a while, I ended up sticking around longer than I had anticipated.

By the end of the night, I had a nice buzz going as I loaded my chair into the passenger seat and climbed into my car. I didn't feel that drunk, just a little drowsy. As I took the freeway back to Pete's place, my eyelids sagged and the car started to swerve as I dozed off. I awoke with a start and pulled back into my lane. Exiting on Rundberg, I came to a red light at a deserted intersection. I watched the hanging light sway hypnotically in the dry autumn wind. It was taking forever to change. I leaned my head against the window and waited, letting my mind drift. The sharp knocking on my window yanked me out of my murky slumber. I looked up and saw a police officer shining his penlight in my face.

"Thanks, officer," I said, waving my right hand and gently easing the throttle forward.

"No, no, no," he said, pointing to the side of the road. "Pull over and park."

He instructed me to get out of the car. I grabbed my chair off the seat next to me and then set it on the ground. I was a little wobbly as I climbed out of my SUV, and the cop assumed I was hammered. He asked me if I had been drinking. I told him that I had, but not very much. I wasn't nervous about admitting the truth because I didn't believe that I was drunk. He started to give me a field sobriety test, shining the light into my eyes.

"I think you're intoxicated," he said. "I can smell alcohol on your breath. I'm going to take you to the station house for a Breathalyzer test."

"Fine," I said.

He cuffed my hands behind my back.

"Are these really necessary?" I asked.

"Follow me," he said, walking to his squad car and opening the back door.

"Uh, officer," I said. "How am I supposed to push myself?"

He unlocked the cuffs and then I transferred myself into his back-seat. We went to the station house and I blew into a plastic tube hooked up to the machine and registered a .12, over the legal limit, and obviously enough to earn you a DUI charge and a night in jail.

I didn't really process what was happening at first. The cops told me I could make one call and said that if I could get someone to post bond, I would be released after I talked to a judge. It was four a.m. when the insistent ringing of the phone prompted Pete out of bed. I explained what had happened and told him where he could find my checkbook. He said that he would take care of it. I asked the officers if I could make one more call and they said sure. I dialed my work and left a message saying I was feeling under the weather and wouldn't be in the next day.

With that lie, the impact of what I had done started to dawn on me. They took me to a jail cell, where I watched silver-dollar-size roaches scurry across the cement floor. The sound of those bars closing made my gut freeze as if it had been packed in dry ice. How could I, the guy paralyzed by a drunk-driving accident, be sitting in a jail cell for a DUI? The irony and idiocy of the event was almost too much to comprehend. I pushed myself back against the water-stained wall and considered banging my head against it. I started thinking about how I was going to explain this to my family and my friends, and a million excuses tumbled into my mind. I was overly tired. I had been under a lot of pressure at my new job. I still wasn't settled from the move. I was sleeping under a table. I was only doing what my friends were doing. The cop was a prick and wouldn't cut me any slack.

But what I was doing was using bits of truth to lie to myself. I was in jail because I had decided to get behind the wheel after drinking and had put both others and myself in jeopardy. I had once again been careless with my life, the same way I had been back when I was injured. I could color it any way I wanted, but that was the real truth. I had been making too many lame excuses lately, and the habit was catching up with me. I thought about all of Igoe's jail time. It suddenly became painfully obvious to me how he must have felt after the accident and in the years that followed when he couldn't get his drinking under control. It had been so easy for other people to judge him harshly for that, and the thought made me afraid, because I hadn't really behaved any differently. I had been drinking all these years too, often to excess. I'm now old enough to realize that alcohol wasn't the real problem for either of us; it was just a symptom. Alcohol is just an inanimate object. It's not good or evil. Sometimes drinking can be fun and social and crazy, but here's the catch: You have to be responsible for yourself, because every moment in life is an active one. It doesn't matter if you're angry, upset, lonely, overworked, overwhelmed, or addicted. You still have free will, and you never know how the actions of this minute will impact the next minute, the next day, and maybe even the rest of your life.

I wish I could tell you I learned some powerful lesson that night sitting in a jail cell, but I didn't—at least not right away. I actually decided to hide my DUI conviction, my court-ordered Alcohol Anonymous classes, and my eighteen months' probation from my parents and most of my friends. I was afraid of being judged. The first time they will hear about it will be in this book. I am not proud of that, but that's the truth. In the end, I hope that owning up to this incredibly poor decision will count for something. I've made a lot of mistakes in my life, some bigger than others, sometimes more than once. Some mistakes are forgivable. Others aren't. But that's life, and you can't rewrite your past. The good news is that we often have more than one chance to do the right thing. We grow only when we are honest with ourselves about our actions and choose to learn from what has happened by examining the part we played. And that's what I'm trying to do right now.

after my dui, i decided to quit drinking for a while and concentrated on getting back into shape. I designed a fitness boot camp for myself to prepare for the upcoming season, and I went so far as to shave my head down to the scalp, a physical display of my changed attitude and rededication to my sport. I restricted my diet, consuming mostly proteins, fruits, and vegetables and avoiding carbohydrates and fatty foods like cheese. It was tough to do, because the BBQ and Tex-Mex in Austin is some of the best in the country. I had always tried to watch what I ate so I wouldn't get what's known as the quad belly, but now I wanted to put only the best fuel in my body so it would be ready for peak performance.

At practice, I made a conscious effort not to question Gumbie's coaching and to follow his lead and execute his plays. It was a lot easier to do this time around. With Pate gone, I had moved into the starting rotation and was running the offense as the high pointer. I took this responsibility seriously and worked at becoming not only a reliable team player but also a leader on the squad. Gumbie helped me to further evolve my game and become even more of a scoring threat. I had always been a good passer, but he helped me improve my ground attack against the half-court defense. Any time you put the ball in the air, you're increasing your odds for a turnover. Gumbie instructed me to hold on to the ball more often, and we worked on dodging opponents and breaking traps, punching holes in the defense, sneaking my chair through the closing windows created by moving picks, and getting across the goal line.

In my spare time, I increased my time spent at the gym. Gumbie had told me that he thought my upper body was becoming too buffed and was actually starting to slow me down. I put my vanity in check and spent hours lifting lighter weights but with more reps, working to develop my strength instead of size. I shed some bulk and slimmed down, which made me lighter, faster, and harder to contain. Surprisingly, it didn't affect my power. Over time, I started to consistently score goals in the double digits as the Stampede moved up in the national rankings.

The better I played, the better I felt about myself, and my confidence continued to grow. Austin was starting to feel like home. I had moved out from under Pete's kitchen table and had gotten a place of my own. My job was going well at C. Faulkner, and I was getting to work on higher-profile projects, helping to design office buildings and private residences. I was figuring out the best venues for live music, and I was getting to know the most talented tattoo artists in town. Over the years, I had become addicted to ink and had extended my tribal tattoos from my back to my arm, shoulder, and leg. And I had a new girlfriend. Her name was Jessica. Strangely, we had met at the funeral of a mutual friend, but the attraction was too much to ignore. She was a petite punk rock girl in glasses who favored wearing combat boots, spiked belts, and tight tank tops. She grew up just outside Austin and was interning at a morgue. She had a slightly off-center sense of humor and would tell her friends she couldn't believe she was dating a jock.

By the time the tryouts came for the World Championships in Sweden, I had no problem making the final cut. Pate had come back to play for this tournament, so I knew I probably wouldn't be part of the starting lineup, but I was cool with that. I had realized that just making the team was an honor in itself, and if I paid my dues, I would eventually get my shot. If making the team had been a quick and easy process, I wouldn't have valued it the way I should have. Because it had taken me so much struggle and sacrifice, it meant that much more to me.

Team USA would be one of twelve teams traveling to Gothenburg, Sweden, to compete for the title, and everyone was gunning for the Americans. We had won the gold medal at the 2000 Paralympics in Sydney and were favored to win in Sweden. The United States had dominated the sport for the past decade, winning eleven consecutive international competitions. But we had a new rival this year. Joe Soares had made his move north to coach the Canadian national team. Because he had played for the United States for so many years, he was familiar with our strategies. His knowledge and passion for the game would make them a formidable opponent, one that we could not afford to take lightly.

Canada's bid to become the world's best wasn't the only element adding to the drama. Everything we did was now being captured on camera. Two young independent filmmakers had made the trek with us to Sweden and were planning on making a documentary about quad rugby. Their names were Dana Adam Shapiro and Henry Alex Rubin (producer Jeff Mandel was holding down the fort in New York). Dana, who was then a senior editor at *Spin*, was writing an article about us for *Maxim*, one of my favorite publications. Some of the players and coaches thought that having them around was a distraction, but I didn't. Dana and I had spoken beforehand, and he and Henry seemed like stand-up guys to me. They assured us that they weren't trying to make a "PBS-style, cue-the-violins" type of film. They wanted to smash stereotypes about people in chairs by making a movie that portrayed us as normal people and fierce athletes. I was into it. I had been spending years trying to show the world that quads are no different from anyone else.

No one was surprised when, after several days of intense competition, Team USA found itself matched up against Canada in the finals. This tournament would be the first time that Soares would be facing the United States since he jumped ship. The rancor that the teams had for each other was palpable, and we were all cagey as Coach Kevin Orr gave us the pregame pep talk in our locker room, instructing us to maintain our composure at all costs and keep our mouths shut.

"They are going to be talking all kinds of trash," Orr said. "Joe is going to say whatever the hell Joe says. I don't care. The only reason why Joe went to Canada is to beat the United States. And we're going to take care of business. We are going to kick the shit out of them!"

Before the game we gathered in a circle for our traditional cheer: "One, two, three...USA...Rugby!" The teams were evenly balanced from the tipoff, and the chair contact was so brutal that spectators were watching through parted fingers. Pate was on the floor, so I was supporting the team from the bench, ready to go in whenever they needed me. At one point, Canada was breaking toward our end and Pate saved a goal by demolishing the player from behind with a vicious spin that made head meet hardwood. The Canadian flailed his arms in the air like a beetle on its back and said something to Pate that I couldn't hear, but it looked like the players were about to brawl. Both teams pushed off the sidelines, ready to start throwing punches, but the refs broke it up. Pate rolled by our bench and I slapped him five.

"Cheap crap!" Joe screamed from his side. "Motherfuckers!"

We traded goals for all four quarters and with twenty ticks on the clock and the score tied at 24–24, Canada surged forward and backed us against our goal. We held fast, but they connected on a backdoor flip pass and went up a point. With ten seconds remaining, USA's Brian Kirkland burned down the court and shotgunned the ball to an open Andy Cohn to tie the game at the buzzer. The ball unfortunately ricocheted off Andy's hands, and for the first time in the history of quad rugby, the Americans lost the finals. Joe and his Canadians went bananas, banging their hands against their spoke guards, hugging each other and hollering like lunatics as Dana and Henry's cameras recorded every excruciating detail of our humiliating defeat.

while competing in sweden, it became clear to me that the final piece of the puzzle of what I needed to improve myself as a player was chair speed. I went to Kevin Orr, who would be coaching the Paralympics team in Athens in 2004 (with Gumbie as his assistant coach), and asked for his help. Orr also coached a team called the Lakeshore Demolition from Alabama (which basically had been undefeated in club play that year) but came from a wheelchair track background and was an expert in biomechanics. He watched me sprint some laps and said that power wasn't my problem—I clearly had plenty of upper-body strength—but my stroke was slowing me down. I was starting my push too far back on my wheel and coming off too early, compromising my rotation. He gave me a layman's physics lesson while adjusting my shoulders forward, telling me to bend at the waist and lean over the axle into each push.

"You want to look at your wheel like a clock," Orr told me. "You should essentially be pushing off at 1:00 and then continue your hands to 4:00 or 5:00 and then snap off the bottom."

I had been starting my push at around 11:00 and releasing around 2:00 or 3:00. Orr explained that every time I cranked my hands back and hit the wheel at the 11:00 position to propel myself forward, I was actually interrupting momentum and decreasing my speed instead of building it. That small rise in speed would make a huge difference, helping me to nose my chair in front of opponents and get into a position where they couldn't block me. I knew I would never be a burner on the court, but I was now fast enough to get where I needed to be.

the next year was pretty much a blur.

The first round of tryouts for the Paralympic team was held in June in Birmingham, Alabama, at the Lakeshore Foundation, a 126,000-square-foot modern-looking two-story facility with multiple pools, basketball courts, a 200-meter track, a sports science lab, and other amenities all geared to meet the needs of disabled athletes. A select group of twenty-six players were invited to compete over five days. This time, I made sure my rugby chair was in perfect working order and I had my head on straight before I left Texas. I kept my cool, avoided injury, and just played my game. When the roster was whittled down to sixteen players, I made the cut.

Back in Austin, the Stampede was having its best season ever and so was I. We had been giving Lakeshore a run for their money all year as the league's top team, and I had been earning distinction at various tournaments, including four most valuable player awards and one best in class. At the USQRA nationals in Louisville, Kentucky, that spring, we played Lakeshore in the finals, and my team and I were determined to win the championship for Gumbie. The game came down to the wire, but we pulled out a victory in the fourth quarter and earned the Stampede its first national championship. At the awards ceremony, I was given a wooden plaque for winning the USQRA's 2003–2004 Athlete of the Year Award. I was stunned. It was my sport's top honor, and I had been singled out from five hundred players.

But the most memorable moment for me came when, after another round of tryouts at Lakeshore, Orr read the twelve final names for Team USA at a press conference. I was pretty sure I had made the squad but couldn't relax until I heard him say, "From Austin, Texas, Mark Zupan." I wheeled into a line with my fellow teammates as the cameras snapped. We huddled up, placed our hands in a circle, and gave our "One, two, three . . . USA . . . Rugby!" shout.

Afterward, I called my parents to give them the good news. It had taken me almost eight years and a lot of growing up, but I had finally reached my goal.

I was going to Athens.

the final seeding for the Paralympics was going to be determined at a summer invitational up in the picturesque mountain city of Vancouver, BC. Since they had won Sweden, Canada was ranked number one in the world, but we were nipping at their heels. This would be our last chance to reclaim what we thought was our rightful position, and we were primed for a win. This time around, I was on the floor for the tipoff, and the game was another nail biter. Each team was unable to stop the other from scoring, and the lead seesawed back and forth.

With fifteen seconds left, the game was tied 32–32 and we had possession. Kirkland once again motored the ball down the court. As time was running out, two defenders trapped him, and he dished the ball into my open space. I cranked my arms over my wheels like a locomotive and won the loose ball, scooping it up gingerly with my left hand and transferring it to my lap. I had a big defender riding my back, trying to wedge his grill into my wheels to slow me down and run out the clock. I continued to sprint toward the goal line like a mountaineer running from an avalanche. My opponent's chair hammered my left side and sent me skidding sideways, but he couldn't stop me. My two wheels found the goal line literally at the buzzer, and we won, beating the Canadians 33–32. This time, the Americans were the ones going ape shit. Athens was only three months away, and we were once again the world's top-ranked team.

team usa continued to bond and develop its chemistry after we moved into the dorms at the Lakeshore facility in Alabama to train for the Paralympics full-time (the good folks at C. Faulkner were kind enough to give me a leave of absence from work). In our daily practices, Kevin Orr and Gumbie pushed us to our physical limits on the court, and from the lines we were running it looked like I would be starting in Athens, along with Norm from my Austin team, big, bald Brian Kirkland, and Cliff Chunn, a wiry and wily veteran 2.0 who had played on Team USA in Atlanta way back in 1996 and again when we took the gold in 2000 in Sydney.

Birmingham isn't exactly a thriving metropolis, and there wasn't a whole lot to do after the sun went down. A group of us would gather in someone's dorm room to socialize and play some poker. It was funny, because no one had enough hand function to shuffle the cards. We had to get a special machine that would do it for us: you push a button and the cards whirl into a random order. I really got to know my fellow teammates, and most of them were pretty good gamblers. Bob Lujano was a regular on poker night, and he would always end up pushing all his money into the middle and going for broke. He just couldn't help himself, and if you think about it, that's kind of how all of us had been living our lives—all in.

I had also been selected to be an official spokesperson for the US-QRA at this time, and I was traveling around the nation to speak to newly injured individuals at rehab hospitals. I obviously knew what it was like to be just like them, and I wanted to be able to reach out and offer them just a little bit of hope for the future. You wouldn't believe how some of their eyes would light up when I would play a USQRA promo video and let them sit in my quad rugby chair. Their questions would crack me up. They would ask why we didn't wear helmets or pads, or if there was any special technique for falling when you get slammed out of your chair.

"Just don't lead with your head," I would say.

During one of these visits, I made the offhand comment that I had accomplished more in my chair than I had done in my able-bodied life. The true sentiment of the statement caught up with me later. I thought about what would have happened to me if I hadn't injured myself. My career in sports would probably have ended when I graduated from college at FAU. But here I was, twenty-eight years old and a world-class athlete, playing at a level that I never thought would be possible. I had been good in college, but not Olympic good. I played out another scenario in my head. I probably wouldn't have realized my academic potential the way I did at Georgia Tech if it hadn't been for the chair. Who knew if I would even have graduated from college? That's when it occurred to me: I had not only been fortunate enough to attain my goals. In some ways, I had surpassed them.

Weeks later, the entire quad rugby team, as well as the men's and women's wheelchair basketball teams, traveled to Fort Belvoir in Alexandria, Virginia, for a demonstration for war veterans wounded in Iraq who were recovering at the Walter Reed Army Medical Center. A lot of people have misgivings about this war, but let me tell you, you forget your personal politics pretty quickly when you are talking to a soldier who lost his arm or leg to a roadside bomb while serving his country. The trip had even more meaning for me because one of my good friends from high school was a Marine stationed near Baghdad. Big Murph was a friend of mine from football, and a day didn't go by that I didn't think about him and say a quick prayer for his safe return.

As I looked at some of these soldiers, I couldn't believe they were eighteen years old, because they looked like fresh-faced kids to me. I was the same age as them when I had broken my neck, but I had been a reckless and somewhat self-centered teenager. That past seemed so long ago—like memories that belonged to someone else. These kids were so different from what I had been, the kind of eighteen-year-olds who had the courage to pick up a weapon and put themselves in harm's way to defend our country, all in the name of freedom and democracy.

Speaking to the soldiers in the cavernous armory, Kevin Orr greeted the group and offered a quick explanation about the sport. He ran through the basic rules and then separated us into teams. As we played, I thought about the debt of gratitude that we owed these men and women who put their lives on the line to fight for their country. Suddenly, the responsibility and the honor of wearing a Team USA jersey took on a whole new meaning.

the 2004 paralympics kicked off on September 17, with five thousand athletes from 145 countries competing for ten days in the second largest sporting event in the world, played in all the same stadiums as the Olympics. During the flight to Athens, most of the players sat silent and stone faced, mentally preparing for what would most likely be the pinnacle of their athletic careers, but there were a few moments of giddy levity when the nervous anticipation took over, like when we tried to convince Bob Lujano to climb up into an empty overhead luggage compartment. He wouldn't do it, even for the $100 cash we pooled together to pay him.

Athens turned out to be another of life's paradoxes, a city that is ancient yet modern, filthy but beautiful as the sun bathed both the Parthenon and the tenement buildings in an indescribable pink-hued light. As we touched down, I reflected on the fact that I had arrived at the birthplace of the Olympic games, and I was overwhelmed and awe-inspired by the thought that I was now part of an incredible history spanning thousands of years, an athletic tradition that had outlasted entire civilizations. This thought made me feel both important and completely inconsequential at the same time.

We were staying at the Olympic village, near the Olympic stadium northwest of Athens, even though we would be playing at the Helleniko indoor arena. The rooms were fine, if spare, but the place was packed with more athletes than I had seen together in one place before; people in chairs, on crutches, missing limbs, all speaking a babble of languages. If the thought of playing in the Paralympics had seemed humbling, the reality hit when I found myself in the center of that crowd, thousands of people who had worked and sweated and sacrificed as much as I had to make it to this moment. To be surrounded by that caliber of competitors is both terrifying and exhilarating. I knew that I was at both the beginning and end of a journey and I wondered if was ready, if I could really be a challenger. I became incredibly invigorated at the prospect of finding out. It was truly an unforgettable moment. For me, being in the Olympic Village must be like what it feels for a Catholic to see the Vatican or a Muslim to arrive in Mecca. This was my church, my salvation, and the closest I'd ever come to really feeling spiritual.

While Team USA were staying together at the Olympic village with the other athletes, my official cheering section was sharing a house near Marathon, hometown of its namesake race. My parents had made the trip, as well as my brother, Jeff, his wife-to-be, Leigh, my cousin Allison, Jessica, Igoe, Cava, and his girlfriend, Ann. I also wanted Nickell and his wife, Jenn, to come along, but they were expecting the arrival of their first child, a little girl they would name Ellie. My dad would go to the market each morning and come back with bags of fresh meat and vegetables, cooking for everyone as they waited for the competition to start.

The first step in our quest for America's third straight Paralympic gold came on September 19, when we faced off against the Japanese team. I expected to be nervous before the game started, but I wasn't. In fact, I felt an unexpected tranquillity, and I think it came from the knowledge that I had done everything I possibly could to prepare for this moment in my life. I had paid my dues, trained hard, listened to my coaches, and put in the hours with my team. I had devoted myself completely, and now all that was left was the execution.

The Japanese gave us little resistance—our constant pressure on defense forced turnovers, and we capitalized on every scoring opportunity. We beat them 41–29, and nine of those goals belonged to me. Next up was a bruising battle against New Zealand, a game that showed the thousands of screaming fans in Helleniko Arena that quad rugby was in fact a full-contact sport. We trailed 8–9 in the first quarter but stepped up our offensive efforts in the second, scoring four more goals than they did, which was a good thing because each squad scored nine goals in both the third and fourth periods, ending with the Americans up 35–32. Our win against the Aussies and then the Germans gave us a 4–0 record and we felt unstoppable.

We met the Canadians a little earlier than we expected— in the semifinals instead of the finals—and we were all confident that we were going to beat them this time around. They had already shown some vulnerability earlier in the week, losing a squeaker to Great Britain. This was going to be our payback for Sweden, and I wanted it to be a game they never forgot. It was a tense time, with everyone on the squad out for blood. We had something to prove, and this one was for all the marbles in a way. Every man there was ready for war.

Minutes before tipoff, Kevin Orr and Gumbie took great pains to make sure we weren't entering this match overly cocky. They tried to rein in our tough talk and bring our minds back to focusing squarely on the game's fundamentals. That, they said, was the key to getting to the finals. "Just relax and stick to our game plan," Orr said as we taped and stretched for the match. "We lost by one goal in Sweden because of mental errors that could have been prevented. We have come a long way to get here. Now let's get out there and win as a unit!"

We knew Soares and Canada would want to make this a defensive battle of wills. What we weren't ready for was the ferocity of the crowd. As I wheeled out onto the wood-floored court, my ears buzzed from the jeers and cheers that echoed off the high ceiling. It was so loud I could feel the vibration in the metal of my chair, with people in the stands stomping, yelling, doing the wave, and generally going nuts. It was a frothing sea of red, white, and blue–Canada's flag being red and white—with stars, stripes, and maple leaves everywhere you looked. People had painted their faces and had hoisted handmade signs, and the stadium had divided itself along national lines.

Our other matches had drawn crowds, but these were quad rugby fans, the kind whose heart and soul were as much in the game as the players themselves. The announcer, in accented English, introduced the players on each team. By the time he got to me, I had found my family and friends in the stands, a clump of reassurance with my parents sitting in the center. I watched my dad when my name was called out over the loudspeaker. I decided then and there that I was going to win this one for him, my mom, my brother, and every one of my friends who had come thousands of miles to see me play. Fuck the Canadians. I was ready for anything they had.

The first few minutes resembled our last two outings, with both teams evenly trading goals, neither able to dominate. I was in the zone, playing my hardest with that laser-focused intensity that comes when you're in the heat of it and training and instinct take over. But the Canadians were right there with us, their offense coming on like a steamroller, out to flatten us slowly. They were using their whole bench, subbing in second-stringers and forcing us to burn up our energy against those fresh guys. We held the line, but the score was tied 7–7 at the end of the first quarter. I hated being tied, and wanted to end the half with us up.

With the clock winding down at the end of the second quarter and us behind by a goal, the ball came my way and I didn't hesitate. I scooped it up, took it into the apron, and scored, my defender on me the whole way. The crowd went insane, creating a rumbling thunder of apprehension and approval that was beyond deafening. But wait. Did I cross the line too quickly? Should I have wasted a little more time? A few seconds remained on the clock, and Canada was already screaming down the floor. They bludgeoned through our defense and scored, making it 12–12 at halftime. In the huddle during the break, the coaches got down to brass tacks. Canada was playing well and we needed to match them, not just with our individual skills but with our teamwork. We needed to cool off and play with our brains. I heard the words, but my heart was pumping so hard I could barely think. I just wanted to be back out on the court.

Early in the third, the game turned ugly for us. We got into some foul trouble, and the momentum began to swing in Canada's favor, with them scoring a series of back-to-back goals. Suddenly, they were crushing our defense, and we were struggling to gain control of the ball. They had two especially tall players, both with good hand function, and were using that height advantage for all it was worth. We bore down, doing our best to thwart their offense, but they kept a lead, and by the end of the third we were down by three goals, 17–20.

Desperate to even the score, we started to gamble on defense, breaking the golden rule of sticking to the basics, and that opened us up to their counterattacks. We forced passes that just weren't there and ended up turning over the ball one too many times. I could feel the frustration rising like bile in my throat, and I channeled it into even more aggressive play. The Canadians knew we weren't giving up, but I saw a smug confidence in their faces that said the game was theirs. I was screaming instructions and encouragement at my teammates so rabidly I could feel my spit flying, and my hits were so hard I vaguely wondered if my chair could take the relentless hammering or if it would suddenly collapse into dented heap of bolts, rubber, and metal.

With four minutes left in the game, Canada went into keep-away mode, not trying to score but looking to maintain their lead and run out the clock. We did everything we could to steal the ball back, but unfortunately their strategy worked. They won 24–20, a trip to the finals and a chance at the gold. The whistle that ended the game was one of the saddest sounds I've ever heard. Up until that moment, losing didn't even seem remotely possible. I couldn't bear to look up in the stands at my family and friends. I could see the same disappointment in the faces of my teammates, and the celebration from the Canadian side was unbearable. The whole place seemed to be singing "O Canada." There's a song I really hate.

We left the court as soon as we could, but Gumbie and Orr weren't going to let us slink away and wallow in our loss. We weren't going to the finals, but the tournament wasn't over for us either. We still had a match against Great Britain for the bronze medal, and the coaches weren't about to let us forget it. We left the locker room with random strains of "O Canada" still hanging in the air. I just wanted to get back to the Olympic village and lock myself in my room, but my parents and Jess were waiting in the hall. Seeing Jess, and the love and empathy on her face, was the last straw. I felt tightness around my throat and in my eyes and lost it. My nose started running like a garden hose, and the tears came out. I buried my head in Jess's sweatshirt, feeling heartbroken. How could my hard work have led to this?

* * *

after a night of soul-searching, we were back on the court the next day to battle for the bronze. We were humbled and bloodied, but sometimes in defeat you find a new strength and purpose. There was no way we were going to lose two in a row or go home without some kind of hardware. It just wasn't going to happen. We had let ourselves down by losing to Canada, but we weren't going to let our country down by going home empty-handed.

The game against Great Britain started with a gut-wrenching similarity to the previous day's match. The Brits came out fast and physical, trying to force us into mistakes. At the end of the first quarter we were tied 11–11, and I'll admit there was some bickering at our bench. But that was all it took. We pulled together, nutted up, and began playing like the team we were—cohesive, skilled, and determined. By half, we were up 22–19. By the final quarter, we had cemented our lead and never let them get closer than a four-point spread. I led the scoring that game, racking up fifteen goals, and we finished out our play in Athens with a 5–1 record.

there's making it to the Paralympics, and then there's winning a medal. The ceremony took place after the New Zealand–Canada finals, which I watched with the guys from Team USA. New Zealand's squad, with my old roommate Curtis, shocked the stubborn Canadians and took the gold. It was great to see an underdog win (and Canada lose). In my book, that's the kind of drama that makes sports so inimitable and exhilarating.

After the final, the three medal-winning teams lined up at the side of the arena, waiting to be called. We were next to the Canadians, but it didn't matter. For a very brief moment, we were all friendly, if not friends. Being the bronze medal winners, the Americans went to the awards area first. Everyone in the packed house cheered, regardless of home-country allegiances. The rivalries were gone for now, replaced by the shared love for the sport and the knowledge that we would be back to fight it out again another day. I wish it would have been "The Star-Spangled Banner" instead of "God Defend New Zealand" playing that day, but still, it was an amazing moment. There was a feeling of camaraderie shared by every athlete and fan as the medals were placed around our necks, and I finally understood the spirit of the Olympics and the Paralympics. They are a testament to the human experience, something that momentarily transcends the differences of nations, cultures, politics, and language.

I felt so much pride and strength that my chest physically hurt, as if it would explode from the emotions. I looked up into the stands and once again found my family and friends. My parents were standing and cheering, with Jeff and Jess right next to them. Looking at my father's face, I was reminded of the last soccer game I had played the night of the accident. I remembered how badly I had wanted to score a goal for him then, to give him a reason to be proud of me. I knew, not mentally, but somewhere deeper, that this moment would be one he would keep with him for his entire life. I cannot express how much that meant to me, to know that something I had done could make him feel that way. I thought about the football game my dad had taken me to early in my recovery and how the crowd had cheered for me. I couldn't even lift my hand over my head that night. While I was humbled by the good intentions of all those people, they had made me afraid and ashamed of my life. That crowd had made me feel small and incomplete. I could remember feeling that way all the time after the accident, but it had been so long since that sadness and regret ruled me that I couldn't imagine ever being that low again. Now, with a medal around my neck, the clapping and cheering was making me sit up higher in my chair because this time, I was sure I had earned it.

My eyes fell on Igoe. He was waving a giant American flag. True to his fashion, he was yelling louder, stomping harder, causing more chaos than anyone around him. Despite the thousands of people in the stadium, in that instant, he was the only person I could see. Although we hadn't spoken about it, we both knew that in two weeks, it would be the eleven-year anniversary of the accident. We had been through more than a decade of turmoil and pain but had both escaped our personal hells and persevered. Somehow, we had remained friends through it all. We were brothers in a way that even blood can't ensure. I knew him better than anyone else in the world, and I was honored to call him my best friend. As I sat there, I wished he were down on the floor next to me, so I could tell him that there wasn't a single moment I would take back or change. I wanted to tell him that my life in a wheelchair was a remarkable one, and it had ultimately helped me to become a person I was proud to be. Igoe stopped yelling, and I swear we were looking right at each other, reading each other's thoughts. At the same moment, we raised our fists in the air in a gesture of triumph.

epilogue

After athens, I flew to Washington, D.C., for another awards ceremony, this time at the White House. I told my friends that if I got to meet George W. Bush, my plan was to give him a nice little pat on the ass, just to see his reaction. I didn't manage to pull that off, but I did shake his hand and have my picture taken with him on October 18 when he welcomed players from the Olympic and Paralympic teams on the South Lawn. On that sunny autumn day, Bush called us "exemplary ambassadors" for the United States. "To qualify for Team USA, you had to set high goals, devote long hours to training, and outperform talented athletes from all across our country," he said. "You faced the toughest competition and the highest pressure in all of sports. When the games were over, America had earned more than a hundred medals. You made us proud."

I framed a picture of the president with his hand on my shoulder and gave it to my father, who is a diehard Republican. He proudly put it on the mantel in their living room. I thought that would be the end of my scrapbook moments for a while, but not long after that, I went to New York City to see a rough cut of Dana, Jeff, and Henry's film. They had decided to call it *Murderball*. I had no idea what to expect. They had been filming us for over two and a half years and had more than two hundred hours of footage that they had pared down to make what was essentially a ninety-minute documentary. Henry had been doing some crazy shit to capture the quad rugby action, like rigging his cameras to the bottom of our chairs, so I was dying to see how the sports sequences would play, as well as the stuff they shot about our personal lives.

I can't say I was anxious the first time I saw the movie— just curious. We had made an agreement with Dana and Henry before they started shooting: if any of us ever felt uncomfortable, we would tell them and they would stop filming. But we never did, because they had earned our trust. Staring at the screen, I could feel Henry and Dana watching me for my reaction, but after a while I barely noticed them because I was so enthralled by the movie they had made. They had totally captured how hard we lived and played and somehow told the stories of our lives perfectly and without any patronizing pity.

"So what did you think?" Dana asked me when it was over.

I didn't know what to say except, "You guys fucking nailed it."

The film had me in tears and made the hair on my arms stand up like when you're listening to a good punk rock song, but I wasn't prepared for the effect it was going to have on other people. Dana and Henry called later to tell me it had been accepted to the famous Sundance Film Festival in Park City, Utah, which was started in the eighties by Robert Redford. It's the best place in the world for an independent movie to get noticed, and just to be accepted to it is an incredible accomplishment. I was invited to attend the festival, and I asked Igoe to come with me. When we arrived in the mountain town, we went to the supermarket to buy some food for the week. The film had already been screening. Two women in their early forties approached us cautiously.

"Oh my goodness," one of them said. "You boys are here together?"

"Uh, yeah," I said, not quite sure why she was talking to us.

"We saw your movie last night," she continued. "It was so inspiring."

"Oh," I said. "Really? Thanks."

"Except I could have done without the sex talk," the other one said.

After they left, I turned to Igoe. "What the fuck was that?" I said. "I have no idea," he said.

In the parking lot, another woman saw us and slammed her car into reverse. She rolled down the window and said, "I just wanted to tell you that I think your movie should be shown in every school. Everyone would benefit from seeing it."

Murderball won the Audience Award at Sundance, and when the film was finally ready to hit theaters, my life changed once again. Suddenly I was being interviewed for magazines and newspapers and appearing on television. THINKFilm partnered with MTV, A&E, and Participant to release the movie. I found myself doing a television special with Johnny Knoxville and Steve-O from *Jackass,* two of the funniest, coolest, and craziest cats I have ever been lucky enough to meet. After a couple of cold ones, Steve-O and I got in a contest to see who could get the best black eye. And that involved getting punched in the face. Hard. Repeatedly. I was going to tell you I won (which I did), but now that I think about it, does anyone really win a black-eye contest?

When I did *The Tonight Show,* Jay Leno walked into the green room and greeted me by saying, "What's going on, Zupan, you big asshole." I thought that was hilarious. That same week, I did *Larry King Live* with some other guys from the movie—Keith Cavill, Scott Hogsett, Bob Lujano, and Andy Cohn. This time around, the interview was a little more serious. After I told Larry King my accident was the best thing that could have happened to me, he was incredulous. He asked me what I thought about stem cell research, and if there was suddenly a cure for paralysis, would I take it? That's a tough question for a quad to answer simply because there is no magic pill, so why even entertain those kinds of notions? It's a big waste of time. But I thought Andy made a good point. "I think we would all listen, but none of us would be the first one to line up and rush in to do that," he explained. His point was that we all loved our lives and who we were. "There's nothing wrong with us that needs to be cured," Andy said.

But it did make me think about what I would want people to take from my experience, and if I had a message. My hope is that when people read this book, they will be reminded that you can stage a comeback even when you think you've lost everything. After my accident, I thought my life was over. I was wrong. It was just beginning. We will all face hardship, pain, difficulty, and death at some point in our short stay on this planet—every single one of us. While tragedy can be a cruel teacher, it can also lead you to understand a truth and beauty that is much greater than yourself, as long as you refuse to quit. Even when you're feeling weak, alone, outmanned, or outgunned, as long as you are breathing, then you are still in the game. Because if a gimp like me can keep playing after everything I've been through, then anyone can.

Months later, *Murderball* was nominated for an Academy Award. As you might expect, rolling down the red carpet in a tuxedo and seeing all the movie stars was pretty amazing, even if we didn't win— fucking penguins. While all the stuff I've been able to do in Hollywood has been great for shits and giggles, I've come to realize that spending time in Los Angeles is like being trapped in a room where the TV is turned up too loud. For me, I'm happiest when I'm playing my sport and hanging out with my friends. I made the national team again and will be traveling with Team USA to play in the 2006 World Championships in Christchurch, where we will most assuredly give Canada (and the Kiwis) a run for their money. Interestingly enough, Gumbie was recently made head coach, and we both have our eyes set on taking home the gold from the 2008 Paralympics in Beijing.

i'm still living in Austin and working as a civil engineer at C. Faulkner, although I've also been traveling around the country on a speaking tour. Igoe is a successful stockbroker in Florida and has become active in raising money and awareness for quad rugby through a Web site we started called Quadfather.net. In May 2006, he convinced all the old Douglas High football buddies—Nickell, Cava, Big Murph, and me— to do the Potomac River Run Marathon together. We asked friends and family to donate five or ten bucks for each mile we completed, with the money going to buy new equipment for the Texas Stampede. Igoe was so into organizing the event, he even designed matching black jerseys for all of us with our names on the back.

Cava, who lives in Virginia, about forty-five minutes from where the marathon was held, was gracious enough to let us stay at his house. The night before the race reminded me of an evening before a big game back when we were at Douglas; the only difference was that now we were a little older and fatter and had to fly in from different parts of the country to be together. As we gathered around Cava's dining room table to load up on carbs, the conversation quickly went from who would win the race to a friendly free-for-all of insults and recriminations. At one point, I was trying to convince everyone to run together and cross at the finish line at the same time (my secret plan was to pull a Jeff Sharon and jump ahead at the last second), but no one was buying my bullshit. The only one spared from the tough talk was my dad, who had driven in from Connecticut to cook for us and cheer us on.

Early the next morning, the alarm clock interrupted my anxious sleep. Igoe was already awake, doing up-downs and high-knee running drills around the kitchen while barking about setting a new land-speed record. The air was damp and chilly as we drove to the race site and lined up with the hundreds of other runners. Those of us in wheelchairs started a little earlier than everyone else so we wouldn't logjam the course, which was roughly a six-and-a-half-mile circuit that we would complete four times. Most guys pushing were in race chairs or on hand cycles, but because I had tryouts for the national team the following weekend, I decided to push in my heavy rugby chair. A few miles into the race, I was regretting my decision and cursing my bad judgment. But when I reached the far end of the first lap, I was greeted by the sound of hands banging against plastic spoke guards. I blinked the sweat out of my eyes and saw that a local quad rugby team had set up practice in a parking lot. They stopped playing and yelled my name as I rolled by, and their support gave me an extra boost.

I kept waiting for my friends to catch up, but ultimately Nickell would be the only one who would pass me. We shot the shit for a second and then he was gone. Instead of trying to run together, we had all learned to take life at our own pace. At the end of the twenty-six miles, I was alone and running on empty, but made a point to sprint out the last leg, flying down the alley of standing spectators to where my family and friends were waiting.

afterword
by dana adam shapiro

Here's Jeff Nickell—former high school linebacker, keg-stander, and now a photo-op for fatherhood—describing a typical phone conversation with his old pal Zupe:

NICKELL: Hey, Zupe, what's goin' on?
ZUPAN: Nothin'...

[*pause*]

NICKELL: What's up with rugby? You psyched for Nationals?
ZUPAN: Yeah...

[*pause*]

NICKELL: How's your girl?
ZUPAN: Fine...

[*pause*]

NICKELL: Yeah? And the job?

ZUPAN: Same shit...

[*a great big lull*]

NICKELL: Zupe, um...you *did* call *me*, remember?

On first listen (see above) and at first glance (that mug-shot mug), Mark Zupan does not seem an ideal subject for a documentary. He grunts, growls, scowls, and he's particularly fond of proving that, despite limited finger function, his middle one still works fine. Sure, there was something immediately cliché-crushing about his "hit-me-I'll-hit-you-back" attitude. But when I first interviewed him in the spring of 2002 he seemed like little more than a one-note jock whose only complexity was that, for a carb counter, he drank a lot of beer. No, for a film genre inherently dependent on candor, access, and intimacy, he simply would not do.

I was wrong, of course, which is why I'm writing this afterword. (Well, that and Eddie Vedder wasn't available.) It all began in the spring of 2002. I was a senior editor at *Spin*, looking to direct a documentary. About what, I had no idea. Then one day I came across five words that had no business being in the same sentence: *Quadriplegics. Playing rugby. In Sweden.*

Truth be told, at the time I probably couldn't have pinned Sweden on a map. I was more familiar with quahogs than quadriplegics, and I thought "scrum" was just another euphemism for you-know-what. But *quadriplegics playing rugby in Sweden*? It reminded me of that Woody Allen joke about the veal parmesan incident: "Well, what *was* it doing in his wallet?" My producing partner Jeff Mandel was similarly perplexed. "How can quadriplegics play rugby?" he asked. "And why would they do it in Sweden?"

So I made some phone calls—to the players, the coaches, and finally to an editor friend at *Maxim*. I gave him the pitch: Turns out the 2002 World Championship Quad Rugby Tournament was taking place in Gothenburg, Sweden, and there was not only a bitter rivalry between Team USA and Team Canada, but between quadriplegics and paraplegics in general. Y'see, paras have full use of their hands; quads don't. But quads can get boners; paras can't. And, no, they don't use power chairs. And, yes, they can still have sex. And one of the guys on the team was punched off a balcony; another lost his arms and legs from a rare blood disease; another was accidentally thrown from the back of a pickup truck by his drunk-driving best friend. But, no, it's not depressing or quote-unquote *inspirational*. This wasn't "Wheelchairs of Fire"—the article would be called "Murderball."

The piece was set to run in the November 2002 issue, giving us immediate access and credibility with the athletes (Zupe is a repeat subscriber). Mandel covered the expenses for the film equipment and for somebody who actually knew how to use it, co-director Henry Alex Rubin. And we were off to Scandinavia, in search of a story and a star. The Paralympics were two and a half years away.

One of the first players I interviewed was Mark Zupan, a twenty-seven-year-old civil engineer living in Austin, Texas. He was pretty grumpy on the phone until *Spin* came up (his dream job is to be an alt-rock DJ). Soon we were on a last-name basis, talking music and trading mix CDs through the mail. As the film progressed, I'd call him at his office and play potential soundtrack songs over the phone—Ministry, Ween, the Moldy Peaches. He turned me on to Mike Doughty, and later revealed the first of many cracks in his gruff exterior. He was a George Winston fan. Indeed, the hard-ass was a sucker for the slow jam, and I'd never let him forget it.

Over the next four years we became close friends. When I stayed at his house, my favorite beer was in the fridge. When I was low at the blackjack table, he tossed me a chip. We talked all the time, just shooting the shit and figuring out what shit to shoot for the film—his tenth-year high school reunion in Fort Lauderdale, his father's famous Thanksgiving turducken* dinner in Jacksonville. In the process, his

---

* "A turducken is a de-boned turkey stuffed with a de-boned duck, which itself is stuffed with a small de-boned chicken. The cavity of the chicken and the rest of the gaps are filled with a highly seasoned breadcrumb mixture or sausage meat, although some versions have a different stuffing for each bird. Some recipes call for the turkey to be stuffed with a chicken, which is then stuffed with a duckling. It is also called a chuckey" (from Wikipedia)

buddies became mine, and vice versa. Through countless phone calls, e-mails, and 200 hours of digital footage shot in eight states and four countries, I watched Zupe go from pine-rider to Reebok-sponsored MVP, from wearing old gym shorts to wearing $1,200 jeans in a *New York Times Magazine* fashion spread, and from crashing on an inflatable mattress in my cramped living room to inviting me to crash in his comped suite at the Waldorf. And together with Mandel and Rubin, we'd end up nudging each other in the tux buttons on the red carpet of the 2006 Academy Awards.

Later that night, Zupe turned to me and asked the same question he'd asked repeatedly ever since we were accepted to the 2005 Sundance Film Festival. But by now it had become rhetorical.

"Who'da thunk it?" he said, shaking his head, sipping his beer.

I pointed at him. "*You* did."

"*You did, too*," he said, as if sharing the blame. Then: "Thanks."

"For what?"

"For *doing* it."

"Thanks for *letting* us do it."

We probably could have gone on like that, back and forth, for the rest of the night. But instead we just stopped, uncomfortable with the gush, and called each other "gay." He flashed his middle finger. I mocked his George Winston collection. And then we did what we always do. We ordered another round.